Heroes of the Nations

EDITED BY

H. W. C. Davis. M.A.,

PROFESSOR OF MODERN HISTORY,
UNIVERSITY OF MANCHESTER.

FACTA DUCIS VIVENT, OPEROSAQUE
GLORIA RERUM.—OVID, IN LIVIAM, 265

THE HERO'S DEEDS AND HARD-WON
AME SHALL LIVE.

CICERO

Taf. X.

CICERO.

FROM A BUST NOW IN THE ROYAL GALLERY IN MADRID.

CICERO

AND

THE FALL OF THE ROMAN REPUBLIC

BY

J. L. STRACHAN-DAVIDSON, M.A.

FELLOW OF BALLIOL COLLEGE, OXFORD

——

G. P. Putnam's Sons
London & New York

First Published 1894
New Edition 1925

Made in Great Britain by
THE BOTOLPH PRINTING WORKS
GATE STREET, KINGSWAY, W.C.2.

PREFACE

MORE is known of Cicero than of any other person of the ancient world, and almost in proportion to the knowledge is the controversy of opinion concerning him. I formerly attempted a discussion of some disputed points in articles in the *Quarterly Review* (1879 and 1880) on the writings of Mr. Froude and Mr. Beesley. Some paragraphs from these articles are incorporated in the present volume. Here, however, my business is not to criticise but to narrate, and I have refrained even from the confutation of Drumann, with whose utterances I find myself at issue on almost every page.

In writing Roman history it is impossible to escape from the influence of the genius of Mommsen. Sometimes by suggestion, sometimes by repulsion, his presence is always felt. I have likewise more especially to acknowledge the aid which I have received from the comments of Tyrrell and Purser, of Boissier, and of Watson. As a lecturer, constantly using Mr. Watson's *Letters of Cicero* for my text-book, I naturally appropriate the result of his labours, and cannot always clearly distinguish how much of my material is borrowed from him.

CONTENTS.

iii

ILLUSTRATIONS.

---

[1] Duruy's "*History of Rome.*"

[2] Cohen and Feuardent, "*Description Historique des Monnaies Frappées sous l' Empire Romain.*"

[3] Babelon's "*Description des Monnaies de la République Romaine.*"

him, committed his orations to writing after their
delivery, and gave them to the world. These
speeches are public documents which were a living
force in the practical politics of Rome; we must not
expect absolute candour in words thus spoken and
written for a purpose; but it is much to know what
were the assertions, the sentiments, and the reason-
ings which rang in the ears of the Romans themselves at this momentous crisis of their fate. Still
more important for the purpose of our story are the
private letters, and especially the letters to Atticus.
We have before us the very words in which Cicero
recorded his thoughts from day to day in all the
confidence of intimate friendship. Cicero was not
a man of cool and cautious temperament, afraid to
commit himself to opinions, accurately weighing and
discounting probabilities beforehand, or occupying
by anticipation the province of the philosophical
historian. From the letters of such a one we should
have learnt comparatively little. We have to deal
with a man of lively mind, quick to receive impres-
sions, rushing to conclusions, garrulous in expression,
and sensitively responsive to the prevailing temper
or drift of opinion. In communing with Atticus
he never pauses to make his writing self-consistent
or plausible. Reasons "plentiful as blackberries"
crowd through his mind as he writes, and the
reasons of to-day will often not fit in with those
of yesterday. There is no reticence, no economy of
statement; every passing fancy, every ebullition of
temper, every varying mood of exultation and
depression, every momentary view of men and

things, finds itself accurately mirrored in these letters. The time lives again before us in the pages of
Cicero, and, thanks to him, he and his contemporaries are for us not mere lay-figures but actual flesh
and blood.

Marcus Tullius Cicero was born on the third of
January in the year 106 B.C., about the end of the
war with Jugurtha. His forefathers had inhabited
from time immemorial the town of Arpinum in the
Volscian mountains which part Latium from Campania. Cicero was therefore a tribesman of the
hardy race whose wars with Rome filled the early
pages of Latin history. Some would have it * that
he was a descendant of Aufidius or Attius Tullius,
the Volscian partner and rival of Coriolanus. The
struggle with Rome had ended more than 200 years
before Cicero was born ; after generations of gallant
resistance the Volscians of Arpinum were reduced
to the lowly position of " citizens without the right
of suffrage," living under Roman law and serving
in the Roman legions without political privileges
either in their own town or in the capital. But the
races predestined to political greatness possess the
faculty of forgetting that which it is best not to
remember ; and this invaluable gift of character was
not wanting to the Volscians. The memory of their
alien origin faded away, and they frankly accepted
their place as humble members of the great Roman
commonwealth. Their ambition now was to attain
the full Roman citizenship, and Rome, at the beginning of the second century before Christ, was still

* Plutarch, *Cic.*, 1.

wise enough to encourage and reward such aspirations. The full franchise was granted to the Arpinates in the year 188 B.C., shortly before the death
of Hannibal and of Scipio Africanus. In the next
generation the Romans deliberately set aside the
wisdom of their ancestors, and adopted a system of
harsh and rigid exclusion in the place of the liberal
practice of gradually elevating aliens to the citizenship, by which the greatness of Rome had been built
up. The punishment for this political crime came
upon them when, a century after the enfranchisement of Arpinum, their Italian allies, after having in
vain sought the citizenship by peaceful agitation, at
length resolved to demand it at the point of the
sword. During the Social War (B.C. 90 and 89) and
during the civic conflicts which grew out of it, Rome
tardily granted to the Italians, in the midst of her
own ruin and theirs, the boon which, if accorded a
few years earlier, would have averted irreparable
disasters from the nation.*

So far, however, as Arpinum was concerned, the
old liberal policy of Rome had lasted just long
enough to secure its inclusion ; and thus it came to
pass that in her hour of peril Rome could reckon
Caius Marius among her citizens. While Cicero was
still an infant, the great soldier of Arpinum triumphed over Jugurtha ; then re-elected
during five successive years (B.C. 104–
100) to the consulship, he crushed by two splendid
victories the invading hordes of the Cimbri and Teu-

Jan. 1, 104 B.C.

---

* See below, p. 11

ARPINUM.
(Itaria.)

tones and saved Rome in this her first conflict with
the German race.

Along with the full Roman franchise the Arpinates
now enjoyed a considerable measure of local self-
government. They were an organised community,
capable of deciding local questions for themselves,
and with their local politics and parties. We get an
interesting glimpse of Arpinum in the second century B.C. from a passing notice which Cicero * gives
of his family two generations back. "Our grand-
father showed great qualities in the administration
of this borough, opposing throughout his life his
brother-in-law Gratidius, who wished to introduce
elections by ballot. For Gratidius raised storms in
a sauce-boat, as the saying goes, just as his son
Marius † did on the high seas. When the matter
was reported to the consul Scaurus, he
remarked to our ancestor : 'Such prin-   115 B.C.
ciples and such firmness, Marcus Cicero, should have
a field for their exercise by our side in the imperial
politics of the capital rather than in the local politics
of your borough.'"

The contrast here marked between the central
unity of Rome and the local life of the township, is
a characteristic feature of these Italian "municipia."
Arpinum was one of the earlier of these "borough-

---

* *De Leg.*, iii., 16, 36.

† This Marius Gratidianus was a partisan of his great namesake
and probably his kinsman by adoption. He was guilty of many outrages during the domination of his faction, and was himself murdered
with circumstances of much brutality by Catiline, when Sulla in turn
triumphed.

towns," but the whole of Italy was after the Social War organised on the same plan. Each community of newly enfranchised Romans had its own institutions, its own magistrates and its own local patriotism, which however did not interfere with the allegiance of every citizen to the city of Rome. " Every burgess of a corporate town," says Cicero,* " has, I take it, two father-lands, that of which he is a native, and that of which he is a citizen. I will never deny my allegiance to my native town, only I will never forget that Rome is my greater Fatherland, and that Arpinum is but a portion of Rome." It will be noticed that while Cicero loves to call himself an Arpinate, and exults to call himself a Roman, he has succeeded in quite forgetting that he is a Volscian.

The insolence of the Roman nobles, especially if they happened to be of patrician blood, might sometimes tempt them to sneer at the modern origin of these municipal Romans. Catiline could speak of Cicero as " a naturalised immigrant," and the young Manlius Torquatus, pleading against him at the bar, could describe his consulship as " the reign of an alien," because forsooth Cicero " came from a borough-town." " I will give you a piece of advice, my young friend," says Cicero in reply † ; " when you are to sue for office, do not use that expression about any of your competitors ; else you may find yourself swamped by the votes of the ' aliens.' "

The statesman who came from a country-town in

* *De Leg.*, ii., 2, 5.
† *Pro Sulla*, 8, 24.

Italy was perhaps more than compensated for the lack of ancestral connection with the city of Rome, by the keen interest which his fellow-townsmen and neighbours took in his political career, by their pride and delight in his exploits, and by their anxiety for the reputation which reflected credit on their native place. In this respect the country-towns were in strong contrast with the civic and suburban districts, such as that of Tusculum, which were surfeited with famous and noble families and were careless about their local worthies. "This is our way," says Cicero,* pleading the cause of a client from his own Volscian district, "and this is the way of our native towns. Why need I speak of my brother and my-self? The very fields, if I may say so, and the mountains were partisans in our elections. Do you ever hear a Tusculan boasting of the great Marcus Cato, foremost though he was in every virtue, or of Coruncanius his fellow-townsman, or of all the famous men who have borne the name of Fulvius? No one ever says a word about them. But if you are in company with any burgess of Arpinum, you will probably have to listen, however little you may like the topic, to something about me and my brother: most certainly you will not get off without some reference to Caius Marius." "Our boroughs," he proceeds,† "lay great stress on the duties of neigh-bourship. In what I say about Plancius I am found-ing on what I experienced in my own case, for we are close neighbours of the Atinates. Most lauda-

* *Pro Plancio,* 8, 20.
† *Pro Plancio,* 9, 22.

ble, or rather I should say lovable, is this feeling of good neighbourship, which keeps the constant fashion of the olden time, not shadowed by thoughts of evil, not practised in untruths, not veneered with false colours, undisciplined in the arts of the suburb and of the city. In all Arpinum there was not a man but strove his utmost for Plancius, not one in Sora, not one in Casinum, not one in Aquinum. All that well-peopled district of Venafrum and Allifæ, all that rugged mountainous faithful plain-dealing clannish land of ours felt that it was honoured in his advancement and dignified in his dignity." Cicero himself shared the feelings which he so finely describes. It is always with a throb of pleasure that he betakes himself to his mountain home. "*Ad montes patrios, et ad incunabula nostra.*" In speaking of it he loves to borrow the language of the home-sick Ulysses as he sets his face toward Ithaca. "Rugged is she, but nurse of a worthy breed of sons; never can I see anything to glad my heart like that land." The little town still stands in the Volscian highlands, and over its gate the traveller may read an inscription which the burgesses have put up to commemorate their two great townsmen Marius and Cicero.

The family of Cicero had held for many generations a place of honour and influence in this little community. They belonged to the upper-middle class in fortune and position, a class which (from a reminiscence of the time when wealth determined the nature of military service) the Romans named "the equestrian order." They had never ventured into the arena of national politics, or aspired to the magistracies of the imperial State. The family house, the actual birthplace of Cicero, was situated some three miles from the town on the banks of the river Fibrenus, an affluent of the Liris. The place may best be described in the words of Cicero himself, who has made it the scene of his dialogue on the Laws. The second book of that treatise opens as follows :—

Atticus. We have had enough walking, and you have come to a pause in your argument. What if we were to cross over and sit down to finish our conversation in the island of the Fibrenus—that, I think, is the name of this second stream ?

Cicero. By all means, for this is my favourite spot whenever I want to think over anything quietly or to write or to read.

Atticus. For my part, this is the first time I have been at the place, and I cannot have enough of it ; I think scorn now of splendid villas and marble pavements and fretted roofs. When one looks at this, one can only smile at the artificial canals which our fashionable friends call their " Nile " or their " Euripus." Just now when you were discussing law and jurisprudence you ascribed everything to nature ; and certainly in regard to these objects at any rate which we seek for the repose and refreshment of the mind, nature is the only true mistress. I used to wonder when I considered that there was nothing in this district but rocks and mountains, (so I gathered from your verses and speeches), I used to wonder, I say, that you so delighted in this spot. Now on the contrary my astonishment is that, when you are away from Rome, you can bear to be anywhere else but here.

Cicero. Nay, whenever I am able to take a long absence from the city, especially if it be at this time of year, I seek this pleasant and healthy spot ; but it is not often that I have the chance. However I have another reason for loving it, which will not affect you so much.

Atticus. What reason, pray ?

Cicero. Well, if the truth must be told, this and no other is the very native land of Quintus and myself : here is the ancient stock from which we are sprung, here are our sacred rites, here our kindred, here countless traces of our ancestors. Just look at this country-house; you see it, as it is now, enlarged by the care of my father, who having weak health passed almost all his life here in literary pursuits; but in this very house, I must tell you, when it was a little old-fashioned cottage, like that of Curius in the Sabine country, I was born. And so there is a something, some sort of lurking feeling and fancy, which seems to make me take a peculiar pleasure in it. And why not? when we remember that the wise man of old is said to have rejected immortality that he might see Ithaca once more.

The early years of Cicero were spent partly in his native hills, partly in Rome. He tells that, as far back as he can remember anything, he recollects the help and the encouragement which his childish efforts received from the poet Archias. Archias came to Rome in 102 B.C. (when Cicero would be four years old) and lived as an inmate of the house of Lucullus. When, forty years later, Cicero appeared as counsel for his old tutor, and successfully asserted his claims to the citizenship before a Roman law-court,* he told the jury that Archias had more right than any man living to claim the benefit of whatever skill in pleading he possessed, for it was Archias who had first implanted in him the love of those studies which had made him an orator. Throughout life Cicero was an omnivorous reader. His theory was that a man who wished to excel in oratory could not study too much nor make his range of culture too wide; and we gather from his descriptions † that he and the group of cousins to which he belonged were trained from the first on this system.

* See below, p. 190.
† *De Oratore,* ii., 1.

CASCADE OF THE LIRIS.

(Duruy.)

Cicero entered on manhood in troublous times. The final defeat of the Cimbri in 101 B.C. and the disturbances at home which cost Saturninus his life in the next year had been followed by a period of comparative quiet. But the precious time had been wasted; the enfranchisement of the Italians had been vainly urged by the great tribune, Livius Drusus, who laid down his life in their cause, and now in the year 90 B.C., the seventeenth of Cicero's life, the obstinate apathy of Rome was rudely disturbed by the revolt of the Italian allies. In this war Cicero served his apprenticeship as a soldier. His references to personal recollections show that he was at one time with the northern army under Pompeius Strabo,* and at another with the southern army under Sulla.† This was in the second year of the war. During the year 90 he remained in Rome and we find in the *Brutus*‡ a full account of the condition of things in the city and of his own way of life there. Cicero was eager to use his new emancipation from boyhood by listening to the speeches of the best orators of the time. But all ordinary business was interrupted by the war; Hortensius, the rising light of the bar, was away with the army; so was Sulpicius Rufus, the most distinguished among the men in middle life, and Antonius, the most famous orator of the seniors; Crassus, the great rival of Antonius, had died the year before. The

89 B.C.

90 B.C.

---

* *Philip.*, **xii.**, 11, 27.
† *De Div.*, i., 33, 72.
‡ *Brut.*, 89.

law-courts were closed with the exception of the
Commission for High-treason. This court had
been instituted by the democratic and equestrian *
parties against those friends of Drusus whose policy
would have averted the Social War, and who were
now accused of having caused it. The noblest men
in Rome were brought to the bar on the charge of
having "incited the allies to revolt." One of the
victims was the orator Caius Cotta. "His exile,"
writes Cicero,† "just at the time when I was most
anxious to hear him was the first untoward incident
in my career." Cicero had to content himself with
listening to the political harangues of the magistrates. Of these there was no lack; Varius, Carbo
and Cnæus Pomponius "seemed," he says, "as if
they had taken lodgings on the Rostra." Cicero attended them all diligently "and every day wrote
and read and took notes."

In the year 88 B.C. he studied the technical part of
his art with the Rhodian rhetorician Molo, who was
then visiting Rome. Philosophical training was supplied him first by the Athenian Academician Philo,
(who fled from the disturbances of the Mithridatic
War and took refuge at Rome in this year) and afterwards by the Stoic Diodotus. Diodotus became for
many years an inmate of Cicero's house, and died
there at last in the year 59, making his great pupil
his heir.

A yet more important aid to Cicero's mental de
velopment was the instruction which he received

---

* See below, p. 35.
† *Brut.*, 89.

from Scævola the augur, the greatest lawyer of his
time. "My father," writes Cicero,* "immediately
after I had put on the dress of manhood, introduced
me to him, instructing me that, so far as I found it
possible and was permitted to do so, I should remain
continually at his side. And so I committed to
memory many of his wise discourses and pithy say-
ings, and strove to learn from his wisdom." After
the death of the augur (probably in the year 87)
Cicero attended on his cousin and namesake Scævola the pontifex maximus, "whom above all others
of our nation I venture to call the most eminent in
talent and in justice." From these men Cicero,
though he never professed the science of jurisprudence, gained such a practical knowledge of the
laws of his country, that he was well equipped for
the duties of an advocate.

The year of Sulla's first consulship (88 B.C.) marks
the close of the Social War and the beginning of
the yet more fatal Civil War which was its consequence. Now for the first time Roman armies were
ranged against one another on the battle-field; the
leaders of the beaten party were executed by public
authority and their heads exposed on the Rostra as
those of enemies of the State. This year saw the
first victory of Sulla, the next year the return of
Marius. Both made havoc amongst the most brilliant orators of Rome. Sulpicius Rufus, Antonius,
Catulus, and Caius Julius (whom Cicero brings together, along with Crassus, as the personages of his
dialogue *De Oratore*) had all perished before quiet

* *De Amicitia*, I, I.

was restored for a time in the year 86. Cotta was still in exile, and for the next three years Hortensius was almost without a rival at the bar. Then with the return of Sulla from the East in 83 the civil wars and massacres began again, ending at last with the re-establishment by Sulla of the oligarchical constitution.

Just upon the close of this period of disorder, about the year 81 B.C., Cicero after his long preliminary training began to speak in the law-courts. He was now about twenty-five years of age. An early speech is preserved to us from a suit in which the young advocate matched himself for the first time with Hortensius. He repeatedly refers to his timidity on this occasion, and says * that when his friend Roscius, the great comic actor, urged him to the attempt, he replied, " that he fears he will seem as impudent as a man who should strive for the palm of comedy with Roscius himself." Elsewhere † he relates that he was ambitious to imitate the two leaders of the bar (for Cotta had now been restored by Sulla), but of the two he considered Hortensius the better model.

Next year Cicero had the opportunity of establishing once for all his own position as a great advocate. During Sulla's reign of terror,
80 B.C.   legalised murder had been an everyday occurrence in Rome, and it was not easy to confine the slaughter within the precise limits which the Dictator ordained. In the midst of the confu-

---

* *Pro Quinctio,* 24, 77.
† *Brutus,* 92, 317.

sion, when the city was full of gangs of assassins
hunting down their victims for the sake of the blood-
money promised by the government, Sextus Roscius,
a wealthy citizen of Ameria, who had served in
Sulla's army and had come to Rome after his victory, was murdered in the street as he returned
home from supper. The assassins were neighbours
and distant kinsmen who had been on bad terms
with the murdered man. These men next applied
to Chrysogonus, a favourite freedman of the Dictator, and induced him to get the name of Roscius
inserted in the Proscription list. His property was
thereupon confiscated and sold *en bloc* at a sham
auction ; Chrysogonus was the buyer, and paid into
the treasury the sum of £20 as the purchase
money of an estate worth £60,000. He then constituted the murderers his agents and employed
them to oust from his father's house the only son
of the deceased, who had remained throughout in
his country-seat at Ameria. Chrysogonus and his
associates now divided the property at their leisure. But they could not feel quite sure that the
son, named like his father Sextus Roscius, would not
one day call them to account. To assassinate him,
now that times were quieter, was not so easy ; so
they adopted the plan of accusing him of being the
murderer of his father. If they could procure his
condemnation on a capital charge, he would, even if
he evaded actual execution by exile, be quite powerless to annoy them in the future. It mattered little
to the promoters of the accusation, that they were
notoriously in possession of the property of the de-

ceased, and that if he had come to his death, as they now pretended, by the parricidal machinations of his own son, his goods could not be liable to confiscation as those of a proscribed person. They calculated that this side of the story would never come out in court. No advocate, they thought, would venture to say a word of the Proscription, of the confiscation of the property, and of its purchase for an old song by Chrysogonus. How could any one insist on these points without openly attacking the Dictator's favourite? and to attack the favourite was to brave the displeasure of his terrible master.

This was Cicero's opportunity. While all Rome lay crushed and silent at Sulla's feet, this young advocate alone dared to set himself in opposition to the Regent's pleasure. In the first five minutes of his speech Cicero had cast away all disguise, and grappled openly with Chrysogonus.

"Chrysogonus asks you, gentlemen of the jury, that forasmuch as he has made himself master of so ample a fortune, which belongs by right to another man, and forasmuch as he is hindered and hampered in the enjoyment of that fortune by the fact that Sextus Roscius lives, he asks you, I say, to relieve his mind from every shade of doubt and anxiety. While Roscius is a citizen, he does not think that he can keep hold of Roscius' rich and splendid inheritance; if only Roscius be condemned and cast forth from society, then he hopes that he may be able to squander in luxury and profusion that which he has won by crime. He begs you, gentlemen, to pluck from his bosom this rooted

distrust which frets and plagues him night and day,
and to lend yourselves to secure him his ill-gotten
gain." *

Cicero modestly ascribes it to his own obscurity
that he is privileged to appear as the champion of
such a cause, while all the leading advocates shrank
from the undertaking; " my plain-speaking may be
unobserved because I have as yet no pretensions to
be a statesman, or it may be pardoned in consideration of my youth—though, to be sure, the notion of
pardoning and even the practice of judging has faded
from the memory of the Republic." †   That day was
the last on which Cicero could plead the security
of insignificance.   He left the court a man of mark
in Rome.   He had done more than save his client;
he had given voice to feelings which all the world
must needs smother in silence ; he had struck a key-
note which vibrated in a thousand hearts, sick of
bloodshed and robbery and terror.

All this required not only great boldness but great
skill.   He was pleading before a bench of senators,
newly re-established in the law-courts by Sulla, who
would not be likely to tolerate from a young man of
equestrian family anything which implied disap-
proval of the Restoration or disrespect towards the
government.   Nevertheless, with the instinct of a
great pleader, Cicero seems to have felt the pulse of
the jury as he proceeded.   He begins by protesting
that he will touch on politics only so far as is absolutely necessary for his case ; he ends by claiming

* *Pro Rosc. Amer.*, 2, 6.

† *Pro Rosc. Amer.*, 1, 3.

2

that he may speak not only for his client but for
himself. " On what seems to me shameful and intolerable, on what, as I think, will touch us all unless
we provide against it, on this I will make my utterance in all the sincerity of my heart and from all
the bitterness of my soul." *

Of Sulla himself, whose carelessness and indifference allow creatures like Chrysogonus to batten on
the Commonwealth, Cicero speaks with an apparent
respect which really covers the sharpest censure.
" Rascally freedmen," he says,† " always try to throw
the responsibility for their misdeeds on their patron ;
but all the world knows that many things have been
done, of which Sulla is only half aware. Are we to
approve then, if some such acts are passed over
because he does not know about them ? We cannot
approve ; but it cannot be helped. Jupiter reigns
above ; yet we have men injured, and cities ruined,
and crops lost by hurricanes or floods or extremes
of heat and cold. We do not attribute these mis-
chiefs to the intention of the god, but to the force
of circumstances and to the magnitude of the uni-
verse over which he has to preside, while we acknowledge his hand in the blessings we receive. And so
it is with Sulla."

But if Cicero affects to screen Sulla under this
contemptuous apology, he condescends to no half-
measures when he deals with his favourite.

" Let the leaders of the party look to it, whether
this be not a sad and shameful conclusion, that

* *Pro Rosc. Amer.*, 44, 129.
† *Pro Rosc. Amer.*, 45, 130.

those who could not bear to see the Roman Knights in the pride of place,* should brook the tyranny of this vile slave. Hitherto, gentlemen of the jury, this tyranny has been exercised in other spheres. Now you see what path it is shaping for itself, at what goal it aims; it aims at your honour, your oath, your verdict, that is to say, at almost all that remains sound and uncontaminated in the State. Think, that on that judgment-seat Chrysogonus believes that he will work his will, that here too he can hold sway. O the misery and the bitterness of it! It is not that I fear that he will have such power. What cuts me to the quick is that he has presumed, that he has hoped to compass, by means of such a bench as that which I see before me, the condemnation of an innocent man. That is the burden of my complaint. Was it for this that the nobility aroused itself and won back the State at the point of the sword? Was it in order that the menials and lackeys of the great should be able to harry the goods and the honour of us and you alike?" †

Of even greater weight are the words of warning with which the speech concludes:

"Men of wisdom, men endowed with the place and the power which you occupy, are bound to apply the appropriate remedies to the disease of which the State is sickening. There is no one of you but knows well, that the Roman people, which formerly had the reputation of being most placable towards its enemies, labours to-day under the curse

---

* See below, p. 34.

† *Pro Rosc. Amer.*, 48, 140.

of cruelty to its own children.   Remove this cruelty
from the State, gentlemen of the jury; suffer it no
longer to work its pleasure in this Commonwealth.
It is a vice which is mischievous, not only in that it
has swept off so many of our fellow-citizens under
every circumstance of horror, but likewise because
by the daily spectacle of painful sights it has made
the tenderest hearts callous to the sense of pity.
For when each hour we see or hear of some fresh
atrocity, even though nature has made us mild of
mood, familiarity with dreadful deeds plucks all
feelings of humanity from our minds." *

In later life Cicero criticised † the style of this his
early effort at oratory, which he found too florid and
exaggerated for his more matured taste.   For all
that, the speech is full of vigour and promise; and
the situation was so critical and momentous, that
every sentence struck home.   Rome was conscious
that yet another brave man and great orator had
been born among her sons.   We can well believe
that "the speech met with such approval, that from
that time no case was deemed too important to be
committed to my charge." ‡

Nevertheless the acquittal of Roscius was soon followed by Cicero's temporary retirement from the
bar.   The circumstances may best be recorded in his
own words § : "At that time my body was very thin
and weak, my neck long and slender; and a frame

---

* *Pro Rosc. Amer.*, 53, 154.
† *Orator*, 30, 107.
‡ *Brut.*, 90, 312.
§ *Brut.*, 91, 313.

like this, if exposed to over-exertion and strain of
the lungs, is reckoned to incur fatal risks. My friends
were the more anxious about me because my practice was to speak without any relief from change of
tones, but always at the full stretch of my powers of
voice and straining my whole body to the uttermost.
They and the physicians urged me to give up speaking at the bar; but I felt that I would rather run
any risks than renounce my ambitious hopes of
being an orator. I reflected, however, that by
changing my style of speaking and by lowering and
regulating my voice, I might both avoid the danger
to my health, and likewise bring my utterances better within compass. It was this purpose of a change
in my habits of speaking that made me resolve on a
journey to Asia. So after I had been two years at
the bar, and had already some reputation in the
courts, I set forth from Rome." Some account of
his studies at Athens and in Asia Minor follows, and
he continues: "Not content with these I came to
Rhodes and resorted to Molo, the same whose pupil
I had formerly been at Rome. Molo was not only
an eminent writer and pleader in actual suits at the
bar, but he had a rare skill in noting and correcting
faults and in conveying instruction. He exerted all
his powers in checking and keeping within bounds
my tendency to exaggerate and to overflow, as it
were, with a certain youthful hardihood and license
of speech. I returned home after two years' absence, not only a more practised rhetorician, but
almost a changed man. The over-straining of the
voice had abated, my style had lost its frothiness, my

lungs had grown stronger, and my bodily frame was
moderately filled out."

Cicero was now fully established as one of the
leaders of the bar along with Cotta and Hortensius,
and was constantly employed in the most important
cases. All three were candidates for
office in the year following Cicero's
return to Italy. Cotta gained the consulship, Hortensius the office of curule ædile, and Cicero that of
quæstor. Under Sulla's constitution twenty quæstors
were elected for each year, and each quæstor when
his term of magistracy was over passed on to the
benches of the Senate, where he had now a seat for
life. Meanwhile Cicero's official duties
sent him to spend the year 75 outside
of Italy. The lot gave him as his province the
western portion of Sicily with Lilybæum for his
headquarters. The other side of the island (though
one prætor ruled the whole) had a separate quæstor
who resided at Syracuse. It is necessary to make
this point clear for the understanding of an amusing
anecdote, which Cicero * tells against himself by way
of illustrating to a jury the small attention paid in
the capital to provincial concerns and provincial
reputations. The experience is one which many an
Indian Commissioner will recognise with a sigh.

" Now, gentlemen, I will make a clean breast of
it, and confess that I thought at the
time that people in Rome were talk-
ing of nothing but my quæstorship. During a
season of dearth I had forwarded a great supply of

76 B.C.

75 B.C.

74 B.C.

* *Pro Plancio*, 26, 64.

grain to the capital. I had been obliging to the
dealers, fair to the merchants, liberal to the country
people, scrupulous towards our allies, and all agreed
that I had been faithful in every duty of my office.
The Sicilians had devised compliments for me quite
out of the common. And so I returned home in
the expectation that the Roman people would come
and lay the world at my feet. But it so happened
that in the course of my journey I arrived at Puteoli,
in the height of the season when it was full of persons of the first fashion. Well, gentlemen, you
might have knocked me down with a feather when
one of these came up and asked, on what day I had
left Rome and what was the last news there? 'I
am returning,' I replied, 'from my province.' 'O
yes, of course,' says he, 'from Africa, I think.' Utterly vexed and disgusted, I said, 'No, from Sicily.'
Then another, who wished to play the well-informed
man, put in: 'What, don't you know,' says he, 'that
our friend here has been quæstor at Syracuse?' Not
to make a long story of it, I pocketed my vexation,
and lost myself among the crowd of those who had
come to take the waters."

Cicero was thirty-two years of age when, after this
adventure, he returned once more to Rome in the year
74 B.C. As a senator, it was time for him to choose
a side and to make his influence felt in the affairs of
state. To gain a clear conception of the political
arena on which Cicero is now entering, it will be
necessary to consider what were the parties and who
the statesmen with whom he was to be engaged.

CHAPTER II.

ROMAN PARTIES AND STATESMEN.

81–71 B.C.

 HEN Cicero entered on public life the government was in the full possession of the "Optimates" or Notables, and of the Senate in which they reigned supreme. These Nobles inherited the splendid traditions of their ancestors who had made Rome great in the century of the Punic and Macedonian wars. At that epoch a ring of great families, some patrician and some

250-150 B.C.

plebeian, had been set in a position of eminence, not by any invidious prerogative, but by the natural process of the working forces of the constitution. Every man was "noble" who could count curule magistrates among his ancestors, and he was most noble whose hall showed the greatest number of family portraits of consuls and censors. Power and influence accrued to the men who had

24

led the Roman armies in their triumphal march over
the civilised world, and this power and influence
they handed on to their descendants. There was
likewise among the Romans a strong public opinion
in favour of a man's sitting in the seat of his fathers.
There was no occasion for the Nobles to assert by
law their exclusive right to the highest offices, for
the electors would hardly look at any candidate who
had not ancestral claims on their attention. It was
perfectly legal indeed, for "the son of a Roman
Knight"—in other words, for one who did not
belong to the official caste—to contend for high
office with a Noble; but he would find that the
stars in their courses fought against the "new man."
"Fato Romæ fiunt Metelli consules"—Providence
always sends the great Noble, the Cæcilius Metellus, to the head of the poll. To dream of clearing
in a single generation the space that lies between
the Roman Knight and the consul is an insolence
which is to be suppressed by the united force of the
Nobility, and which is looked on with disfavour even
amongst the ranks from which the candidate is
struggling to emerge.

Thus the Roman Nobles became in fact though
not in law an hereditary caste of office-holding families. In their best days they had all the great
qualities of an oligarchy—high spirit, steadiness of
purpose, persistence under difficulties, trained sagacity in war and diplomacy. The Nobility represented Rome in a stronger and loftier spirit than any
popular organisation could have done, and the
Romans were proud to follow its lead and to accept

as their own the majestic policy which the Senate announced by word and deed.

During the latter half of the second century the Nobility shows in a less favourable light. It failed to deal with the complicated questions which presented themselves as the result of conquest, especially the agrarian question and the question of the Italian allies. Thus the statesmen who undertook to solve these problems naturally drifted into opposition, and from opposition into revolution. The Roman constitution gave fatal facilities for such a development. It had the theory of popular sovereignty without any machinery for realising that sovereignty in fact. The power of the people was nullified by the dangerous fiction that the whole nation could assemble in the Forum, and that an affirmative answer to the question put by a magistrate to such a casual gathering made the proposal into law, absolute and indefeasible. The machinery, like that of the French *plébiscite*, was fitted not to express the popular will, but to give opportunities for a despotism. Unlimited power would be lodged in the hands of any magistrate who could organise the city rabble, if only he were unchecked in his right of initiating proposals. To avoid this consequence, the Romans gave the legal power of initiative, not to one man or to any body of men collectively, but to each one of a number of annual magistrates, consuls, prætors, and tribunes, and they further gave to each of them singly an absolute right of veto over the action of any or of all his colleagues. The result was to throw

150-100 B.C.

the constitutional control into the hands of the permanent advising board, the Senate of Nobles. Constitutional usage obliged the magistrate to employ his power of initiative only in accordance with the advice of the Senate; if he declined to do so, his action was at once paralysed by the veto, and he must either submit * or else incur the guilt and danger of an actual breach of the law. Thus, so long as a single tribune remained loyal, the Senate would govern Rome in peace.

The whole constitutional fabric rested on the absolute sanctity of the veto. In the controversies of the Gracchi and their successors with the Senate, this ultimate safeguard of the constitution was violated and so the Revolution began. But while they impaired the oligarchical constitution, the democrats failed in all efforts to set up a new one in its place. Notwithstanding its formally recognised sovereignty, the Assembly was too uncertain and too little representative of the whole people to be able either to check its leaders or to give them any effective support in the hour of danger. The demagogues were for the moment irresponsible despots in the midst of a dependent crowd, and for that very reason they had no reserve force of organised public opinion on which to fall back. The democracy in its impotence turned to a military chief, and attained by this evil alliance a brief supremacy under the leadership of Marius and of his successor Cinna.

---

* As for instance Scipio Africanus was obliged to do when he tried to override the Senate in his first consulship, 205 B.C. ; see Livy, xxviii., 45.

But the revolutionists proved themselves unworthy
to rule ; they resorted to bloodshed and plunder ;
they governed yet more despotically than their
rivals had done, and without the softening effect of
ancestral custom and historic dignity to relieve the
naked harshness of their domination. This party
fell ingloriously and without regret before the swords
of Sulla's veterans when he returned from the East
in 83 B.C.

An unlimited power for the reconstruction of the
State was lodged in the hands of Sulla. Avowedly
the partisan of a Restoration, he attempted little
that was original in substance, though many of his
regulations were new in form. He desired to revive,
so far as possible, the Rome which had been before
the Gracchi with such variations in detail and such
safeguards against revolution as seemed to be suggested by the experience of the last half-century.
The senators were henceforth to have exclusive
possession of the jury-courts, the corn-distributions
instituted by Gracchus were abolished, and the
tribunate which had been used as an instrument of
revolution was strictly curbed. The constitutional
obligation which lay on the tribune to use his initiative power only with the approval of the Senate, was
no longer left to be enforced by the uncertain and,
as it had proved, insufficient sanction of the veto,
but was raised to the level of positive law ; the proposal of a bill to the Plebs was now null and void,
unless it had received the previous assent of the
Senate. Within the Senate itself precautions were
taken to prevent any one man from aspiring to rise

above the little circle of his peers; the offices of the
State must be held at fixed intervals, and no man
might hold the same office twice except after the
lapse of ten years. Free popular election of the
magistrates was still allowed. Long experience had
shown that this was not really dangerous to the
supremacy of the Nobles, and that the influence of
the great families would secure them a practical
monopoly of the highest offices.

Such was the constitution of the Republic when
Cicero became a senator. His bold defence of Roscius had marked him out as a future leader of opposition. Indeed, from his position and circumstances
he could not well be otherwise. His sympathies
were naturally on the side of the equestrian order
from which he had sprung, and that order was now
in a state of discontent and hostility to the government. For an explanation we must look back a
little in the history.

The Roman Nobility was, as we have seen, a Nobility of office; and public opinion as well as positive
law prescribed that this official caste should confine
itself to the business of war and government, and
should hold aloof from trade and banking, and more
especially from speculations connected with state-
contracts. All these fell into the hands of another
set of families, which constituted in its turn a sort
of high mercantile caste. As the armies of Rome
spread her power over the shores of the Mediter-
ranean, her commerce increased likewise, and so did
the complexity and magnitude of her financial
arrangements: all this added to the importance of

the second order in the State. Its members were necessarily men of wealth and substance, and necessarily likewise they were men who renounced the chances held out to ambition by the official career of magistracy. The new order borrowed a name from the centuries of Knights, which had originally formed the cavalry of the State, and for which a high property qualification was required. Every Roman who was in possession of the requisite property (about £4000),* and who had never held a magistracy or sat in the Senate, now called himself a "Roman Knight." The phrase implies pretty much what we mean when we speak of a "private gentleman." The consolidation of the order is due to Caius Gracchus. He gave the Knights outward signs of distinction, the narrow hem of purple on the tunic, the gold ring, and the right to reserved seats, immediately behind the senatorial stalls, in the theatre; he multiplied their influence and their gains by ordering the collection of the taxes of Rome's new province of Asia to be farmed out to them; and above all he gave them a controlling power over the Nobles, by bestowing on them the exclusive right to sit as jurors in the criminal courts.

This order occupied a position midway between the ruling senatorial families and the mass of the

---

* Throughout this volume I count 100 sesterces as equal to £1 sterling, and an Attic talent as equal to £250. This is a rough compromise between the weight of gold and the weight of silver in the sums named. In the ancient world gold was worth only about twelve time its weight in silver.

people. It was strong enough to give a preponder-
ating power to whichever of the extreme parties it
might favour for the moment; and, as its interests
were in many respects identical with those of the
Commonwealth, it seemed as if this influence was
likely to be used for good. To men of substance,
engaged in commerce and banking at Rome and
throughout the civilised world, public order and the
maintenance of credit were matters of prime importance. Whenever the democratic
factions resorted, as under Saturninus, 100 B.C.
to riot and bloodshed in the streets, the Knights
took sides with the Senate against the disturbers
of the peace. When the slackness of the Senate
allowed piracy to get the upper hand in the Medi-
terranean or when its leaders pocketed Jugurtha's
bribes, while he was cutting the throats of Roman
merchants in Africa, the Knights bestirred themselves and gave valuable support to the democratic
opposition. Unhappily there were other considerations which touched them more nearly. In the first
place the State-contracts were their monopoly, and
the equestrian order was apt to be the humble servant of whichever party promised the best bargains.
Scarcely less important were its interests in the
provincial administration. The Roman Knights
trafficked with and lent money to the subjects of
the Republic; they had control of the lucrative
slave-trade; they collected from the provincials the
taxes which had been farmed from the Roman treasury, or which had been pledged to them as security
for debt by the local exchequers of client kings and

conquered civic communities. All controversies
arising out of these matters fell under the cognisance
of the Roman governor. If he were contemptuous
of the traders and tax-collectors, these might find
endless difficulties in exacting their dues ; if he were
subservient, they were able to reap a rich harvest
from the subjects. In every commercial transaction
with a provincial the Roman Knight considered
himself a privileged person, who might stand on the
strictest letter of his bond, if it suited his purpose,
or again, if he found it convenient, might play fast
and loose with the law. Atticus once asked Cicero's
advice on behalf of a provincial who was unable to
pay his way. "Good heavens," writes Cicero in
reply, "has the man lost his wits? Does this
Greek think that he is privileged to commit acts of
fraudulent bankruptcy, just as if he were a Roman
Knight?"*

"Publicans," or farmers of the taxes, have always
laboured under an evil reputation. It is related that
to pass a wet day at a French country-house it was
once agreed that each of the company should tell a
story of robbers. Voltaire was of the party, and when
it came to his turn he said, "Ladies and gentlemen,
there was once a Farmer-General." "Well," said his
hearers, "and what next?" "What next? What
more do you want? We were to tell of robbers."
The Roman tax-farmers had at least an equal claim
to the title. Cicero is a very friendly witness when
the Roman Knights are concerned, and we may be
sure that he is within the truth when he tells us that

* *Ad. Att.*, iv., 7, 1.

a conscientious governor was often sorely perplexed by their demands.   When his brother was governor of Asia, Cicero wrote to him : " If we set ourselves in opposition to the publicans we alienate both from ourselves and from the State an order, to which we are under obligations, and which by our efforts has been attached to the constitution.   If on the other hand we give way to them in everything, we shall be parties to the utter ruin of those over whose safety and even whose interests it is our bounden duty to keep guard.   This is (if we are to look the business in the face) the one great difficulty in your administration." *

We now see why the control of the jury-courts was a matter of prime importance for the equestrian order.   In the province they were at the mercy of the governor ; they required that he should be at their mercy when he came to stand his trial at home.   There was the closest understanding between the Roman Knights in the provinces and their fellows on the bench in the Forum.   " In former days," says Cicero,† "when the equestrian order sat on the juries, evil and extortionate magistrates in the provinces were always the humble servants of the tax-farmers; they were civil to the agents of the companies ; whenever they saw a Roman Knight in their province, they followed him up with favours and compliments.   These efforts did not after all do much to help those who had been guilty of malpractices ; but on the other hand

---

* *Ad Q. F.*, i., 1, 32.

† In *Verr.*, iii., 41. 94.

many a one found it fatal to him to have acted in any way against the wishes and interests of the order. There was observed among them a strict understanding that any one who had thought himself at liberty to treat with indignity a single Roman Knight should be treated as a malefactor by the whole order." These equestrian juries were naturally disliked and feared by the Nobles. It was against them that the famous appeal of the great orator Lucius Crassus was urged. "Snatch us away from this torture; tear us out of the jaws of those whose cruelty cannot be satiated with our blood; suffer us not to be in bondage to any, saving to yourselves as a nation, to bear whose yoke is within our endurance and within our duty." *

106 B.C.

To secure this control over the official class was the first object of equestrian policy; the second was as purely selfish and far more perverse. The Roman Knights claimed for themselves an immunity from all State-prosecutions. The senators, such was their contention, are the governing class, and against them alone should such prosecutions be directed. Cicero puts their pretension as plausibly as he can when pleading at the bar for an equestrian client.†
"There is a charm in the most exalted rank in the State, in the curule chair, the fasces, the commands, governments, priesthoods, triumphs, and, last of all, in the effigy which hands down your memory to posterity. Along with these come some anxieties,

---

* *De Orat.*, i., 52, 225.
† *Pro Rab. Post.*, 7, 16.

and a greater responsibility to laws and tribunals.
We have never thought lightly of your prerogatives
(so the Roman Knights argue), but we have chosen
instead this life of quiet and leisure ; as there is no
glory to win in it, so let there be no trouble to
molest it." This limitation was introduced not only
in the case of the court which dealt with extortion
in the provinces, but also into the trial of charges
for judicial corruption. A senator, who gave false
witness or conspired to bribe a jury or himself took
money for the condemnation of an innocent man,
might be put on his trial for the offence ; any other
citizen was irresponsible. This monstrous immunity
was not only publicly defended by Cicero,* the
favourite champion of the equestrian order, but was
acquiesced in even by its greatest enemy, Sulla, who
"when he reconstituted the court for the trial of
these offences, forasmuch as he had found the
Commons of Rome free from such responsibility
did not venture to entangle them in fresh liabilities."†
Any one who presumed to interfere with these
cherished exemptions and prerogatives incurred the
deadly enmity of the Roman Knights. Livius
Drusus, the patriotic tribune of 91 B.C., had committed this unpardonable offence, and, in order to
thwart him, the Knights turned against the Italian
allies, whose cause Drusus defended, and thus involved Rome in the disaster of the Social War.‡ On

---

* See below, p. 185

† *Pro Clu.*, 55, 151.

‡ See above, p. 12.   We shall see later on how the equestrian
order turned against Cato for the same reason.

this occasion, as on many others, those who might
have controlled both the extreme parties and enforced moderation on both, preferred to sell their
support to whichever of the combatants best served
their private interests and class privileges.

When the contest with the allies developed in the
years 88 and 87 into the first Civil War, the equestrian order patched up its differences with the
Italians; but the alarm which Drusus had spread in
its ranks was still the governing principle of its
policy. In fear and hatred of the Nobility the
Knights espoused the democratic cause. They saw
with satisfaction their haughty rivals fall beneath
the daggers of Marius, and pressed forward to buy
up the confiscated properties. A terrible day of
reckoning was in store for them. The full brunt of
Sulla's savage retaliation fell on the equestrian order,
twenty-six hundred of whose members found their
names in the Proscription Lists.* Sulla reduced the
survivors to political insignificance by expelling them
from the jury-courts, and at the same time he deprived them of dignity and precedence by withdraw-
ing their valued privilege of special seats in the
theatre.

The equestrian order was naturally the enemy of
the constitution established by Sulla; and, decimated
though it had been by the Proscriptions, its influence
was still considerable. The enfranchisement of the
Italians had filled its ranks with worthy
90-81 B.C. recruits. In each new municipal town
and district were to be found substantial and honour-

---

* Appian, *Bell. Civ.*, i., 103.

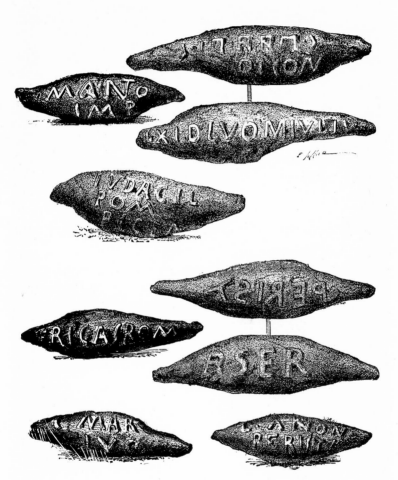

SLING MISSILES FOUND AT ASCULUM.

SOME OF THESE DATE FROM THE SOCIAL WAR.

(*Duruy.*)

able families, whose members were now Romans, but Romans without ancestral nobility ; not belonging by birth to the official caste, these naturally found their place in the second order of the State.

The Roman Knights, not being personally engaged in politics, sought their spokesmen and representatives among those members of the senatorial order who were most in sympathy with their feelings and interests. At this time their most prominent champion was Marcus Licinius Crassus, a man of high nobility and now in the ^{74 B.C.} prime of life. He had fought on the side of Sulla in the Civil War, but he had no loyalty to his caste ; as the richest man in Rome and the foremost in all lucrative speculations, he was the natural representative of the capitalists and bankers. Cicero himself was fast rising into the position of a second leader of the party. He had fully resolved to win his way by his own talents and energy to the highest grade in the State. For the last three generations only one " new man " had succeeded in attaining the consulship, and this one was his fellow-townsman, Caius Marius. In aspiring to reach the same goal Cicero must necessarily offend all the proprieties of good society, and must be sure that the ruling families would exert themselves to exclude him. He describes the struggle as he looks back on it in the inaugural speech of his consulship.* " I am the first ' new man ' whom you have raised to the consulship after an interval which reaches back almost beyond our recollection and the present generation ; I have

* *Contra Rullum*, ii., 1. 3.

shown you the way into that stronghold which the
Nobility has held with its garrison and fortified with
every device ; you have breached the defences of
that stronghold, and have willed that they should lie
open to merit in the future."

The professional rivalry between Cicero and Hortensius at the bar was sharpened by the circumstance
that the one represented the " new men " and the
other the ruling Nobility. The one naturally led
the assault and the other defended the barriers of
political and social exclusiveness which Cicero had
resolved to pass. We may catch a glimpse of the
situation in a passage * where the younger advocate
challenges the behaviour of the high society of
Rome, tolerant to the mis-doings of those within the
charmed circle, cold and rigid towards all outsiders—
" Is it not intolerable, Hortensius, to see that your
friendship and that of the rest of the great and noble
allows an easier approach to the wickedness and
effrontery of Verres, than to the virtue and incorruptibility of any one of us. You detest the industry
of ' new men,' you look down on their frugal life, you
think scorn of their purity, and for their genius and
their manliness you wish it stifled and crushed out.
Verres is your favourite."

The survivors of the Marian party were of course
bitterly opposed to the constitution set up by the
conqueror ; but they had exhausted themselves in an
abortive attempt at revolution under
78 B.C.   the conduct of Lepidus immediately
after Sulla's death.   They gathered around Crassus,

* In *Verr.*. iii., 4, 7.

so far as he showed himself in opposition ; but much
their ablest man and the one already marked out for
their future chief was the young Caius Julius Cæsar.
Wild and profligate and immersed in debt though
he was, his native genius, his manly beauty and the
charm of his manners and conversation already won
the hearts of men and women and made him the
most popular man in Rome.   Though a patrician of
the very bluest blood, claiming descent from Æneas
and the kings of Alba, he was closely connected by
family ties with the democratic party.   Julia, Cæsar's
aunt, was married to Marius, and he himself had
taken to wife Cornelia, the daughter of Cinna.
Cæsar, like Cicero, and under circumstances of
greater danger, first showed his mettle by daring to
oppose the will of Sulla ; the threats of the Dictator
failed to terrify the young man into divorcing Cornelia, and he was obliged to fly for his life.   His
powerful friends and relations afterwards extorted a
reluctant pardon from Sulla, who warned them that
"in that young dandy there lay hidden many
Mariuses."

Young as he was, being four* years junior to
Cicero, Cæsar from the first judged and acted for
himself.   He saw that the movement of Lepidus in
78 B.C. was premature and destined to fail, and he
refused to throw in his lot with it.   He urged that
the various provisions of the complicated constitution of Sulla should be assailed one by one, and that
the rehabilitation of the tribunate was the first point

---

* I adopt Mommsen's conclusion that Cæsar was really born in the
year 102.   Most authorities make him two years younger.

to aim at. The personal disqualifications which
Sulla had attached to all who had ever held this
office were removed by a law of the orator Cotta in
his consulship 75 B.C. ; and another ordinance of the
Dictator was repealed by the renewal of the dis-
tributions of corn to the people.

In estimating the forces with which the government had to reckon, we must not forget the newly
found power of a professional soldiery. During the
three generations which elapsed between the first
consulship of Marius and the battle of Actium the
Roman armies were organised on a principle inter-
mediate between the militia system of the earlier
Republic and the permanent standing armies of the
Empire. The soldier, during this period of transition, is a volunteer and not a conscript. He is no
longer a citizen serving his time in the ranks, but a
professional. On the other hand he is under no
permanent contract with the State, and hardly feels
himself to be its servant. He has enlisted under a
particular general for a particular war, which now
often extends over many campaigns, and to his
general alone he looks for promotion and for reward.*
There now comes into prominence the personal
" sacramentum " or oath of military obedience which
the soldier swears to his own commander. The
" sacramentum " and not loyalty to the State is his
point of honour, and the circumstances under which
this allegiance may be lent or recalled or trans-

---

* The mischief of the want of a regular system of retirement and
pension is set forth by Mr. Fowler in his *Life of Cæsar* in this series
(p. 107).

ferred are points to be argued with the lawyer-like precision which the Romans carried into all their transactions whether with men or gods.

The power of this mercenary soldiery had been abundantly shown by Sulla, who revealed the fatal secret that with a victorious proconsul and a veteran army lay the last word in political contests. When Sulla had completed his work of restoration, it was from the same quarter that danger to his oligarchical constitution was most to be apprehended. Yet Sulla did nothing or little to guard against the peril. The best safeguard would have been a strong central executive in Rome, wielding the whole military force of the empire and strictly responsible to the Senate. But this seemed too hazardous an experiment. Sulla weakened the magistrates at the seat of government, lest they should be too strong for the Senate, and shut his eyes to the fact that he thus renounced control over the far more dangerous magistrates on the frontiers.

As yet the mercenary soldiery was only half conscious of its powers ; nevertheless the fact that a new military force had grown up was one of the main elements in the political situation. The blind hopes and wishes of the soldiers needed a representative, and this representative was found in the person of the young commander Cnæus Pompeius Magnus. Born in the same year as Cicero, and son of the consul under whom Cicero had served in the Social War (p. 11), Pompey was twenty-three years of age when Sulla returned from the East in 8, B.C. By his own influence and reputation with the soldiers,

Pompey raised three legions in Picenum, out-
manœuvred the superior forces opposed to him, and
affected a junction with Sulla's troops in Southern
Italy. The Dictator treated the young soldier with
marked distinction; he employed him in independent commands, he yielded in spite of all constitutional objections to his demand for a triumph, and
saluted him with the title of "the Great," which
Pompey bore henceforth as a surname. After Sulla's
death Pompey in turn lent his sword to defend the
constitution against the attacks of Lepidus. Nevertheless the union between the general and the government was never hearty or sincere; and this was
mainly because the oligarchs would not take the
trouble to bind Pompey to their cause. It was
intolerable to them that any man should claim the
exceptional position which Pompey had occupied
from the outset, and which he had no intention of
relinquishing. It was contrary to all rules that a
young man, not yet of senatorial age, who had filled
none even of the minor magistracies of the State,
should be invested with one extraordinary command
after another, that he should be general-in-chief of
armies, and triumph like a legitimate consul. Pompey was not really a dangerous man : he had no
designs against the State, and no love of the hazards
and dislocations of revolution; he asked for nothing
better than to be the armed protector of a Republican government; but he considered himself a privileged person, for whom every-day rules were not
made, and he was fully resolved not to reduce
himself to the rank of an ordinary noble as the

principles of oligarchy required. The difference was one which might have been easily settled with a little tact on both sides ; but this was wanting, and the influence of Pompey must be considered as potentially at least on the side of the opposition.

These then were the forces which threatened the established order of things when Cicero became a senator. We have yet to consider what was the character of the government itself, and who were its chief supporters. An oligarchy, governing by a permanent and practically hereditary chamber, such as was the Roman Senate, is exposed to many risks and dangers. It is apt to injure itself by over-exclusiveness, cutting off the supply of able recruits from below, and thus impairing the efficiency in administration which is the chief title of such a government to rule. The great prizes which are to be distributed among its members give occasion to cliques and cabals within the privileged ranks. Self-conceit shuts the eyes of the Nobles to dangers, and leads them to disregard public opinion outside their own ranks as the mere babble of the multitude ; lack of sympathy and intelligence makes them slow to read the necessities of the time, and they are apt to be affected by a certain lordly apathy which prevents their seriously exerting themselves to frame a policy or to adapt themselves to changing social conditions. These are all natural and inherent defects which every oligarchy has to dread. These dangers may be aggravated by habits of luxury and by the absence of political responsibility. Never, perhaps, was an oligarchy set in the midst of such dangers

and temptations as those with which Sulla had
surrounded the ruling families of Rome. He had
carefully stopped all the channels through which
public opinion could legitimately find utterance, and
had freed the Nobles from all responsibility except to
their own order. The fear of equestrian juries and of
tribunician license had at least brought it home to
the governing class that they were not the whole
State. Now there was nothing to disturb their
repose. Sulla's constitution staked all on the hope
that within this ring of families there should be a
constant succession of vigorous administrators and
able officers capable of guiding the State in peace
and war. But the system was little calculated to
produce the men required to work it. The Roman
Noble was encouraged to spend his youth in luxury
and extravagance. If he were easy-going and careless, he sank into the class of elegant triflers of whom
Cicero says—" they are so stupid that they seem to
think that though the Commonwealth may go to
ruin, their fish-ponds will be safe." If he had
ambition, then the wilder his expenditure on shows
and largesses, the more surely he might look forward
to his election as prætor and as consul. Here was
the opportunity to restore his shattered fortune.
The world was divided into provinces, each of which
was destined to be prey of one member after another
of the official caste at Rome. The short period of
eleven years between the dictatorship of Sulla and
the first consulship of Pompey has for its typical
administrators the three men whose names Juvenal
selects out of all past history when he wishes to

gibbet the most shameless and notorious plunderers
of the provinces—Dolabella, Antonius, and Verres.*
We must turn again to Cicero for a summing up of
the condition of the subjects of Rome under this
dreadful yoke. " All the provinces are mourning,
all the free states are complaining, every principality
utters its protest against our greed and our insolence ;
within the bounds set by the Ocean there is no spot
so distant or so retired that the lewdness and evil
dealing of our nation have not found the way
thither. The tribes of the earth overpower the
Roman People beyond its endurance, not with force,
not with arms, not with war, but with their sorrow,
their tears, their lamentation." †

One more cause of demoralisation must not be
forgotten. The Roman oligarchy owed its present
position to the sword of Sulla, and had founded its
domination on the slaughter and robbery of all its
principal opponents. Such a past is enough to sap
the vigour of any body of politicians ; it leads them
to look to mere brute force to clear a way for them
out of their perplexities ; it seems to absolve them
from the necessity for wisdom and prescience and
statesman-like capacity, and teaches them to evade
the task of finding a solution for political problems.

Rome still possessed in her ruling order some men
of respectable ability, who in easy and quiet times
might perhaps have conducted the business of the
State creditably, though they were unequal to deal
with the tremendous issues of their own day. Such

---

* Juvenal, *Sat.*, viii., 105.

† In *Verr.*, iii., 89, 207.

was Quintus Hortensius Hortalus, whom we have already seen as a leader of the bar ; Servilius Isauricus who did good service in Cilicia in the years 78–76 ; Metellus Pius who at the head of an army in Spain displayed a moderate soldier-like capacity, though he was overshadowed by his younger and more vigorous colleague Pompey ; Servius Sulpicius Rufus, a young man of amiable character and blameless life, who was already becoming famous as the most learned lawyer in Rome ; Quintus Lutatius Catulus, a distinguished and respected nobleman already past middle age, and lastly one man of more brilliant parts, Lucius Licinius Lucullus. Lucullus after his consulship in 74 B.C. was entrusted with the command against Mithridates of Pontus, who had again resolved to try the fortune of war with the Roman People, and who was now supported by the powerful king of Armenia. In this war Lucullus showed a boldness and skill which we may almost call military genius, but this was marred by a carelessness of disposition and an incapacity for dealing with men, which effectually prevented his becoming a great statesman.

A more interesting personality than all these was just rising into notice. Marcus Porcius Cato, a descendant of the famous censor, was the youngest of the four great men whose fortunes were involved in the fall of the Roman Republic ; he was born in the year 96 B.C.,* ten years after Cicero and Pompey,

---

* The date commonly given is 95, but we know that he was quæstor when Catulus was censor (Plutarch, Cato Minor, 16, 4), *i. e.*, in 65 B.C., and he must therefore have passed thirty at the beginning of that year.

and six years after Cæsar.   Plutarch tells us a story
of his childhood, which seems like a foreshadowing
of his whole life.   He was nephew of the great
Livius Drusus, and happened to be with other
children at his uncle's house, when the question of
the enfranchisement of the allies was beginning to
be mooted.   Pompædius Silo, an emi-
nent Italian who was present, laugh-   91 B.C.
ingly canvassed the children for their vote and
interest in his cause ; and all readily consented except
Cato.   He had somehow got it into his obstinate
little head that to yield to the demands of her allies
would be unworthy of Rome.   When coaxing failed,
Pompædius held him out of the window and threatened to drop him ; but no, " he would not, and he
would not."   If the fate of Italy had rested with
this urchin of five years old, he would have died
sooner than allow her to be saved from the Social War.

The same unbending temper, inaccessible to
reason, to fear, or to favour, characterised Cato
throughout.   He always did that which his conscience told him was right, irrespective of consequences, and his very narrowness made him a power.
He was the only Roman whom Cæsar condescended
to fear and to hate.   He might unconsciously do
Cæsar's work for him ; in fact, his shortsightedness
caused him repeatedly to throw the game into
Cæsar's hands ; but he could neither be bought, nor
conciliated, nor coerced ; and such a man was highly
provoking to Cæsar.   In aims, in character, and in
conduct, alike in their qualities and in their defects,
the two men were hopelessly antagonistic.   Cato's

whole life was a tacit condemnation of Cæsar, and his voluntary martyrdom was a keenly felt reprobation of the Dictator and all his works. Cæsar pursued him even in his grave with a lampoon.

Cato's obstinacy, his narrowness, and his impracticability will find ample illustration in the following pages, and I need not dwell on them here. But we must not forget the other side of the picture. In an age of the most unbridled license of speech, an age which would have been inclined to leave, "not even Lancelot brave or Galahad pure," the character of Cato stood alike above censure and above eulogy.* The common sense of the Romans recognised in him a man over whose actions corrupt or self-seeking motives had no power, and whose sole thought was of duty. He became to them a sort of embodiment of the public conscience; "to earn the approval of Cato," was a synonym for pure and righteous action. Rome was the better for having a living standard of integrity set before her eyes. An advocate, though he might quake at the thought of having him for a juror, hesitated to challenge Cato, for such a challenge seemed an acknowledgment that his case was a bad one. In the year 54 B.C. certain candidates for the tribuneship, who wished for once to have a pure election, agreed each of them to deposit a large sum with Cato, which the depositor was to forfeit if his proceedings seemed to Cato deserving of blame; "if," exclaims Cicero,† " there is really no bribery this

---

* Cujus gloriæ neque profuit quisquam laudando, nec vituperando quisquam nocuit, quum utrumque summis prædati fecerint ingeniis. —Livy, *Fragm.*, 44 (Madvig).

† *Ad Att.*, iv., 15, 8.

time (and people seem to think that this will be so),
Cato singlehanded will have proved of more avail
than all the laws and all the courts." He was likewise through life the champion of the helpless provincials,* and in the last terrible struggle he lifted up
his voice, though in vain, against the harshness and
cruelty of his associates. Cato's want of tact and
judgment often made him a sore trial and vexation
to his friends ; but these weaknesses were on the
surface ; at heart the man was sound, honest, and
fearless. His faults have deserved to be forgotten
by posterity, and his virtues have been claimed as a
possession of the world for all time. It has proved
true for him, that "The path of duty was the way to
glory."

The fortunes of Rome were chequered during the
years following the Restoration which was the work
of Sulla. Lucullus, as we have seen, won some
brilliant victories in the East. Spain was disturbed
by a remnant of the Marians under Sertorius. By
the aid of native allies Sertorius resisted for long
years with varying success the efforts of Metellus
and Pompey. His assassination by one of his Roman
comrades caused the collapse of the Spanish insurrection, and the country was effectually subdued by
Pompey. Meanwhile the government had on its
hands two contests of a very dangerous and irritat-
ing nature. It was too timid or too supine to organise a powerful and centralised fleet, or to supply
Italy with a proper garrison. The result of the first

* A quo uno omnium sociorum querellæ audiuntur.—*Ad Fam.*,
xv., 4, 15. Plutarch, *Cato Minor*, 53, 4.

error was that pirates swarmed over the Mediterra
nean. A half-hearted attempt was made to create
a High Admiral in the person of Antonius, but he
proved both corrupt and incapable; he plundered
the subjects of Rome remorselessly, and was defeated by the pirates. After this, the Senate desisted
from its efforts. Still nearer home, a serious danger
befell the Romans in the slave insurrection headed
by Spartacus. The great plantations worked by
slave-labour, which were so convenient and profitable to the wealthy Nobles, filled Italy with men
whose extreme misery made them ready for any
desperate attempt; and bold bandit chiefs were
reared for them in the gladiatorial training-schools,
which for the purposes of the game were obliged to
cherish in their victims habits of endurance, contempt of pain and death, and a sense of honour to
be kept bright in spite of social degradation. Cicero
has described how " gladiators, barbarians or criminals though they be, stand to the stroke; how those
who have perfected themselves in their calling will
rather take the wound than avoid it by foul play;
how manifest it is that their first object is to do
their duty to their master and to the public. Even
when sinking under his wounds the man sends a
message to his master to know whether he has any
further orders; if his master thinks he has done
enough,* he should be glad to be allowed to lie down
and die." Spartacus, a gladiator of this type, escaped from his barrack and soon collected round
him an army recruited from among the slaves of

* Reading " si " with Tischer. *Tusc. Disp.*, ii., 17, 41.

Southern Italy. After defeating over and over again the Roman magistrates and their hasty levies, the insurgents were at length crushed by Crassus, and their leader fell in battle. This was in the year 71 B.C.; at the same moment Pompey returned with his army from Spain, and extirpated the remnants of the rebel force.

COIN STRUCK BY ITALIANS IN SOCIAL WAR.
SABELLIAN BULL GORING THE ROMAN WOLF.

(Duruy.)

CHAPTER III.

CICERO AS AN ADVOCATE. ATTICUS. CICERO'S FAMILY.

71–67 B.C.

OMPEY and Crassus were not good friends, but a common interest now drew them together. Pompey claimed a triumph for his victories in Spain. The claim was irregular. Pompey had never been consul or prætor. He had therefore no legitimate " auspices " to hallow his success, and so was not properly qualified for the religious ceremonial of the triumph. In former days the great Scipio himself had asked in vain for a triumph under similar circumstances. But Pompey had already a precedent in his own case,* and it was short-sighted pedantry on the part of the Senate to refuse what even Sulla had been obliged to concede. Pompey likewise demanded that the privilege should

* See above, p. 42.

be granted him of overstepping all the minor magistracies and being at once accepted as a candidate for
the consulship. To the restrictions of age prescribed
by the law he might well reply, as Napoleon did on
a like occasion, " a man grows old on the field of
battle, and that is where I have been." Here again
the government, which might easily have won the
support of Pompey, foolishly haggled over the price.
The Nobles had soon reason to regret their obstinacy.
The democrats grasped the opportunity
and called on Pompey to put himself at   71 B.C.
the head of the opposition. Pompey and Crassus
availed themselves of the pretext of their intended
triumph to march their united armies to the gates
of Rome. The Senate, which had no troops available, was forced to an ignominious surrender ; the
necessary decrees were passed, and Pompey and
Crassus were elected consuls for the year 70 on the
understanding that they were to satisfy the two
great sections of the opposition, the democrats by
the restoration of their former legal right of initiative
to the tribunes, and the Knights by placing them
once more on the judicial bench.

In this great assault on the constitution of Sulla,
Cicero naturally went with the equestrian order and
took the side of Pompey and the opposition. He
frankly accepted Pompey for his political leader, and
the bond thus knit between them, though often subjected to severe strain, was never wholly broken.
Whether Cicero heartily approved of the restoration
of the tribunate, or whether he merely acquiesced in
it as part of the bargain between the factions, is un-

certain. His references to the change at the time, are slight,* but they seem to imply satisfaction. Even in later years, when he had himself suffered from the unbridled power of a tribune, he contended, though somewhat faintly, that Pompey was justified in his policy.† He urges that, though the power of the tribune is doubtless excessive, yet " the violence of the people is a force yet more savage by far and more uncontrollable, and this is sometimes under greater restraint, if it has a leader, than if it has none ; for the leader considers that he advances at his own peril, whereas the popular impulse takes no account of danger." " Pompey," he continues, " was bound to have regard not only to what was most desirable, but to what was necessary. It was the part of a wise citizen not to leave to some pestilent demagogue the credit of a measure, which was not so very dangerous in itself, and which was too popular to be resisted."

But if Cicero were dubious or neutral in respect of this portion of the programme of the opposition, it was far otherwise when he dealt with the reform of the jury-courts. Here he was heart and soul with the order from whose ranks he had sprung. He felt that it was a mere mockery of responsibility to bring corrupt governors before a bench of their peers, who were too often their accomplices. It was easier indeed to point out the faults of the present system than to provide a remedy. Pompey's

---

* In *Verr.*, v., 63, 163, and 68, 175.

† In the treatise *De Legibus* (iii., 10, 23), written about eighteen years later.

measure had the merit of settling once for all this much disputed question by a compromise which divided the juries between the orders in the proportion of one of the senatorial to two of the non-official class. But though useful in quieting the rivalry between the orders, it is doubtful whether the new law did much to make the courts more pure or more impartial.

Cicero rendered an important service to the party of reform by breaking through his usual practice of accepting briefs only for the defence, and by bringing to trial the most flagitious of all the offenders, Caius Verres, the notorious prætor of Sicily.

I will not attempt even a summary of the appalling misdeeds of Verres. Every calamity which the lust, the cruelty, and the rapacity of a tyrant could inflict on his slaves, was endured for three years by the miserable Sicilians. Cicero's description of the governorship of Verres serves as a sort of high-water mark to show to what a pitch of iniquity men set above the fear of responsibility may attain, when granted absolute power over a subject population. I prefer to dwell on a matter which could be treated by the orator with lighter touches.

The name of Verres is perhaps best known and remembered as that of the most inveterate pillager of all the great army of unscrupulous art-collectors. Nothing which was at once beautiful and portable escaped his fingers. From the plate at the tables where he was invited to dinner, up to the most ancient image of Ceres in her native seat of Henna, which was believed to be sanctified by the very

presence of the goddess herself, all was swept into
his net. Sometimes he added insult to injury by
compelling his victims to accept a trumpery sum, as
purchase money for their ancestral heirlooms or for
the tutelary gods of their cities. He appropriated
even the statues which the Carthaginian conquerors
in former days had carried from Sicily and which
Scipio had restored, as a monument of the magnanimity of Rome, to their first possessors. The bases
with the name of Scipio alone remained to tell the
story. The historic pictures on the walls of the
temple of Pallas at Syracuse were torn from their
site; the gates of the same temple, supposed to be the
finest in the world, were stripped of their embossed
gold and ivory, and their marvellous Gorgon's head.
Of the statue of Sappho from the prytaneum of Syracuse Cicero says,* " this gave you so fair an excuse
that one is almost obliged to allow it. This master-
piece of Selanion, so perfect, so graceful, so exquisite,
how should it be in the possession of any individual
or of any State, saving only of our most elegant
and accomplished Verres? Any one of us, not born
to such good fortune, has no business to be particular;
if he wants to look at anything of the sort, let him
go to the Temple of Happiness, to the Monument
of Catulus, to the Portico of Metellus; or let him
bestir himself to obtain admission to the suburban
villa of one of you fine gentlemen; or let him content himself with the sight of the Forum, if Verres
lends any of his treasures to the ædiles to decorate
it on great occasions. But Verres must have these

* In *Verrem*, iv., 57, 125.

things at home; Verres must have his mansion and his country seats crammed with the spoils of temples and cities. Will you bear any longer, gentlemen of the jury, with the fancies and luxuries of this clown, who by nature and education seems formed in body and mind to be the porter of works of art rather than the collector?" In the meantime the occupation of the Syracusan guides was gone; they used to take strangers round to show the art treasures of the city, now they could only point out the place where each had stood, before the prætorship of Verres. The end of Verres is characteristic. Condemned and driven into exile, he still clung to some of his darling stolen goods; twenty-seven years later he was in possession of some vases which attracted the attention of Antony, and for their sake Verres' throat was cut in the last great Proscription.

Before leaving this subject I must say a few words on Cicero's treatment of art and art-criticism. We find in his writings all the appreciation of a cultivated gentleman for painting and sculpture; and in his earlier letters to Atticus he continually commissions his friend to purchase statues and bas-reliefs in Greece, and expresses the greatest delight in what Atticus sends him. But in this speech, in order to point the contrast against Verres, he appears as the representative of the sterner and simpler of his countrymen, who regard the new-born interest of the Romans in art as a sign of degeneracy, the lowering of the imperial race to the petty skill and effeminate tastes of the Greek or the Asiatic. The

sentiment has found expression in the immortal
verse of Virgil—

> Excudent alii spirantia mollius æra ;
> Credo equidem vivos ducent de marmore vultus :
> Orabunt causas melius, coelique meatus
> Describent radio et surgentia sidera dicent ;
> Tu regere imperio populos, Romane, memento,
> Hac tibi erunt artes, pacisque imponere morem,
> Parcere subjectis et debellare superbos.

In Cicero the affectation of indifference is merely
playful and is not long sustained ; but while it lasts
it is very pretty fooling, and affords an excellent
specimen of the "mendaciuncula," or mystifications,
with which, as he tells us,* an advocate is permitted
to season the gravity of his discourse.

The following description,† which comes at the
very beginning of this section of the speech, will
give a sufficient idea of Cicero's manner.—" In the
house of Heius there was in the place of honour a
shrine, an inheritance from his ancestors, of great
antiquity, in which there were four admirable statues
of the finest style of art and famous of their kind,
such as might give pleasure not only to this virtuoso
and connoisseur, but to any one of us—to any ' ig-
noramus ' as he would say. One of these was a
Cupid in marble by Praxiteles—you see that in
getting up my case against Verres I have learned
the names of the artists. . . . On the opposite
side was a Hercules, excellently moulded in bronze ;

---

* *De Orat.*, ii., 59, 241.
† In *Verr.*, iv., 2, 4, *seq.*

this, unless I am mistaken, was the work of Myron
—yes, Myron was the name, I am sure. In front of
these gods were small altars which sufficiently indicated the sanctity of the shrine, and furthermore two
bronze statues, of no great size but of exquisite
beauty, in the form and dress of young girls with the
hands raised to support some sacred object, which
they bore on their heads after the manner of Athenian maidens; 'Canephoræ' was what they were
called, but what was the name of the artist? who
was it?—thank you for reminding me; the artist was
named Polycletus." It would be absurd of course
to take all this seriously; it is merely as playing the
part of the antique and unsophisticated Roman, in
which character Cicero is posing for the moment,
that he must affect to have learned the names of
Myron and Polycletus and Praxiteles as an incident
of the getting up of his lawyer's brief.

Notwithstanding the notoriety of Verres' crimes,
the Nobles of the Senate seem to have looked on
him with favour. His provincial command, conferred originally for one year only, was extended
for two succeeding years. The great family of the
Metelli supported him both at home and in Sicily,
where all the machinery of the government was set
in motion to detain witnesses and to suppress evidence. Hortensius put not only his eloquence but
his powerful influence at his disposal, and Verres
seems to have fully expected that between influence
and bribes he would be able to secure an acquittal.
"Those," he observed, "had reason to be alarmed
who had plundered only enough for themselves; he

had taken so much that there was plenty for others as well "; * " he had so ordered the three years of his Sicilian prætorship, that he should do exceedingly well for himself if he put the proceeds of the first year into his own pocket, while he handed over the second to his advocate and supporters, and reserved the third, that fattest and most lucrative year of all, entire for the jury." †

His chances would have been much improved, if he could have put off the delivery of the verdict till after the beginning of the new year, when Hortensius would be consul with a Metellus for colleague, and another Metellus would be called to preside as prætor at the trial. By the help of intervening festivals he hoped to be able to spin out the trial over this date ; but Cicero outwitted him by making a very short opening speech, and leaving his case to be proved by the witnesses. The evidence was so overwhelming that Verres abandoned his defence and retired into exile.

In the meantime public opinion was running high against the corruption of the senatorial juries. If we may trust Cicero's representation, it was this which gave force to the whole attack against the constitution of Sulla. " The Roman people," he says, ‡ " though beset with many distresses and many anxieties, yet seeks for no reform in the State so eagerly as for the restoration of the old firmness and the old integrity of the juries. It is because they

---

* *Actio Prima,* 2, 4.
† *Actio Prima* 14, 40.
‡ *Divinatio,* 3, 8.

cannot trust the courts that they clamour for the tribunician power; it is because the courts are corrupt that another rank of men is demanded for the bench ; it is from the iniquity and the ill-fame of the jurors that the censorship, which was once a name of dread, is now asked for, is now a popular cry and calls forth cheers of approbation."

And again *—"this point did not escape that wise and eminent statesman Quintus Catulus, who when asked his opinion in the Senate by our noble and gallant consul on the question of the tribunician power, which was before the House, began his speech with these weighty words : ' that the senators have handled the courts corruptly and scandalously, and that if they had been content to satisfy public opinion by their verdicts, the Roman people would not be so anxious for the tribunician power.' Finally Cnæus Pompeius himself, in the first speech which he made as consul elect before the gates of the city, when he indicated (as most people expected) that he would restore the tribunician power, elicited a hum and murmur of approval from his audience ; but when in the course of the same speech he said, ' the provinces are pillaged and harried, and gross and scandalous verdicts are returned ; I hope to find a remedy for this state of things ' ; then the Roman people gave voice to its feelings no longer by indistinct utterances but by downright shouts of applause."

Cicero aided this movement by publishing the full and detailed exposition of the crimes of Verres,

---

* *Actio Prima*, 15, 44.

which he would have delivered as a second speech
if the trial had run its full course. The speech is
thus a political pamphlet, setting forth the misdoings
of senatorial governors and the corruption of senatorial juries. The influence on opinion of Cicero's
published pleadings was such as to make the orator
a great power in Rome. "His speeches," writes
Mr. Tyrrell, "discharged the highest work now done
by our best newspapers, magazines, and reviews. To
gain Cicero was what it would be to secure the advocacy of the *Times*; or rather what it would be
were there no other paper, review, or magazine but
the *Times*, and were the leaders of the *Times* written
by Burke and Sheridan. . . . They put the
public in possession of the circumstances in each
case, and taught them to look on these circumstances with the eyes of the speaker and his party;
they converted resistance into acceptance, and
warmed acceptance into enthusiasm; they provided
faith with reasons, doubt with arguments, and triumph with words."

Cicero was now the foremost among the advocates
of Rome, for Cotta had died, and Hortensius passed
through a period of eclipse, from which however he
seems to have emerged later on. This is Cicero's
own account of the matter in the *Brutus*.* "After
his consulship (I suppose because he saw that he
was beyond comparison the first speaker among the
consulars and took no count of those who had not
attained that dignity), Hortensius relaxed the efforts
which he had exerted from his boyhood up, and

---

* *Brut.*, 93, 320.

HORTENSIUS.
(From Bernouilli's Röm. Ikon.)

being well off in every way chose to pass his time
more agreeably, as he thought, or at any rate less
laboriously. Just as the brilliancy fades from the
colouring of an old picture, so the first, the second,
and the third year each robbed him of something
not noticeable by a casual observer, but which an
educated and discerning critic could detect. As
time went on, he continued to deteriorate in his
delivery, especially in readiness and sustained flow
of utterance, until he became every day more unlike
his old self . . . By the time that I was made
consul, six years after his own consulship, Hortensius had almost effaced himself. Then he began
again to take pains; for now that he and I were
equals in rank, he wished us to be equals in everything. Thus for the twelve years following my consulship we two were engaged in the most important
cases with unbroken friendliness. I always considered him superior to myself; he put me first."

The most notable case in which Cicero was engaged during the period immediately before his
consulship was his defence of Caius Cornelius, who
as tribune in the year 67 B.C. had attempted to check
the practice, by which the Senate granted dispensa-
tions from general laws under peculiar circumstances.
The permission to Pompey to stand for the consulship in 70 B.C. is one instance of the kind, and
Cæsar's request for a triumph in 60 B.C. is another.
In pressing his bill through its earlier stages Cornelius had certainly been guilty of irregularities;
still he had not persevered in illegal courses, but
had withdrawn his measure and substituted another,

which was unanimously accepted, recognising the
prerogative of the Senate but guarding against its
abuse.   Nevertheless when he went out of office he
was put on his trial for riot and Cicero appeared as
his counsel.   His speech, now unhappily lost, is
adduced by Quintilian * as the great example of the
power of fervid eloquence. " In defending Cornelius
Cicero wields arms which are not only potent but
flash resplendent.   If he had contented himself with
instructing the jury on the merits of the case, and
speaking sensibly and clearly and in good Latin, he
would never have brought the Roman people, as he
did, to utter their enthusiasm not by cheers alone
but by clapping of the hands.   It was because he
was lofty and majestic and splendid and overpower-
ing that he wrung that applause from them   .   .   .
I fancy that those who heard him were transported,
and cheered because they must, not because they
chose; like men beside themselves who had lost
consciousness of where they stood, they burst forth
into those expressions of delight."

Cicero's reputation as an advocate was now so
great that, " his doors," as Plutarch tells, " were
thronged with clients, no less than those of Crassus
and Pompey who were then the most famous persons in Rome, the one for his wealth the other for
his military renown."   He adds that " Pompey
courted Cicero, and the support of Cicero contributed much to Pompey's power and reputation."

This influence was at first exercised only indirectly,
for Cicero never addressed the people, nor, so far as

---

* Quintilian, *Inst. Orat.*, viii., 3, 3.

we know, the Senate, until after he was elected
prætor in 66 B.C. At this period of his life Cicero is
above all things a pleader at the bar, and it will be
interesting to see what are his own notions of the
duty of an advocate. They are just those which
the practical necessities of pleading have prescribed
to modern lawyers. The advocate speaks as the
representative of his client ; it is not his business to
weigh the case as a judge, but to put as strongly as
possible those points which are in favour of his
client, and to extenuate those which make against
him. It once fell to Cicero's lot to speak in defence
of a man named Aulus Cluentius who lay under
strong suspicion of having bribed a jury to obtain
the condemnation of his enemy. The case was a
notorious one, and had been referred to as such by
Cicero, when three years previously in his speech
against Verres he was inveighing against the corruption of the courts. The counsel opposed to Cluentius took advantage of this circumstance to claim
the authority of Cicero's sentence against his own
client. Cicero's argument in reply is very much
what an English barrister would plead on a similar
occasion. " There remains one most weighty judgment, which to my shame I was nearly forgetting to
notice, for it is that of no less a person than myself.
Attius read out of some speech or other, which he
said was mine, an appeal to a jury to give a righteous
verdict, in which I referred to some verdicts of evil
fame, and amongst others to that of the court over
which Junius presided ; just as if I had not said myself in opening this speech that the verdict in ques-

5

tion lay under grave imputations, or as if when I was
discoursing of the corruption of the courts I could
at that time have passed over this case which was
then in every one's mouth. If I said anything of the
kind, I was not speaking from ascertained inquiry
nor was I giving evidence in the witness-box, and
my remarks were such as the occasion demanded
and not to be taken for my final sentence and judgment. . . . It is a great mistake to suppose that
in our speeches, which are delivered at the bar, you
have our deliberate judgments on record. All such
speeches are the utterances not so much of the
counsel as of his brief and of the case. For, if the
case of a litigant could speak for itself, no one would
employ a pleader. Now we are employed to utter,
not that which we are to lay down on our own responsibility, but that which is prompted by the
requirements of the case in which we are engaged." *

Side by side with this passage we may set another
from the *Brutus* † in which Cicero's ideal of the
qualities of the forensic orator is more fully set
forth. " To have studied more subtilely than other
men that literature wherein the fountain-head of
perfect eloquence is to be found ; to have embraced
philosophy the mother of all good deeds and good
words ; to have learned the Civil Law, a matter
most necessary for private suits and for the technical
skill of a pleader ; to hold in your memory the story
of Rome, whence you can summon, when need is,
most authentic witnesses from the tomb ; to be able

* *Pro Clu.*, 50.
† *Brut.*, 93, 322.

shortly and neatly to turn the laugh against your
antagonist, and so give some repose to the minds of
the jurors and lead them away a little from stern-
ness to a smile; to be able to take a wider sweep
and transfer the argument from the particular man
and the particular time to the consideration of the
universal principle involved; to know how to give
pleasure by a slight digression; to be able to stir
the soul of the juryman to anger or to move him to
tears, to carry him with you, this is the special prerogative of the orator, in whatever direction the
case demands."

With the year 68 B.C. begins the great series of
Cicero's letters; but they are at first brief and
scanty; it is not until after his consulship that they
become our main guide and authority for the history. This will be a good opportunity to speak of
Cicero's chief friend and correspondent, Titus Pomponius Atticus.

The family of Atticus had held its place for
generations in the equestrian order, but unlike that
of Cicero it belonged from the first to the purely
Roman stock.* He was closely connected with the
tribune Sulpicius Rufus, who became the victim of
Sulla in his first attack on Rome in the year 88.
The young Pomponius is said to have been in some
danger on this occasion, but this did not deter him
from aiding the flight and supplying the needs of
the younger Marius, who was proscribed at the same
time by Sulla. Sick of the civic bloodshed, which

---

* These and the following details are derived from the Life of
Atticus by his contemporary and friend Cornelius Nepos.

as he doubtless foresaw was destined immediately to be renewed on a more horrible scale, he transferred his home and his money to Athens, where he resided for the next twenty-three years. On his return to Rome in the year 65 he still declined to take any active part either in the administration of the State or in the decision of the great issues of the time. His manhood coincided almost exactly with the period of the Civil Wars (88–31 B.C.); yet through them all he claimed, and his claim was allowed, to stand neutral. It was not an exalted part to play, and such apathy is a danger to any commonwealth; yet, as he bowed his head to each new master, the victory was always a little less savage, and the humiliation of the conquered a little less bitter, because Atticus was friend with all parties and could make his influence felt on the side of moderation.

His ample wealth was husbanded by skilful management and by frugal habits of life. Cornelius Nepos tells us that to his own knowledge Atticus' household expenses came to only £30 a month. His money was always at the disposal of his friends in difficulties, and especially when the fortunes of their party were at a low ebb. As he had aided Marius in his hour of danger, so he befriended the Pompeians who were in need of money for their hurried flight at the beginning of the second Civil War. He helped and protected Terentia when Cicero was in exile, and Fulvia and her children when Antony was defeated at Mutina.

We have here to consider mainly his life-long

friendship with Cicero. This intimacy began when they were fellow-students in youth, and it lasted to the end. In Atticus Cicero found the friend exactly fitted to supplement his own qualities. The warm impulsive heart of the one sought repose in the easy-tempered, stable, appreciative nature of the other. The impetuous, indiscreet man of genius needed a calm, sympathising and absolutely safe companion, in whose ear he could breathe all his fears and hopes and doubts; through all the years of their inter-course never a word escaped through Atticus which could add to Cicero's embarrassments. It is from this perfect confidence that the letters to Atticus derive their peculiar interest and their peculiar value. Cicero is no more likely to deceive Atticus than a patient is likely to lie to his physician; the statement of the circumstances which he lays before his coun-sellor may sometimes be erroneous, but it is never wilfully misleading. Cicero set the highest value on the judgment of his friend. At critical seasons he writes to him every day, and sometimes as much as thrice in a day. His dependence is quaintly ex-pressed, in a passage where he describes his per-plexities just before the outbreak of the Civil War. " Imagine the scene; the consul names me—' I call on Marcus Tullius.' What am I to say? ' Wait a little if you please, till I can go and consult Atticus'; alas there is no evading the question in that fashion." *

Moderate, sagacious, and cautious, with an on-looker's insight into the game, Atticus was admira-

---

* The paragraph preceding this sentence will be found in its place, page 320.

bly fitted to support and to control the far greater
intellect and finer character but less equable temperament of his friend. His advice is commonly towards
a safe course, and he has a constitutional dislike of
hazardous ventures. He particularly objected to
Cicero's rash opposition to the triumvirs in the year
56, and if his advice had been followed Cicero would
have escaped the humiliation which befell him after
the conference of Luca.* So in the years immediately following, Atticus counselled submission and the acceptance of Cæsar's
overtures for friendship.† Nevertheless he is keenly
interested not only in the safety but in the good
fame of his friend. He recognises that while the
Roman Knight, the man of business and of letters,
may be permitted to make his own preservation and
his own ease the first object, a very different standard of conduct is set up for the consular. He sees
that by the lofty tone of his speeches and writings
Cicero has given hostages to public opinion which
must not be forfeited. Atticus may go out to the
fifth milestone to greet Cæsar, as he
returns after driving Pompey from
Italy; but at the same moment he encourages
Cicero "so to bear himself that Cæsar may have
cause to respect him rather than to thank him, and at
all risks refuse to allow himself to be dragged to
Rome."‡ Though Atticus was staggered by Pompey's

55-51 B.C.

49 B.C.

* See page 273.
† See page 320.
‡ *Ad. Att.*, ix., 18, 1. Cicero's action under this advice is de-
scribed below, page 338.

desertion of Italy, and though at first he counselled neutrality with a view to mediation of peace, yet when that hope failed it was with his full concurrence that Cicero betook himself to Pompey's camp. Immediately after the assassination of Cæsar, Atticus could see, though both Cicero and Brutus were blind to it, that, whether   44 B.C. or no Cæsar's acts were to be confirmed, it was ruinous policy to allow a public funeral to his body, and that passions would thus be excited which would be fatal to the general amnesty.* And once more when six months later Cicero is on the point of retiring to Greece, we find Atticus ready to brave his friend's displeasure by telling him plainly that public opinion will accuse him of deserting his post. Cicero, obedient to the call, returns at once to face Antony in the Senate.† If it had not been for Atticus, the First Philippic would never have been spoken.

In private life, as in public, Cicero always leaned on Atticus. All domestic jars (and Cicero's family often caused him uneasiness) are reported at once to his friend, who always plays the part of sympathiser and sometimes that of peace-maker. All his business transactions likewise went through Atticus' hands, and the letters are full of references to them. Cicero was very careless about money-matters; if a house or a farm or a statue took his fancy, he bought first and afterwards considered how he was to find the money. Thus though his fortune was never compromised, hardly even seriously

---

* *Ad Att.*, xiv., 10, 1.
† See p. 392.

embarrassed, he is constantly in small difficulties;
such a bill has to be met on such a day and there
are no funds, unless that other sum which he is expecting, be paid up to date, which is unlikely.　On
such occasions Cicero gets alarmed about his credit,
and writes to Atticus to raise money for him at any
cost or to sell his property at any sacrifice rather
than allow him to appear for a moment as a defaulter.
Atticus never grudged trouble on behalf of his
friend.　We always find that, one way or another,
he manages to meet the call, and a few months'
economy or a legacy, opportunely falling in, sets
Cicero's affairs straight again.

One business relation between the friends has a
more permanent interest.　Atticus had a large retinue of slaves, born in his house, whom he carefully
educated and trained to act as his literary assistants.
"His household staff," says his biographer,*
"though insignificant for purposes of display, was
admirable so far as use was concerned.　It comprised
a number of highly educated slaves, excellent
readers and copyists enough and to spare; indeed
there was not a footman but was able to fulfil both
these tasks with credit."　They were experts in the
art of binding, cataloguing and arranging, and were
at home among bookcases and titles.　Atticus lent
their skilled assistance to repair the damage done in
Cicero's library while he was in exile, and Cicero
was delighted with their work: "Since Tyrannio
with their valuable aid has put my books in order,
the house seems to have a soul breathed into it." †

---

* Nepos, *Vit. Att.*, 13.
† *Ad Att.*, iv., 8, a. 2.

After completing his own library, Atticus set his slaves to work to make extra copies of his books, for which he found a ready sale. Before he left Athens we find that he had a whole library to dispose of, and that Cicero marked it for his own.* " By no means pledge your offspring to anyone else, though you meet with a wooer never so ardent. I am keeping all my odd moneys for that object, and I look to those books as the stand-by of my old age." Cicero's own compositions naturally passed into the workshop of his friend, and Atticus became his publisher. There was no copyright either of author or publisher, but the labour of Atticus' literary slaves doubtless brought in handsome returns to their master. Cicero commonly had the benefit of Atticus' criticisms while each work was in progress and looked with anxiety for his " red pencil marks." † His suggestions on the Second Philippic are known to us from Cicero's letter in reply. When Cicero has put the last hand to a book, he sends Atticus word " now you may begin copying out." ‡ When he resolves to cancel the first version of his *Academics* and to recast the dialogue with a fresh set of interlocutors, he writes,§ "You will easily console yourself for the loss involved in those copies which you have had written out to no purpose. The new version is more brilliant, more concise, better in every way." Sometimes these relations cause a momentary unpleasantness, as when Cicero finds that copies

---

* *Ad Att.*, i., 10, 4.

† *Ad Att.*, xvi., 11, 1.

‡ *Ad Att.*, iv., 13, 2.

§ *Ad Att.*, xiii., 13, 1.

of the *De Finibus* had got abroad without his leave before he had put in his final corrections, and before the presentation copy had been sent to Brutus to whom the treatise was dedicated.* Though Cicero was not aware of it, the same thing must have happened in the case of the *Academics*, for of the two surviving books one belongs to the revised and the other to the suppressed version. Boissier remarks,† that here we have publishing in its inchoate stage. Originally, whoever wished for a book must borrow it and get it copied at his own risk ; here we have a private gentleman employing his special facilities to make copies for sale among his friends ; in the next generation the Sosii family, the publishers of Horace, make the bringing out and selling of new books a regular trade.

Atticus survived Cicero eight years. With the triumph of Antony all Cicero's friends were in danger. Atticus had to fly for his life, and took refuge with Volumnius, an officer of
42 B.C.
Antony's, whom Atticus had himself concealed and protected, while his enemies were in power a few months previously. When however Antony heard of Atticus' kindness to Volumnius and to his own wife and children, he caused word to be sent that he had removed from the Proscription list not only his name but, for his sake, that of his friend Gellius Canus who was in hiding with him.‡ From that time

---

* *Ad Att.*, xiii., 21, 4.

† In an interesting little monograph entitled " Atticus, éditeur de Ciceron " (Paris, 1863). I am indebted to this work for the substance of the whole of the preceding paragraph.

‡ Nepos, *Vit. Att.*, 10.

forward Atticus was on intimate terms both with
Antony and Octavian ; true to his usual practice he
kept up his friendly relations with both till the end
of his own life, though at that time
the two were preparing for another   31 B.C.
civil war.   Meanwhile he had accepted the interest
of Antony * to obtain for his daughter Cæcilia Attica
the most splendid match in Rome. He married her
to Agrippa, the prime friend and coadjutor of Octavian ; and Atticus lived to see his little grand-
daughter Vipsania, the only issue of this marriage,
betrothed in her cradle † to Tiberius, the stepson
and destined successor of Augustus. Their child
again was Drusus, who was appointed the colleague
of his father Tiberius, and who but for his premature death would himself have been emperor of the
Romans.   The high society of Rome considered it
a blot on the nobility of Drusus, that there were men
alive who could remember his great-grandfather, a
simple Roman Knight. ‡

But to return to Atticus himself.   Can we forgive
the man, who after enjoying for half a century the
most endearing friendship with Cicero, could forget
all and live on as the genial companion and favoured
adherent of the men who had murdered him ? Atticus might plead that he had never failed Cicero
while he lived, and that he could do him no good
now, whereas there were living friends whom he
might still help and save.   When once his own

---

* Nepos, *Vit. Att.*, 12.
† Nepos, *Vit. Att.*, 19.
‡ Tac., *Ann.*, ii., 43, 7.

peace was made with the triumvirs, he was privileged
to offer a shelter to the proscribed, and his estate
in Epirus became a sort of unchallenged sanctuary.
After the battle of Philippi we find him at the same
work, and his biographer * mentions the names of
many republicans who owed their lives and fortunes
to Atticus.　For all this, the human instinct of
Homer is true, when he marks it as a grievous and
a dreadful thing that Priam must needs stoop to
what never man had borne to do before, and that
he should put his lips to the hand which had slain
his son. †　This instinct did not touch Atticus.　In
his youth he made himself so charming to Sulla,
that the proconsul, while he remained at Athens,
could never bear to have him out of his sight; he
refused Sulla's pressing invitation to come back with
him to Italy, on the ground that in the opposite
camp there were friends against whom he could not
lift a hand ‡; but of the dead friend Sulpicius Rufus,
whom Sulla had murdered, he took no account.　So
it was again in his old age; and better would it
have been for Atticus, if his name had remained on
the Proscription List.

Atticus cannot have been a selfish man, for he
spent his life in doing good to his friends, at the
cost of unceasing trouble and sometimes of serious
danger.　He must have been a lovable man, for
every one loved him, and such affection is not to be
gained except by a kindly and tender heart.　But

---

* Nepos, *Vit. Att.*, 11 and 12.

† Homer, *Iliad*, xxiv., 506.

‡ Nepos, *Vit. Att.*, 4.

AGRIPPA AND AUGUSTUS.
(*Cohen.*)

MARCUS AGRIPPA, SON-IN-LAW OF ATTICUS.
(*Cohen.*)

DRUSUS CÆSAR, SON OF EMPEROR TIBERIUS.
GREAT-GRANDSON OF ATTICUS.
(*Cohen.*)

lest they should do something to discredit the
family. It is needless to say that he confides his
alarms to Atticus. One such communication may
serve to illustrate the elder brother's uneasiness.
When Cicero quitted Cilicia after his year of governorship (50 B.C.), it was a difficult question, whom
to leave in charge of his province; he finally resolves
that he will not pass over his quæstor, officially the
second in command, in favour of the higher standing
and greater experience of his brother. In writing
to Atticus, after a long string of arguments for this
decision, he concludes *—"So much for reasons
which we can give to the world; next one for your
private ear. I should never have a moment's peace
for fear he should do something hasty or insolent or
indiscreet, for such things will happen in this world.
Then there is his son, a boy, and a boy with a
mighty good opinion of himself; what a vexation it
would be; and his father will not hear of sending
him home, and is displeased at your suggesting it.
Now as for the quæstor, I don't pretend to say
what he may or may not do, but then I plague myself much less about it."

On one occasion (see below, p. 342) a darker
cloud came between the brothers; but though the
evidence looks black against Quintus, the complete
reconciliation which followed allows us to hope that
what looked like baseness proved to have been only
ill-temper and indiscretion. In death they were not
divided; and Cicero's nephew, too, redeemed a

* *Ad Att.,* vi., 6, 4.

worthless life by a heroic end.　In the last dreadful days of the Proscription, the two brothers set forth together on their flight.　Quintus returned with his son to Rome to procure supplies for their journey, and the two fell into the power of the head-hunters. They died like worthy Romans, each striving to sacrifice his own life for the preservation of the other.*　Young Marcus, the son of Cicero, alone survived.　Like his uncle he was a gallant soldier, and he did good service both under Pompey and under Brutus ; but with the Civil War his credit ended ; thenceforth he was known chiefly as the hardest-headed toper in Rome.　Nevertheless in his case too " the whirligig of time brings in his revenges."　The pious historian † deemed it a clear case of the special interposition of Providence, that Marcus Tullius Cicero was consul in the latter part of the year 30 B.C., and that so it fell to his lot to announce in the Senate the tidings of the final defeat and death of Antony, and to decree the destruction of Antony's statues and the legal damnation of his name.

---

* Dio Cassius, xlvii., 10.

† Plutarch, *Cic.*, 49, 4.

CHAPTER IV.

CICERO AS A MAGISTRATE.

69–63 B.C.

WHILE the case against Verres was still pending Cicero had been 70 B.C. elected curule ædile, and in the year 66 B.C. he served the office of prætor. He had no difficulty in his contest for this magistracy, and he tells Atticus that he need not put himself out of the way to come to Rome to help him. There appear to have been two abortive attempts at a voting before the election was actually carried through, and on each occasion it was clear that Cicero was at the head of the poll.*

Meanwhile political agitations were astir which brought Cicero for the first time to the front as an orator dealing directly with the affairs of the State.

* *Pro Leg. Man.*, 1, 2.

6

* *Pro Leg. Man.*, 16, 54.
† Dio Cassius, xxxvi., 23, 5.

was passed. Pompey was then unanimously appointed to this great charge, and the Senate was
directed to give him all assistance in detail, an instruction which the Nobles did not now venture to
disregard.*

The public confidence in Pompey was marked by
an immediate relief in the corn-market, where famine
prices had been ruling, and this confidence was
abundantly justified by the result. Pompey made
his preparations instantly for a systematic campaign.
Personally and by aid of the fifteen lieutenants
whose services he commanded, he swept the Medi-
terranean from west to east, and drove back the
pirates into their Cilician harbours where he soon
compelled their surrender. Before the end of the
summer his task was accomplished, and the seas were
open. His triumph was due partly to the overwhelming force which he displayed at every point,
partly to the mildness and clemency with which he
received submission. Many of the freebooters
were glad to abandon resistance and to accept pardon
from Pompey's hands. He planted thousands of
them in Cilician colonies, and granted them lands,
that they might not be driven by poverty to resume
their old trade. The anxiety of the Cretans to
make their submission to Pompey, rather than to
Metellus, the proconsul of the island, nearly brought
on an armed collision between the two generals.

In an age when, as Cicero says, † " the Roman soldiers had destroyed more cities of their allies, which

---

* Dio Cassius, xxxvi., 37, 1.
† *Pro Leg. Man.*, 13, 38.

were assigned to them for winter-quarters, than cities
of the enemy, which they had taken by force of
arms," Pompey succeeded in protecting the peace-
able provincials against his troops. His own self-
restraint set them an example, and likewise enabled
him sternly to repress any outrages on the part of
his subordinates. The integrity and single-minded-
ness of the commander contributed not a little to his
great and startling success. "Whence came, do you
suppose, this incredible rapidity of movement? It
was not any preternatural strength in his oars-men,
nor any magic art in navigation, nor any new cur-
rents of wind which bore him so swiftly to the ends
of the earth. It was, that those impediments, which
check the progress of other commanders, never
stayed him. Greed never made him swerve from
his path for any prey, nor lust for any beauty, nor
any pleasant spot that he should loiter there, nor
any famous city that he should be curious about it,
nor any toil that he should repose after it; and for
the statues and pictures and all the adornments of
Grecian towns, which others think are made for them
to carry off, he would not so much as go to look at
them." *

The glories of Pompey's success are heightened
doubtless by all the skill of the orator; but the success itself was complete, indubitable, and overwhelming, and it was the more welcome from the long
period of distress and humiliation to which it put an
end. In the meantime affairs in the East were fast
approaching a serious crisis. Lucullus could conquer

* *Pro. Leg. Man.*, 14 40.

in the field, but he could not manage his troops, who were now in open mutiny against him. Acilius Glabrio had been sent to succeed Lucullus, and the soldiers considered this sufficient to discharge them of their allegiance; although the new commander delayed his appearance they refused to obey the old one. Mithridates with the assistance of Tigranes had again begun to make head against the Romans; he had cut off and overpowered a division of the Roman army under Triarius before Lucullus could come to its assistance; he had recovered the greater part of his kingdom of Pontus, and was pressing hard upon Cappadocia. It was evident that the Romans had acted prematurely when they decreed the recall of Lucullus under the belief that the war was practically over; and Glabrio and Marcius Rex, the governors on whom would fall the responsibility of defending Asia were obviously not strong enough for the task. Everything seemed to portend a great disaster in the East, and all eyes turned towards the victorious proconsul of the seas and coasts. Manilius (one of the tribunes of the year 66 B.C.) gave voice to the general wish by a proposal that the command against Mithridates should be assigned to Pompey.

A disturbance in Asia was not so much a matter of life and death to the mercantile class at Rome as was the blockade of the seas and coasts by the pirates. Still the interests of the Roman Knights both as merchants and as tax-farmers were seriously affected by the threatened danger, and they expected relief from the same hand which had just rescued them from the more pressing and intolerable calamity.

COIN OF CNÆUS POMPEIUS MAGNUS.
(*Babelon.*)

MITHRIDATES.
(*Duruy.*)

COIN OF CNÆUS POMPEIUS MAGNUS, AND ONE OF HIS LEGATES.
HEAD OF PALLAS.
(*Babelon.*)

They applied to Cicero, as their natural representative and champion, to support before
the People the proposal of Manilius.* 66 B.C.
Thus it was that for the first time Cicero, now
vested with the office of prætor, came forward on
the Rostra and lifted up his voice no longer to a
bench of jurors but to the assembled Roman People.

To the Nobles, this heaping of fresh honours and
powers on the head of the man they detested was a
bitter necessity, against which they rebelled to the
end. Had they possessed sagacity to penetrate the
character of Pompey, they might have known that
he could be safely trusted with these powers; but
they seem never to have truly gauged either his
greatness or his weakness. If he had been indeed a
man possessed with the vulgar ambition to make himself a despot, this last additional grant would, no
doubt, have concentrated in his hands force sufficient
for the overthrow of the free State. It might well
be argued that the Republic ought not to be thus
laid at the mercy of any citizen, however loyal. But
such arguments were discredited by having been
used the year before against the Gabinian law.
Cicero's rejoinder † is crushing : " What then is the
burden of Hortensius' speech ? That, if all power is
to be placed in the hands of one man, Pompey is the
most worthy recipient ; but that such a grant ought
not to be made to him or to anyone else. That
argument has grown stale ; it has been refuted, not
so much by words as by events. For you, Horten-

---

* *Pro Leg. Man.,* 2, 4.
† *Pro Leg. Man.,* 17, 52.

sius, who advise us now, employed last year all your wealth of words and all your marvellous faculty of oratory in a studied and weighty speech in the Senate against that worthy citizen Aulus Gabinius, when he proposed his law for appointing a single commander-in-chief against the pirates; and again from this place, where I now stand, you spoke at length against that law to the People. Well, suppose that —Heaven help us!—the Roman People had then listened to your counsels rather than to its own instinct of self-preservation and to the cogency of fact, should we this day be enjoying this glorious present, and this Empire which we hold over the wide world? For how could you call that an Empire, when legates and prætors and quæstors of the Roman People were taken captive? When neither the State nor its citizens could touch the supplies which should have come to them from all the provinces? when every sea was so closed to us that we could conduct no business, private or public, across the water? . . . And so the Roman People judged that you, Hortensius, and the rest who agreed with you, spoke in all sincerity what you believed to be for the best; but it preferred, when the public safety was at stake, to obey the call of its own sufferings rather than bow to your authority. And so one law, one man, one year has not only freed us from that distress and that reproach, but has made us at last to be in very truth what we claimed to be, lords by land and by sea over all peoples and nations."

The result could not be doubtful. The law of

Manilius was carried by acclamation, and Pompey
was invested with powers hardly inferior to those
afterwards enjoyed by Augustus. For the next five
years he remained in the East, marching, fighting,
and organising. Meanwhile affairs in the capital
went on their course without his active intervention; but amidst all the shifting scenes of parties
and all the conflicts of statesmen, the presence in
the background of the power of Pompey is never
forgotten; it is felt that whatever men may do at
home, his must be in the end the deciding will.

Among those who most envied the great position
of Pompey was his former colleague Crassus. Crassus was anxious to win for himself some exceptional
command which might hold in check the power of
his great rival. It seems probable that
Cæsar, who was now dazzling the world **65 B.C.**
with the extravagant splendour of his shows as
ædile, encouraged these aspirations of Crassus, and
that the democratic party, as a whole, followed
his lead. Though they had supported Pompey in
the struggle over the Gabinian and Manilian laws,
the democrats seem to have recognised more clearly
than the Optimates, that the great soldier would not
readily fall in with the plans of a revolutionary party.
Crassus and Cæsar looked to Egypt as the scene of
their * operations. Crassus was censor this year, and
he proposed to enrol Egypt in the list of provinces
on the ground that it had been left to the Roman
People by the Will of the last king. This king

---

* Plutarch, *Crass*, 13, 1. Suetonius, *Jul.*, 11.

(Ptolemy Alexander II.) had died sixteen years before, in 81 B.C.; but with characteristic hesitation the Senate had never declared whether they considered the bequest valid or whether they meant to accept it. Meantime an illegitimate member of the family, nicknamed Auletes, or "the Piper," had usurped the throne, where he had been tolerated, though never acknowledged, by Rome.* The plans of Crassus with regard to Egypt were frustrated by his brother censor Catulus and by Cicero,† who as a matter of course opposed all measures directed against Pompey. The most that Crassus could do was to induce the Senate to despatch a young partisan of his, named Cnæus Piso, with an extraordinary command to Spain, where he hoped that he might raise an army to serve as some sort of counterpoise to that of Pompey. This scheme too fell through, for Piso was assassinated, some said by partisans of Pompey, not long after his arrival in his province.

The mission of Piso to Spain is connected with a strange story in which we hear for the first time the name of that Lucius Sergius Catilina, who was destined two years later to cross Cicero's path with momentous consequences to them both. This "first conspiracy of Catiline," as it is called, is assigned to the end of the year 66 and the beginning of the year 65 B.C. Crassus and Cæsar are said to have been implicated in it. A plot which never came to overt acts

---

* See below, p. 102.

† Mommsen (*Rom. Hist.*, v., ch. 5) points out that the fragments of the speech "De Rege Alexandrino" prove it to have been delivered at this time.

is a fruitful theme for speculation, and modern writers have expended much ingenuity in discussing it. The evidence is so inconclusive, and the story, as told, contains so many contradictions and improbabilities, that I prefer to pass it over as wholly or almost wholly apocryphal. An assassination or a massacre, more or less, makes no great difference in our estimate of Catiline or even of Crassus; but it is satisfactory not to be obliged to fix this stain on the great name of Cæsar.

Having served the prætorship in 66 B.C. Cicero was eligible for the consulship of the year 63 B.C. For a year before the election, that is to say from about Midsummer 65 to Midsummer 64 B.C., his thoughts and efforts were constantly directed to the attainment of this great prize. From his own letters, and from his speeches on behalf of clients, and likewise from the " canvasser's pocket-book " of instructions (*Commentariolum Petitionis*), which Quintus Cicero * wrote out for his brother's use, we get a vivid picture of a contested election at Rome.

Questions of party or policy hold but a small place in these contests. There is nothing answering to the modern " caucus," and it is rarely that we hear of the selection of candidates who are to forward the interests of a party or can claim its united support. It was not even expected that a competitor for office should put forth any political creed or announce what " platform " he adopted ; rather it seems to have been considered proper for the aspirant to office,

* The genuineness of this little treatise has been questioned, but not, to my mind, on sufficient grounds.

while striving to produce the general impression of statesmanlike qualities, to efface his particular convictions as much as possible, and not to touch on the burning questions of the day * for fear of giving offence to any party or section in the State. The explanation of this strange divorce between politics and electioneering is not far to seek. In modern States there is what the French call " solidarity " between the different members of the executive government, so that votes at elections are practically given for a whole group of men united by common convictions under a common chief, who are to undertake, not only the business of administration, but the responsibility of initiative and the duty of guiding the policy of the State. But in the Roman Republic the function of the magistrate is much more limited. The Senate, and not the magistrate, advises and directs ; and, while he keeps within constitutional limits, the magistrate does not use his formal power of initiative in legislation except under the Senate's instructions. It is noticeable that the revolutionary faction at Rome, which never respected the constitutional rules and always, when it was strong enough, carried through its measures on the bare initiative of a magistrate, had an organisation more resembling that of modern parties, and tried to elect magistrates in order to carry out schemes of policy and legislation by their means. But this is the exception and not the rule. The regular practice is that, as each magistrate has under the constitution

* Q. Cicero, *De Pet. Cons.*, 13, 53.

a personal though limited power co-ordinate with that of his colleagues and not a joint power as member of a Board or Cabinet, so in the contest for magistracies each man is chosen separately and independently and each must " fight for his own hand." An election to the consulship is the advance of an individual in the official career, and the door of admission to the most dignified order in the State, not the triumph of a party or of a principle.   The aspirant does not wait to be adopted as the representative of a party, whether as the reward for past services or in hopes that he will carry out its political programme.   If to high nobility and connections he unites a decent character and tolerable capacity, he drifts naturally to the front *; if he be the son of a Roman Knight, destitute of the advantages of aristocratic lineage, he must force his way by personal exertions.   In either case it is a question " of men, not of measures."

The ideal Roman elector was supposed to look to the merit or " dignity," as it was called of the candidate, resting partly on a man's ancestry, partly on his own services to the State at home or abroad. But " merit " was always liable to be overridden by " favour " ; " each man who votes considers more frequently what claims the candidate has on him,

---

* When Domitius Ahenobarbus was cut out of his hopes of the consulship of 55 B.C. by the unexpected and irresistible candidature of Pompey and Crassus, Cicero exclaimed (*Ad Att.*, iv., 8, b. 2) : " What can be more annoying than for him, who has been designated for the consulship since his cradle, to miss it when his turn comes." After all Domitius was only put off till the next year.

than what claims he has on the commonwealth." *
To gain this personal favour was the first business of
the candidate. To this end he must be constantly
in evidence, and habituate the people to his presence; his face and manner must be familiar in their
daily surroundings. " I perceived," says Cicero of
himself, † " that the ears of the Roman People were
somewhat dull but their eyes quick and keen ; and
so I ceased to trouble myself as to what men might
hear of me from a distance, but took care that they
should see me in person. I lived in public, I fre-
quented the Forum, no one was ever kept from
seeing me by my porter or by my slumbers." In
apportioning their good-will the electors kept a
strict note of what each candidate had done or
was prepared to do in the way of amusing them.
"The Roman people dislikes private luxury, but
it loves public magnificence ; it has no liking for
sumptuous banquets, but it hates shabbiness and
ungraciousness." ‡ Cicero tells of one rich man who
was always unsuccessful in his candidatures, because
he was thought to have shirked the ædileship, and
of another of great family and reputation who

> " lent his ears
> To those budge doctors of the Stoic fur,"

and by an unlucky display of philosophic frugality
on a great occasion lost his chance of the prætor-

* *Pro Plancio*, 4, 10.

† This is the sequel to the story of Cicero's return after his Sicilian
quæstorship, see p. 22.

‡ *Pro Mur.*, 36, 76.

ship. On the other hand there was a feeling that
the man who had sufficiently dazzled the people by
his entertainments would never ask for their votes
in vain. It was on this account that the ædiles ran-
sacked the world for the gift of wild beasts and the
loan of works of art, that Cæsar displayed gladiators
in silver panoply, and that Scaurus invented his
movable theatres, which when the plays were over
were wheeled round, spectators and all, so as to
form an amphitheatre for the exhibition of the fighting. "You have no right," says Cicero,* "to cast
such scorn on the tastefulness of Murena's games or
the magnificence of his scenery, which were strong
points in his favour. Why should I observe, what
is obvious, that it is the populace and the crowd of
ignorant men who are so much caught by games?
There is no great wonder in that. But that is
enough for my argument; for the elections lie with
this same common multitude. . . . Men do enjoy
the games, you may take my word for it, and not
only those who frankly acknowledge their interest,
but those who pretend not to care. This was
brought home to me when I was a candidate, for I
too had the magnificence of a rival's scenery against
me; and if I, who had given three sets of games
myself, was staggered by those of Antonius, do you
suppose that you, who as it happened had not
given any, were not put at a disadvantage by these
very silver fittings of Murena's stage at which you
scoff?"

* *Pro Mur.*, 19 38.

In Cicero's own case it was mainly the influence
gained by his practice at the bar which won him the
consulship. His brother puts this in the forefront
of his advantages : " You will have your fame as an
orator to counterbalance your want of noble birth."
The Roman advocate was forbidden to accept a fee,
but he expected to be repaid by the personal exertions of the client and his friends at the next election ; " you must take care," writes Quintus, " that
they are as good as their word ; you must constantly
remind, ask, exhort and look after them, that they
may understand that they will never have another
opportunity of showing their gratitude." Each
brief undertaken thus formed a centre of influence
and of support for the successful pleader. We hear
much of the aid given by friends and partisans. In
Murena's contested election, for instance, his stepson had feasted his young comrades in the equestrian centuries, his chief engineer had hired seats at
the games for his fellow-tribesmen, a Vestal, his
kinswoman, had placed her stall at the disposal of
the candidate. These proceedings, so Cicero argued
with success, did not come within " the blow of the
law " ; " all such observances count among the
dues of friendship, the gratifications of the humbler
classes, the attentions looked for from a candidate."

The Roman elector expected to be asked and even
entreated for his vote. He was not displeased if
he were asked more than once. This required great
personal exertions on the part of the candidate and
his friends. Quintus urges his brother never to be
out of the way, and never to give anyone the oppor-

tunity to say " that, so far as he was concerned, you might have had what you wished, if he had been asked by you and asked with earnestness and insistence." Nearly a year before the actual election there commenced the process of preliminary canvassing, *prensatio* or " hand-shaking," as it was called. It was a great point for the candidate to be able to address each voter by his name, and to aid him in this he had specially trained slaves, whose business it was to make themselves acquainted with the faces of the citizens and to whisper the name of each in his master's ear as he approached him. " O fie! for shame, Cato!" exclaims Cicero, as he banters the precisian statesman who is trying to upset the election of Murena,* " is it possible that you can do such a thing? are you not deceiving? are you not using your slave's memory to act a lie to your fellow-citizens? is this consistent with principle? can such a practice bear to be weighed in your philosophic scales?" †

As " nothing succeeds like success," it is important for a candidate to produce the impression that he is assured of overwhelming support. He must lose no opportunity of advertising his strength, and for this purpose must collect an imposing array of " followers." To take part in such a following is an attention which the humblest can offer, and on that ground Cicero defends the practice against Cato's strictures. ‡ " ' What need is there,' says Cato, ' for

---

* See below, p. 131.

† *Pro Mur.*, 36, 77.

‡ *Pro Mur.*, 34, 70.

7

followers?' What a question to put to me of all
people, 'what need is there' for that which we
have all of us always practised! The one opportunity, which men of humble rank have of earning
the thanks and repaying the kindnesses of those in
our station, is the service and attendance which they
give in our candidatures. Senators and Roman
Knights cannot spend all the day in following about
their friends when canvassing, and no one expects it
of them. If they call at your house each morning,
and occasionally escort you down to the Forum and
honour you with their company for one turn along
the colonnade, you think that they have shown
ample consideration and observance. Constant attendance is the special task of our humbler friends,
whose time is more at their own disposal, and of
these a kindly and charitable man is sure to have no
lack. Do not be so anxious then, Cato, to rob the
lower classes of their sole chance of showing their
dutifulness; allow those, who look to us for all sorts
of favours, to retain one favour which they can confer on us. If such a one has nothing to give but his
single vote, that seems a petty boon ; if he wishes
to canvass for us, he has no influence. As they say
themselves, they cannot speak for us, they cannot
give security for us, they cannot invite us to their
houses; such attentions they expect to receive from
us, and they think that their only means of acknowledgment is this personal service."

All this elaborate machinery of canvassing was
worked with untiring assiduity by Cicero when he
stood for the consulship. It may be doubted, how-

ever, whether he would have had an easy victory, if
he had not been aided by an external circumstance.
The candidature of Catiline and Antonius began to
alarm the constitutional party. Already during the
early summer of the year 64 B.C. Catiline had begun to
lay the foundations of a desperate conspiracy against
the State. His plans got abroad through the vapourings of one of his associates, a foolish young spendthrift, to his mistress. The woman gave information
to the government, and the Nobles, who had hitherto
looked askance on Cicero's candidature, now withdrew their opposition.* Cicero was returned by acclamation at the top of the poll, and Antonius headed
Catiline by a few votes for the second place. Caius
Antonius was a man of high birth but of indifferent
character and small reputation, who had been closely
connected with Catiline, and who was supposed to
be ready to give at least a passive support to his
plans. Cicero's first effort was to detach him from
the conspiracy, and he purchased his support by
giving up to him the lucrative province of Macedonia.
Thus fortified Cicero entered on his consulship on
the 1st of January 63 B.C.

The year began with an attempt on the part of
the democrats to renew the efforts, which they had
made under the guidance of Crassus
two years before, to win for themselves   63 B.C.
some base of operations independent of the power
of Pompey. This time, the scheme took the well-
known form of an Agrarian Law. A tribune of the

---

* Sallust, *Cat.*, 23.

plebs, Publius Servilius Rullus, proposed that there should be a great distribution of land to the poorer citizens. But where was the land to be found ? As the result, partly of the legislation of the Gracchi, partly of the reactionary measures which had followed their death, the whole of the public land which had formerly been held by the great squatters had ceased to belong to the State. It was now the property of individual Romans, and the agrarian agitators of the Roman Republic, though they often disregarded equitable rights of occupancy hallowed by long prescription, never mentioned the confiscation of what was legally private property. Some fresh public land had indeed been provided for this generation through the appropriation by the State of the lands of towns and individuals that had stood against Sulla, and the occupiers of these lands might well fear eviction. But Rullus protested that he had no such design. He even introduced a clause making all such land the absolute property of the present occupiers, or else paying them its money value in case they preferred to get rid of it. There remained only a small district round Capua, which, because the tenants of this land paid a rack-rent to the State, had escaped distribution in the age of the Gracchi. This Rullus proposed to parcel out, though the Treasury could ill bear the loss of the rent.

But this was the most modest feature of the bill. Rullus' commissioners were further empowered to sell the whole of the property of the Roman People beyond the seas, in order with the money so obtained to buy land in Italy for distribution. The project seems so extraordinary that we could hardly believe it, if the very words of this clause had not been preserved to us by Cicero.* " *All lands, places, buildings* —what is there besides ? Well there is much property in slaves, cattle, gold, silver, ivory, raiment, furniture and so forth. What are we to say ? Did he think it would not look modest if he named all these things ? He has never shown any signs of such scrupulosity. What then ? He thought it would be tedious, and feared that he might omit something; so he simply added, *or anything else.* Everything therefore outside Italy, which has become the property of the Roman People in the first consulship of Sulla or since that date, is ordered to be sold by the decemvirs. I say, Romans, that by this clause all peoples, nations, provinces and kingdoms are granted away and committed to the sole authority, judgment, and power of the decemvirs. For first I would ask, what place in the world is there of which they may not assert that it has become the property of the Roman People ? For when the person who asserts has the power of pronouncing judicially on the question, where need he draw the line in his assertions ? It will be convenient to maintain that Pergamus, Smyrna, Tralles, Ephesus, Miletus, Cyzicus, in fact the whole of Asia, which has been recovered since that consulship, has become the property of the Roman People. . . . Then there is Alexandria and the whole of Egypt; how secretly it is smuggled

* *Contra Rullum*, ii., 15, 38, *et seq.*

in, how all mention of it is avoided, how cunningly it is handed over to the decemvirs.   You all of you know, that it is said that this kingdom became the property of the Roman People under the Will of King Alexander.   Now on this matter I, as consul of the Roman People, not only pronounce no judgment, but decline to express any opinion.   For the question seems to me too difficult, I will not say to decide, but even to discuss.   I see that there are some who assert that such a Will was made, and that the Senate committed itself to the acceptance of the inheritance, when after the death of Alexander it sent envoys to Tyre to claim possession of moneys which he had deposited there.   I remember to have heard Lucius Philippus repeatedly assert this in the Senate; and I take it that almost all are agreed that the person who occupies the throne at present is not of royal birth and has none of the qualities of a King.   On the other side it is maintained, that no such Will exists, that it is unbecoming in the Roman People to seem to be grasping at the possession of kingdoms; that our citizens will be tempted to migrate to that country on account of the richness of the soil and the abundance which reigns there.   Well, on this momentous question who is to be judge but Rullus and the rest of the commissioners his colleagues ? and a famous decision they will make of it surely ! "

Thus under cover of an Agrarian Law the democratic leaders seem to have designed to secure for themselves the control of the powerful province, which would as they hoped enable them to treat

with Pompey on equal terms. This unlimited power
of raising money was supplemented by an equally
wide discretion in spending it.   The decemvirs were
empowered to buy lands and plant colonies in whatever part of Italy they chose, or rather, says Cicero,
to occupy the strategical points of the country with
their garrisons, "keen partisans, eager for violence,
ready for rebellion, who at a word from the decemvirs can be armed against the citizens and let loose
for slaughter." *

Respecting the "Ten Kings," as Cicero calls them,
who were to be set up by the law, two things were
certain : first, that Rullus would, under the machinery
proposed, practically have the nomination of them ;
and secondly, that Pompey was not to be one of
them.   While other existing magistrates were eligible, Pompey was excluded, almost by name, through
a clause which required the personal appearance of
each candidate in the Forum ; "and can you doubt,"
says Cicero, † "that certain persons are seeking for
domination and supremacy over the whole State,
when you see that they keep out that man who, as
they plainly perceive, will be the defender of your
liberties ? "

The bill as it stood was fairly open to Cicero's
strictures.   At the same time we need not suppose
that its promoters were so foolish as to intend to
bring about any immediate conflict with Pompey.
If the bill had been carried, Cæsar would doubtless
have persuaded his colleagues on the commission to

* *Contra Rullum*, ii., 30, 82.

† *Contra Rullum*, ii., 10, 25.

avoid carefully any interference with Asia Minor or Syria or the Greek islands. Possibly he might have made it a merit with Pompey, to refrain from any action which could trench on this, Pompey's undoubted sphere of influence. At any rate the game of the democratic party was to allow Pompey to settle the East as he pleased and to return quietly to Rome, while they established a rival power for themselves in Egypt or elsewhere. Meanwhile they would have ample means at their disposal to provide for their more hungry partisans, and so to put off any premature attempts at revolution.

It may be doubted whether Cicero himself fully understood the plan on which Cæsar was working when he encouraged Rullus to propose this law. The main lines of that plan can now be clearly traced by the light of Cæsar's subsequent action in Gaul; but at the moment they were not so obviously discernible. In the meantime, however, it was quite clear that a blow was being aimed at Pompey, and Cicero justly thought that it was his first business to parry that blow. If the main object of the bill was dangerous to the future peace of the State and the stability of the constitution, the most tempting points for criticism were those which seemed to portend a speedy collision with Pompey. On these Cicero directed his main attack, and the bill was so loosely and clumsily drawn that it was easy to construe its provisions as an outrage on Pompey's dignity. All the sources of revenue with which Pompey had enriched the State, all the kingdoms and cities which he had conquered, and whose affairs he was in the

act of regulating, might be claimed by the rival
power. The very ground on which Pompey was
encamped might be sold under his feet by virtue of
this law. " Pompey," he says,* " is determined that
whatever you decide, he will consider that he must
bear it ; but he will take good care, you may be
sure, that whatever you cannot bear, he will not
permit you to be compelled to bear it longer than
you please."

" Are these," Cicero asks in another place, † " the
plans of sober men or the dreams of wine-bibbers?
Are they the calculations of sense, or the extrava-
gances of lunacy? " The answer doubtless is, that
the promoters of the bill can have hoped to carry a
scheme, manifestly directed against Pompey, only
on the supposition that he was too far off to trouble
himself about their machinations, and that his friends
in Rome would not honestly and fearlessly maintain
his cause. In this they were disappointed ; Cicero
at once came forward, and in a series of spirited and
effective speeches exposed the nature and object of
the scheme. He directs many arguments against
the promoters, but one is really sufficient, namely
that the bill is a studied attack on the position of
Pompey ; with the name of Pompey he always
couples the liberty and the greatness of Rome. He
sums up the whole matter at the end of the third
speech—" Is any one of you disposed for violence,
for crime, for massacre? Not one. And yet it is
for men who will do all these things that the land of

---

* *Contra Rullum,* ii., 23, 62.
† *Contra Rullum,* i., 1, 1.

Campania and the great city of Capua is reserved.
An army is being got together against yourselves,
against your liberty, against Cnæus Pompeius. Capua
is set up against this city ; bands of desperate ruffians
against you ; the ten chiefs against Pompey."

When once the bill was put in its true light, as
an act of war on Pompey, public opinion declared
against it. Cicero was listened to with marked favour by the multitude.—" They gave up to him,"
says Pliny,* " the Agrarian Law, that is to say, their
own bread." One of the other tribunes announced
that he would veto the bill, and its chances were
so hopeless that Rullus presently withdrew it of his
own accord.

The next six months may be passed lightly over.
The consul is recorded to have pacified by a conciliatory speech the popular resentment
against Roscius Otho, who four years
previously had restored to Cicero's friends, the
Knights, their reserved seats in the theatre. A little
later we find him resisting an attempt to remove the
political disabilities with which Sulla had affected
the children of those who had been put to death in
the great Proscription. Cicero acknowledged that
the proposal was humane and righteous, but he succeeded in persuading not only the people but the
very victims of the existing law themselves, † that it
was ill-timed. Strange to say, the same considerations seem to have kept Cæsar during his consulship
and the triumvirs during their period of supremacy

January to June.

---

* Pliny, *Hist. Nat.*, vii., 30, 116.
† Pliny, *Hist. Nat.*, vii., 30, 116.

from meddling with Sulla's arrangement, and it was
not until the year 49 B.C., while the second Civil War
was in progress, that this relic of the first was removed.

Cicero does not appear to have taken any part
against a harmless but popular measure proposed by
the tribune Labienus, which restored to the people
under certain restrictions the power of electing the
members of the great priestly colleges. The first
effect of the change was to place in strong light the
overwhelming personal popularity of Cæsar. The
supreme dignity of Pontifex Maximus was now
vacant, and Cæsar, though as yet he had served no
office higher than the ædileship, appeared as a candidate, and was elected by a great majority over
the heads of all the most distinguished members of
the senatorial party, including the aged and revered
Catulus.

Labienus and Cæsar were next found united in a
fanciful project, which seems to have been intended
as a sort of manifesto of principle on the side of the
democratic party. Thirty-seven years previously
the tribune Saturninus had been put to death in
consequence of an armed riot during which he had
seized on the Capitol. The Senate by special decree
had empowered the Consul Marius to act against
him, and on the strength of this decree Saturninus
and his associates had been overpowered and massacred. Cæsar and Labienus now affected to re-
habilitate the memory of Saturninus and to protest
against such proceedings on the part of the Senate,
by bringing to trial an aged senator named Caius

Rabirius, who had avowedly taken part in the attack
on Saturninus, and who, as his accusers asserted
(though he seems to have proved the contrary), had
actually struck the fatal blow. For the purpose of
this trial an imposing though somewhat childish display of constitutional antiquarianism was provided.
On the one side there was furbished up the "rugged
formula of the old law," * which was said to have been
invented by King Tullus Hostilius for the trial of
that Horatius who stabbed his sister for lamenting
her lover, the fallen champion of Alba. On the
other side an equally obsolete contrivance enabled
the prætor Metellus Celer to break up the assembly
by striking the red flag on the Janiculum, which in
old times was the sign that the Etruscans were at
the gates, and that the burghers must run to arms.
Cicero spoke to the people on behalf of Rabirius;
but the proceedings were not intended to be very
serious; the assembly was allowed to disperse, and
Labienus and Cæsar, though they might have brought
on the case again another day, let the matter quietly
drop.

Only two legislative measures bore the super-
scription of Cicero's name as consul. The first was
a law heightening the penalties for corrupt practices
at elections. An opposing advocate once wittily
suggested that Cicero must have passed it "in order
to furnish his perorations with more touching appeals
to the feelings of the jurors." † The second measure
relates to honorary or, as they were called, "free

* " Lex horrendi carminis," Livy, i., 26.
† *Pro Plancio,* 34, 83.

embassies," which enabled a senator to travel in the provinces at the public expense. A law was passed by Cicero limiting the power of the Senate to grant such commissions. They were now never to be extended beyond the period of one year. Cicero tells us * that he wished to abolish them altogether, but was thwarted by the opposition of a tribune.

I have hitherto noticed those actions of Cicero, as consul, which had no direct bearing on the Catilinarian conspiracy. So far we have the record of a useful and creditable but by no means a brilliant year of office. We must now turn to the more stirring events which have made Cicero's consulship famous in the history of the world.

* *De Leg.*, iii., 8, 18.

CHAPTER V.

CICERO AND CATILINE.

63 B.C.

IN describing the conspiracy of Catiline we lie under one grave disadvantage. Atticus was by Cicero's side throughout this period, and no letters passed between them; and so the detail of events, as they appeared from day to day, is wanting. We cannot, as in each subsequent crisis of Cicero's life, reconstruct an absolutely trustworthy picture of his plans, his hopes, and his fears. We cannot say positively what Cicero knew or believed about Catiline at the moment, but only what the consul chose to announce to the world. Our main authority is the collection of four speeches which Cicero delivered to the Senate or the people during the last two months of his consulship. The accounts of the later writers, Appian, Plutarch, and Dio Cassius, are probably founded to some extent on Cicero's own story as told

in the lost treatise on his consulship.   Besides these
we possess the monograph of Sallust on the Catilinarian conspiracy.   This as the work of a contemporary
and a Cæsarian is of especial value.   We have the
satisfaction of finding that the writer on the Cæsarian
side gives substantially the same account of the conspirators and their plans as that which we gather from
Cicero's own speeches.   In presence of this agreement
we may feel pretty confident that we have a story
trustworthy and correct in its main outlines.

Lucius Sergius Catilina was a member of an ancient
patrician family which had been famous in the early
days of the Republic, but which had long fallen into
obscurity.   None of its members had attained the
consulship during the last two hundred years, and
the name of the Sergii is scarcely mentioned in the
history of the period when Rome was conquering
and ruling the world.

During the Civil War Catiline had been a partisan
of Sulla and had taken an active part in the bloody
work of the Proscription.   His brother was one of the
victims, and a dark story ran that the infamy which
Lepidus earned in later years had been anticipated
in the first Proscription, and that Catiline was himself responsible for the insertion of his kinsman's
name in the list.*   Since then he had risen through
the various magistracies till he attained the government of Africa as pro-prætor.   After his return he
was accused of extortion on evidence which Cicero,
though he thought of accepting a brief for the

---

* Plutarch, *Sulla.* 22, 2.

defence, evidently believed to be overwhelming.* He was acquitted by the jury, but according to Quintus Cicero † the verdict cost him a ruinous sum in bribes. At any rate we find him immediately afterwards overwhelmed with debt, and ready for desperate methods of extrication. He had by this time completely deserted his old party and was among the most violent members of the opposition. The hopes which the democrats had of useful service from him are attested by Cæsar's action when in 64 B.C. he brought to trial the assassins of Sulla's Proscription. Everyone knew that Catiline had been a ring-leader amongst these; but Cæsar, who throughout his life let by-gones be by-gones whenever he had any present purpose to serve, screened him from punishment. In private life Catiline was known to be both dissolute and unscrupulous. He had many of the qualities necessary for a revolutionary chief—a powerful frame, a fearless temper, great capacity for endurance, a ready tongue, and a faculty of adapting himself to his company and winning familiarity with good and bad alike. At the same time he was hopelessly deficient, as the event showed, in the most essential qualifications of a leader, the cool head, the keen eye for the real forces to be dealt with, and the power of co-ordinating means to ends.

We have seen that in the years of Pompey's absence the democratic party under its recognised leaders Cæsar and Crassus was engaged in fruitless

---

* *Ad Att.*, i., 1, 1, " si judicatum erit meridie non lucere."
† *De Pet. Cons.*, 3, 10.

attempts to establish itself as a power independent both of the Senate and of Pompey. This was the object of the attempt of Crassus, as censor, on Egypt in 65 B.C. and of the Agrarian Law of Rullus in 63 B.C. It must be supposed that Cæsar and his associates counted on the political shortsightedness of both Pompey and the Senate to frustrate any cordial action between the two until the new power should have grown too strong to be successfully resisted. A consummation closely resembling this actually resulted some years later when Cæsar established himself in Gaul, so that the project must be deemed not wholly chimerical, if only the first step could be safely taken. This first step was however prevented on both occasions, by Catulus and by Cicero. In the meantime the democrats had striven hard to gain possession of the consulship. Catiline and Antonius were supported by all the efforts of the party against Cicero in 64 B.C. and Catiline again at the next year's elections. An active and unscrupulous man like Catiline, once possessed of the consulship, would have been able to help forward the long-cherished schemes of the party, and if at the same time he could have found means to shake off the burden of his debts and to provide for himself in the future, he might easily have been induced to confine his operations within the limits prescribed by his more sober coadjutors. Crassus and Cæsar could have kept Catiline quiet by flinging him a rich province to worry, just as Cicero converted Catiline's associate Caius Antonius by the gift of Macedonia.

The frustration of these plans brought to light the

8

weak point in the position of the democrats. They
had within their ranks men who could not afford to
wait, to whom the want of immediate success meant
absolute ruin; these could not be withheld from attempts which in their failure brought discredit on
the democratic party, but which, if they had succeeded, would have destroyed that party altogether
and profited no one but Pompey. At the head of
this desperate class was Catiline himself, and around
him were other men of high family whom reckless
luxury and extravagance had brought to the verge
of bankruptcy and ruin. If these men could see
their way clear to a political revolution, they might
hope to restore their fortunes in a general scramble
for the good things of the government; but, if they
were debarred from this chance, they were resolved
to fall back on counsels of despair, and, as Catiline
afterwards put it, " to extinguish the fire which would
consume them by bringing down the roof-tree on the
top of it." * The evil precedents of Marius and of
Sulla appealed with fatal seductiveness to these
ruined aristocrats. A civil war, a massacre, a proscription, a confiscation appeared things possible and
hopeful. They could point to men who in the late
troubles had suddenly emerged from poverty to
enormous wealth and from obscurity to domination.†
Their power of judgment was impaired, partly by the
dazzling contrast of these hopes with their present
embarrassments, partly by the deluding atmosphere
of secret cabals in which the vapourings and day-

---

* Sallust, *Cat.*, 31, 9.   Cicero, *Pro. Mur.*, 25, 51.
† Sallust, *Cat.*, 37, 6.

dreams of one hour are apt to become the fixed
ideas of the next, and above all perhaps by the im-
patience of weakness which, when once men have
begun to conspire, makes them feel that suspense is
intolerable and that something, no matter what, must
be done. To eyes so blinded the occasion seemed
not unfavourable. The noble conspirators, though
their fortunes were hopelessly undermined, still kept
up the show of wealth and profusion, and could
command the services of armed slaves, of clients and
of retainers. Rome was full as Sallust tells us * of
fugitive rascals from all the world; the remnant of
the sufferers by the last revolution likewise lingered
on there in hopeless poverty. These would be ready
enough for deeds of bloodshed; and the mass of the
populace crowded together in a great city without
industry, pauperised by doles of State corn, puffed
up with the conceit that they were the masters of
the world and yet painfully conscious that they
gained little either in comfort or in dignity by their
pre-eminence, would, it was thought, welcome a disturbance in which they might hope to gain, while at
the worst they had nothing to lose. In the country
towns of Italy the conspirators though they might
number in their ranks some Italians of good position † who had been drawn into the vortex of fashionable life in the capital, would find little favour
with the rank and file of the citizens, who were
sounder and more industrious than the masses in
Rome itself; but they counted that the country-folk

* Sallust, *Cat.*, 37, 5.
† Sallust, *Cat.*, 37, 4.

would be slow to move, and that they would have
time to strike the great blow before a sufficient force
could be raised against them.   On the other hand
Sulla had stored up for them an ample supply of
revolutionaries in the very men whom he had intended to be the guardians of his government.   The
veterans * of his Asiatic army were richly rewarded
from the spoils of the conquered party, and were
planted out as colonists over Italy : it was supposed
that their interests had been effectually bound up
with the maintenance of Sulla's ordinances.   But
these professional soldiers seem not to have made
good farmers.   Some of them had sold their holdings and gone to swell the pauper population of
Rome, others remained, having squandered their
donatives and involved themselves in debt, and
these naturally looked for a fresh call to civil war as
the best means of restoring their fortunes.

While these resources lay ready to the hand of the
conspirators, the forces at the disposal of the government were invitingly weak.   There was no garrison and no tolerable police force in the city of Rome ;
the officers and public slaves who attended the
magistrates might be overpowered by a resolute gang
of assassins, especially if their attention could be
distracted by the alarm of fire in various parts of the
city.   The only efficient army of the State was far
away with Pompey in Asia, and all the troops available were a few cohorts in Cisalpine Gaul and the
scanty retinue of two commanders, Lucius Lucullus

---

* Sallust, *Cat.*, 28, 4.

and Marcius Rex, who were waiting for their triumphs outside the city gates.

On these considerations the schemes of this party within a party were based. A military force was to be raised in Upper Italy which was to advance as quickly as might be on the city; its approach was to be the signal for fire-raising within the walls, which would, it was hoped, give the opportunity for a sudden assault. Catiline was to seize the government with the same title of consul, which Marius and Cinna had borne, there was to be a general abolition of debt and recall of condemned criminals, and the old story of massacre and confiscation was to be renewed.

It will now be clear how widely the plans of Catiline differed from those of Cæsar. The revolution projected by the great leaders of the democratic party was an elaborate and far-reaching scheme. It recognised the fact that Rome was no longer the chief strategical point, and that the first requisite was a base of operations in the provinces. A remote country such as Spain or Egypt would be the best fitted for the silent equipment of an armed force which might eventually co-operate with partisans at home. To train an army for civil war and generals fit to command it must needs occupy, if not so long a stretch of time as Cæsar afterwards employed in the same task in Gaul, at least several years of hard fighting with enemies who were to be sought on the frontiers of the Empire. In the meantime the rival interests in Rome were to be alarmed as little as possible; the Senate and Pompey were to be left to

counteract each other by their mutual jealousies, and
the Roman Knights were to be kept quiet by being
allowed to see Crassus, the greatest of all the
moneyed men, at the head of the movement.
Viewed as a plan of revolution, the defect in this
scheme lay not in the general lines on which it was
framed, but in the great difficulty of getting it
launched. Catiline's plan on the other hand presented a fatal facility in its initial stage, but it led up
necessarily to a result the very contrary of that
which Cæsar hoped to accomplish. Its first effect
was to produce a cordial union between the Senate
and the equestrian order. Now one of two
things must happen : either these two united would
be strong enough to deal with Catiline—this of
course was the actual result,—or else the senatorial
government would collapse and Catiline would be
able to carry out his full programme and establish in
Rome a revolutionary government of the same
bloody type as that of Marius and Cinna. The conspirators forgot that in one essential point their
situation differed from that of which Cinna had
taken advantage. The revolutionary movement of
87 B.C. had been possible because Sulla and his
army were engaged with Mithridates. It took Sulla
three years to dispose of his great enemy, and until
this was done, happen what might in Italy, he could
not stir.* A three years' respite was thus allowed to
the new government, and it was only by its own folly
that it did not use the time in building up a military

---

* See above, pp. 14 and 28.

and political power against which Sulla would have
found it hard to contend. But what chance was
there of a similar respite for Catiline? Mithridates
was already driven from Asia and Pompey was ready
to set sail immediately. A massacre in Rome would
have brought the Nobles thronging to his camp; he
would have returned with his veteran army; his
name would have rallied all Italy to his standard,
and the hasty levies of the insurgents, led by men
not one of whom had ever commanded an army in
the field, would have been swept like chaff before
him.* The difference between Cæsar and Catiline
reminds one of the choice placed before the peasant
of the Scottish legend, who found himself in the
presence of a magic sword and horn, and whose fate
was to depend on whether he first drew the sword
or first blew the horn. Cæsar avoided the challenge
to Pompey until he had provided himself with a
weapon. The fate of Catiline, even had his first
effort succeeded, would have been that of the peasant in the tale, who was torn in pieces by the spirits
whom his blast evoked—

> " Woe to the fool that ever he was born,
>   That did not draw the sword before he blew the horn."

It is obvious that Crassus, however willing he may
have been to use Catiline as a tool in his designs
against his rival Pompey, can have had no sympathy
with his schemes of national bankruptcy, and we

---

* Their plan for holding Pompey in check was in keeping with the
folly of the whole movement; they dreamed of pouncing on Pompey's
children and having them for hostages.—See Plutarch, *Cic.*, 18, 1.

may be sure that Cæsar was no less averse to a movement which would have united the Senate and
Pompey, the constitutional and the military power,
once for all firmly together, and would have post-
poned indefinitely the chances of revolution.   Both
Crassus and Cæsar got wind of the plot which was
formed inside the ranks of their party.   They did their
best at first to gain for Catiline an official position
which would have enabled him to dispense with actual
armed rebellion; when this failed and it was manifest that the conspirators would proceed with their
further designs, Cæsar * and Crassus both warned
Cicero of the danger and gave him such information
as they possessed about the plot.   The subsequent
utterances of both may be cited in evidence of the
reality of the conspiracy and the imminence of the
danger.   When Cæsar fourteen years later wrote of the
"*ultimum Senatus Consultum*" that the State had
never had recourse to it saving when "the city was
almost in flames and the audacity of malefactors was
striking terror into the hearts of all men," † he must
have been understood by all Rome to refer to Catiline.   Crassus is still more explicit.   A year after
Catiline's death he declared in the Senate : ‡ "I owe
it to Cicero that I am a senator, that I am a citizen,
that I am a free man, that I draw the breath of life;
whensoever I look on my wife, on my home, or on
my country, I behold a blessing for which I am
indebted to him."

---

* Suet., *Jul.*, 17.   For Crassus see below, p. 123.

† Cæsar, *Bell. Civ.*, 1, 5.

‡ *Ad Att.*, i., 14, 3.

The election of consuls for the next year, which probably took place in July, gave the first opportunity for violence. Catiline was once more a candidate. Manlius, a veteran centurion of Sulla's army and a confederate of Catiline, came to Rome with a gang of his associates to organise a riot at the polls, in the course of which the consul was to be assassinated.* In view of this danger Cicero obtained a decree temporarily postponing the elections, and next day (the day for which the polling was originally fixed) he publicly questioned Catiline in the Senate † with regard to seditious and inflammatory words which he was reported to have addressed to his partisans. Catiline showed a bold front: he replied "that there were two bodies in the State, the one weak with a feeble head, the other strong without a head; to this he would take good care that a head should be supplied." Cicero thought that the challenge should be taken up at once, but he could not on this occasion carry the Senate with him. The resolutions passed were mild and colourless, and Catiline strode forth from the Senate-house triumphant.

Cicero's own precautions proved, however, to be sufficient. When the day of election arrived, he appeared as returning officer on the Campus Martius, guarded by a strong body of friends, and the gleam of a corselet which could be seen between the folds of the consul's civic gown proclaimed his danger to the world. The popular feeling was deeply stirred; Catiline saw that an attack on that

---

* Plutarch, *Cic.*, 14, 2.
† *Pro Mur.*, 25, 51.

day would be hopeless, and kept quiet. The voters gave their voices against him, and Silanus and Murena were elected consuls. Manlius returned to Etruria; the last hopes of the confederates for a triumph by means of simple riot or assassination were over, and they fell back on their reserved project of military insurrection. During the next months their forces were silently enlisted in Upper Italy; by the month of October they were ready for action.

On the 21st of October * Cicero announced in the Senate that open rebellion was imminent, and that the 27th was fixed as the day for the rising. Next day (the 22d) the statement of the consul was taken into consideration, and the Senate resolved to proclaim that a state of civil war had begun, † thus recognising in the consul the power to use extreme measures of resistance, which were permissible only when the commonwealth was in danger. This " Extreme Decree," as it was termed, was expressed in the words, " Let the consuls see to it that the State takes no harm." Under this modest form the magistrate was commissioned to exercise, though always on his own responsibility, whatever force he might deem necessary for the salvation of the Republic. While Cicero guarded Rome, the consul Antonius and the prætor Metellus Celer were directed to take the field against the insurgents. Manlius appeared in arms, just as Cicero had announced on the 27th of October at Fæsulæ in

---

* Cicero, *Cat.* i., 3, 7.

† The precise date (October 22d) of the *Ultimum Senatus Consultum* is fixed by the note of Asconius in Cicero's *In Pisonem.*

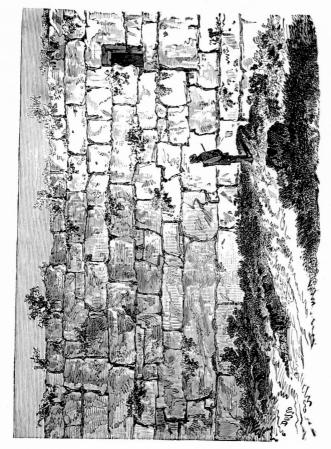

WALLS OF FÆSULÆ (FIESOLE).

(*During.*)

Etruria. Catiline had planned a massacre of the nobles in Rome on the next day * (the 28th), and had intended to seize the stronghold of Præneste † three days later on the 1st of November. Cicero announced both projects to the Senate beforehand, and completely frustrated the attempts. So far he had checked the enemy at every point, but he had not succeeded, as yet, in forcing him to disclose himself.

Though the forces of his confederates were actually in the field and Catiline had arranged shortly to put himself at their head, he thought proper to occupy the intervening days with a clumsy display of innocence, offering himself to the custody of one magistrate after another, and finally taking up his quarters with Marcus Metellus, whom he begged to keep watch over his movements. ‡ Cicero tells us § that down to the time when Catiline actually joined the rebels in Etruria—" there are men in this House, who either do not see what is hanging over us, or seeing it pretend not to see, who have nourished the hopes of Catiline by the mildness of their proposals, and have given strength to the new-born conspiracy by refusing to believe in it ; and there are many outside, not only of the bad but of the simple, who have followed their lead, and who, if I had taken extreme

---

* Cicero, *Cat.* i., 3, 7.   This is perhaps the occasion on which, as Plutarch (*Cic.*, 15, 1) asserts, Crassus brought to Cicero a number of letters which had been left at his house, warning him and other senators to keep out of the way.   The story closely resembles that of the letter to Lord Monteagle about the Gunpowder Plot.

† Cicero, *Cat.* i., 3, 8.

‡ Cicero, *Cat.*, i., 8, 19.

§ Cicero, *Cat.*, i., 12, 30.

measures against Catiline, would have called my action cruel and tyrannical." Something like a dramatic exposure of the childish pretences of Catiline was desired by the consul, and for this his adversary soon gave him an occasion.

On the evening of the 6th of November a meeting of the conspirators was held at which it was agreed that Catiline should forthwith set out from Rome and take command of the troops raised by Manlius, leaving the other chiefs of the conspiracy to continue their operations in the city. He would fain have Cicero disposed of before his departure, and two of his associates, Cornelius and Vargunteius, promised to procure him this satisfaction. They were on sufficiently friendly terms with the consul to be able to make their way into his house as morning callers, and they arranged to take advantage of this opportunity to murder him the first thing next day. Cicero, however, was well served by his spies. Next morning the murderers found the door barred against them, and a number of the principal senators assembled to witness the discomfiture of the men whose presence verified what Cicero had announced beforehand as to their names and their purpose. Next night the conspirators met again and decided that, notwithstanding the failure of the assassination, Catiline's departure could no longer be delayed.

On the following morning (Nov. 8th) Cicero summoned the Senate to the temple of Jupiter Stator on the Palatine. Catiline himself, who was resolved not to throw off the mask until the very last moment, had the audacity to be present. This was

Cicero's opportunity. He knew that Catiline was about to join the insurgents, and he wished to emphasise this his first act of overt rebellion. He wished likewise to have the correctness of his own information publicly attested, and to avoid the supposition that Catiline's hypocritical protestations had duped the consul, and that his escape from Rome was a success scored against the government. He therefore turned upon him in the tremendous invective which has been preserved to us under the title of the *First Catilinarian Oration.* The opening words—"Quousque tandem abutere, Catilina, patientia nostra?"—are perhaps more universally known than any other sentence from an ancient author, and the whole speech well merits its fame as a masterpiece of passionate and defiant eloquence. Throughout, Cicero assumes the tone of one who has complete command of the situation. He mocks at Catiline's affectation of innocence, he reveals all his actions and projects before his face, charges him with all that had occurred at the secret meetings of the conspirators during the last two nights, and explains to him where his comrades are to meet him on the road, how the silver eagle which is to serve as their standard has gone on before, and how Manlius awaits his arrival. As consul, Cicero has ample evidence and ample precedent for ordering him to execution on the spot, but it does not suit his convenience to do so. "I will have you put to death, Catiline," he says,* "but it shall be later on, when it will be impos-

---

* Cicero, *Cat.*, i., 2, 5.

sible to find anyone so vile, anyone so abandoned, anyone so like yourself, as to deny that I am justified in the act. So long as there is anyone left to plead for you, you shall live ; and you shall live, as you live now, hemmed in by my guards—many and trusty they are—so that you cannot stir a finger against the State : the eyes and ears of many, when you least suspect it, shall in the future as in the past spy out your ways and keep watch on your actions."

If Catiline wishes to keep up the farce for a few hours longer and to represent himself as an innocent man driven friendless into exile by the threats of the consul, Cicero will humour him so far. " Go," he says,* " I order you ; go into banishment, if that is what you want me to say. And if," he continues,† " you wish to blast the name of me, whom you are pleased to call your enemy, withdraw in very truth into some distant land. I shall scarcely be able to survive the ill-fame which will attach to me, if you allow yourself to be driven from the country by the command of the consul. But if you wish to be the instrument of my praise and my reputation, then set forth with all your crew of reprobates, betake yourself to Manlius, summon all criminals to your standard, sever yourself from every honest man, declare war against your country, glory in the act of impiety, that it may be clear that you have not been thrust forth among strangers, but that you have sought the company of your fellows. You will go at last," he

* Cicero, *Cat.*, i., 8, 20.
† Cicero, *Cat.*, i., 9, 23.

adds,* "well I know it, to that camp whither your
unbridled and insane desires have long been sum.
moning you. It is no painful task that I impose
upon you but an inexpressible pleasure. For this
mad adventure it is, that nature has fashioned you,
that choice has trained you, that fortune has spared
you. You never loved peace, nor even war unless it
were war as a pirate. You have found for yourself
a gang of ruffians, recruited from among broken men,
whom not only all luck but all hope has deserted.
In the midst of such a crew how you will take your
joy, how you will triumph in delight, how you will
revel in satisfaction, when in the whole circle of your
associates you never hear the voice of one honest
man, nor see one honest man's face."

That night Catiline left the city for Etruria. Next
day (Nov. 9th) Cicero addressed a speech (the *Second
Catilinarian Oration*) to the Roman People, in which
he announced the departure of Catiline, and laid
before them the whole situation. He exults in the
thought that he is now permitted to fight with the
traitor in the daylight. "For this one leader of this
intestine war, I have beaten him beyond a doubt.
No longer will his dagger play against my breast. I
have done with the perils which I have had to face
on the Campus and in the Forum and in the Senate-
house and even within the walls of my own home.
He has lost his vantage ground now that he is
driven from the city. We shall wage a fair war
with none to hinder us against a declared enemy.
Unquestionably we have ruined the man and tri-

* Cicero, *Cat.*, i., 10, 25.

umphed over him, now that we have drawn him from his secret ambush into open piracy." *

Cicero answers to the people, as he had already done to the Senate, the criticisms which he fears will be made on his policy in allowing the rebel captain to put himself at the head of his forces. He protests that though he would have been justified in killing him, yet that his execution would have been useless to the commonwealth. Catiline's associates would have declared his innocence, would have made a martyr of him, and would have used the outcry against the consul in order to carry out Catiline's schemes more effectively. Now that he has set himself in arms against the State, no one can any longer pretend to disbelieve in his conspiracy, and so not only he but his accomplices whom he leaves behind can be safely dealt with. To these last Cicero addresses significant words of warning. "They are conscious," he says,† "that all the resolutions of their council of the night before last have been reported to me. I exposed them all yesterday in the Senate. Catiline took fright and departed. What are they waiting for? Nay, but they are much mistaken if they think that my lenity is going to last for ever. . . . One boon I will still grant them; let them go forth, let them start on their journey, let them not suffer their Catiline to pine with grief for want of them. I will show them the road : he has gone along the Aurelian Way ; if they will but make haste, they may catch him up towards

* Cicero, *Cat.*, ii., 1, 1.

† Cicero, *Cat* , ii., 5, 11.

evening. . . . One word more; either go they shall, or keep quiet; or else if they remain in the city and do not mend their ways let them look to receive their deserts." Further on * he returns to the same theme—"If my mildness heretofore has seemed to anyone to argue want of vigour, I would reply that it has been waiting till this which lay concealed should spring to light. For the future I can no longer forget that this is my native land, that I am the consul of all these Romans, that it is with them that I have to live or for them that I have to die. There is no guard set upon the gates, no ambush upon the road. If anyone wishes to go forth, he can use his own discretion. But if anyone dares to stir a finger in the city, if I take him, I will not say in any accomplished act, but in any attempt or effort against the nation, then I say that I will make him feel that in this city there are consuls who will not sleep, there are magistrates who will do their duty, there is a Senate which will stand firm, there are forces in arms, there is a prison which our ancestors established to be the scene of vengeance for heinous and red-handed crime."

With this warning Cicero left things to run their course in the city. Outside, the armies of Metellus Celer in the valley of the Po and of Antonius in Etruria were hurriedly reinforced by fresh levies. Meanwhile Catiline had fulfilled Cicero's predictions by joining the band of Manlius at Fæsulæ. Disguise was no longer possible, and he assumed the dress and title of consul in open rebellion against the

* Cicero, *Cat.*, ii., 12, 27.

9

State. The Senate replied by declaring Catiline
and Manlius enemies, and summoning those who
had followed them to disperse. Rewards had already been offered for the denunciation of their
confederates within the city. Sallust tells us * that
these decrees produced no effect. None of the conspirators in the capital came forward to give evidence, and none of those in the field deserted their
standard. Catiline's force now amounted to ten
thousand men. He felt himself strong enough to
refuse the aid of the runaway slaves who would
gladly have flocked to him. He feared that their
presence might alarm those who looked with indifference or with favour on his movement, and so
spoil his chance of support from the populace of the
capital.

While the forces were thus mustering on either
side, Cicero was annoyed by a foolish and ill-timed
contest among his own followers. At the recent
consular election Silanus and Murena had headed
the poll with Servius Sulpicius Rufus for third and
Catiline for fourth. A law had been lately passed
increasing the penalties against bribery, and Cato,
the sworn foe of electoral corruption, whose characteristic it was to be instant in season and out of season, must needs choose this moment, when all the
fortunes of the commonwealth were at stake, to
divide the friends of the constitution by trying to
unseat Murena on a charge of bribery and treating

Cicero protested against the folly of throwing the
city again into the confusion of a contested election ;

* Sallust, *Cat.*, 36, 5.

he offered himself as counsel for Murena, and delivered on his behalf a speech * which is a very model of playful and persuasive eloquence, the more pleasant because it comes as an interlude in the grim tragedy of the Catilinarian orations. The serious arguments of the consul as to the political necessities of the time are relieved by a sportive attack on the technical subtleties which form the stock in trade of the lawyer Sulpicius, and on the precisian doctrines which Cato has imbibed from his Stoic tutors. " I must tell you, gentlemen, that those eminent qualities which we observe in Marcus Cato are all his own ; what we sometimes find wanting in him is to be set down not to his nature but to his master, Zeno, whose doctrines have been caught up from learned tutors by our most talented friend, and that not as a topic for discussion, which is the usual way, but as a rule of life." Cicero laughed the jurors into a good humour by a ludicrous application of Stoic maxims to the practical exigencies of Roman politics, and they unanimously acquitted Murena. The additional peril which Cato's obstinate purism would have created was thus happily averted. It is difficult to realise that this witty and sparkling speech was uttered by a man in hourly danger of his life, and with all the responsibilities of a tremendous political crisis weighing upon him. " What a merry man we have for consul," was Cato's remark, as he listened from the accusers' bench. It never seems to have occurred to Cato, that Cicero's merriment was pressed into the

---

* Some extracts from the *Pro Murena* will be found above, pp 94-98.

service of the State, and that his own austerity was helping on the projects of the very men whose execution he was himself to urge a few days later.

The trial of Murena took place in the month of November.   Meanwhile the conspirators in the city anxiously awaited the appearance of Catiline and his army.   Their chief was Publius Cornelius Lentulus Sura, who had been consul in 71 B.C., and had been afterwards expelled from the Senate by the censors. He had recovered his seat by being again elected to the prætorship, and was now serving that office. He appears to have been a man of flighty and credulous temperament.   He lent his ears to designing soothsayers who persuaded him that a Sibylline oracle had foretold the domination in Rome of three Cornelii.   Part of the prophecy, they said, had been already fulfilled by Cinna and Sulla, and Lentulus was marked by fate to be the third.   Other senators and knights of good family, Autronius, Gabinius, Statilius, Cassius, and Cethegus were associated with him. Cethegus was supposed to be the most energetic of the conspirators and always urged immediate and violent measures.   Cicero had failed as yet to get evidence of any overt act which would justify the arrest of these men, but at length their own folly gave him the desired opportunity.

There were present in Rome at this time some envoys from the Allobroges of Transalpine Gaul. The Allobroges were overwhelmed with a burden of debt to Roman money-lenders and were ready for any desperate action.   In the meantime they had sent an embassy to Rome to beg some relief from

the government. These Gallic envoys were introduced to Gabinius by a certain freedman named
Umbrenus, and Gabinius and the rest conceived the
wild idea of associating the Allobroges in the conspiracy and inducing them to supply Catiline with
cavalry for the invasion of Italy. The Gauls at first
listened with sympathy; but on further consideration they reflected that they might gain more by
betraying their tempters to the government than by
engaging seriously in so desperate a cause. They
accordingly took counsel with Fabius Sanga, the patron of their tribe, who at once gave notice to Cicero.
The Allobroges were instructed to continue their
negotiations with the conspirators and to obtain from
them if possible written documents. With incredible stupidity Lentulus and his associates fell into the
trap. They gave the Gauls letters in their own hand-
writing, addressed to the senate and people of the
Allobroges, undertaking to perform what they had
promised verbally to the envoys, and urging the
Allobroges in turn to send the assistance which their
envoys had promised. The Gauls were to visit Catiline on their way north, and they bore with them a
letter from Lentulus to Catiline in which he advised
him to admit the slaves into the ranks of his band.

By the evening of the 2d of December all was
settled, and the Allobroges started on their homeward journey that night. They were accompanied
by Volturcius, one of the confederates, and attended
by a considerable escort. Cicero was duly informed
of all this, and made his preparations accordingly.*

---

* Cicero, *Cat.*, iii., 2, 5.

The great northern road from Rome crosses the Tiber at the Mulvian Bridge some two miles above the city. Cicero set two of the prætors in ambush with armed bands in farm-houses on each side of the water. These waited until the Allobroges and their companions were crossing in the darkness; then advancing simultaneously they occupied the two ends of the bridge. Thus not only were the letters seized, but the whole party was caught on the bridge. They were conveyed to Rome and deposited at the consul's house about daybreak (Dec. 3d). Cicero forthwith summoned to his presence Gabinius, Cethegus, Statilius, and Lentulus. Messages were likewise sent to some of the principal senators, who hurried to the consul's house. Contrary to the advice of these, Cicero declined to open the letters. He preferred at once to convoke the Senate, so that the evidence might come out in open court. In the meantime, acting on a hint from the Allobroges, he sent one of the prætors to search the house of Cethegus, where a store of swords and daggers was soon found. These were immediately seized.

As soon as the Senate had assembled, Cicero took Lentulus by the hand and led him into the House. This show of gentle force exercised by the consul in person was considered due to the dignity of the prætor; the other conspirators, being but private men, were arrested with less ceremony. Volturcius was first admitted to give evidence under promise of pardon, and detailed the instructions with which he was charged for Catiline, who was to be urged to advance as soon as possible on Rome, so as to be before

the city during the festival of the Saturnalia; this
would be the most convenient opportunity for his
accomplices to co-operate with fire and sword within
the city.   Next came the Allobroges with their evidence as to the messages and letters with which they
had been entrusted, and as to the promises which
Lentulus had made them on the strength of his
Sibylline oracle (see above, p. 132).   When confronted on this point, Lentulus' assurance forsook
him, and he did not venture to deny the charge.
But the most overwhelming evidence was that of the
letters themselves which lay still unopened on the
table.   The accused were called upon, one by one,
and each acknowledged his own hand and seal before
the thread was cut and the correspondence inciting
to a Gallic invasion of Italy was read to the House.[*]
After this there could be no question as to the guilt
of the prisoners; and to close the mouths of all ob-
jectors for the future Cicero directed that the evidence should be taken down word for word by certain
trustworthy senators, and then immediately copied
out and published.   The fidelity of the document
was thus guaranteed by its being at once subjected
to the criticism of those who had heard the evidence,
and it was impossible to maintain with any plausibility that the record had been tampered with afterwards.[†]   The Senate next[‡] resolved by an unanimous
vote that Lentulus should be required to resign his
magistracy, and that he should then be remanded

---

[*] Cicero, *Cat.*, iii., 5, 10.

[†] *Pro Sulla*, 14, 41.

[‡] Cicero, *Cat.*, iii., 6, 14.

with the rest to safe-keeping. Cethegus, Statilius, and Gabinius were already secured, and orders for arrest were issued against five other ring-leaders, of whom however one only, Cœparius, was actually caught. The prisoners were guarded in the houses of magistrates and senators, two of them being committed to the charge of Cæsar and Crassus. By this choice of guardians the consul meant to indicate that he put no trust in the rumour which made Cæsar and Crassus accessories to the conspiracy, but regarded them as loyal and trustworthy citizens. After thus providing for the custody of the prisoners, the Senate with equal unanimity passed a vote of thanks to Cicero because "by his courage, wisdom, and forethought the commonwealth had been delivered from the greatest dangers." At the same time a solemn Thanksgiving was voted to the gods for having blessed the efforts of the consul "to rescue the city from conflagration, the citizens from massacre, and Italy from war." Thanksgivings had often been decreed for the success of commanders in the field, but Cicero was the first to whom it had ever befallen to receive such a recognition of his services in the city.

Late in the afternoon of the same day (Dec. 3d) Cicero assembled the people and recounted to them the events of the last twenty-four hours. This speech, the *Third Catilinarian Oration*, is our main authority for the incidents which have been already detailed. The statements are fully confirmed not only by Plutarch but by Sallust, whose master, Cæsar, voted on this day in agreement with the rest of the Senate; we are justified in concluding from this unanimity that the facts were absolutely plain and notorious and that there were not two opinions as to the guilt of the accused. Thus Cicero's first object was fully attained; the conspirators in the city, whose machinations had hitherto been hidden from the public, were now caught in a flagrant act of rebellion, and an act which had conspicuously failed. In presence of their egregious folly Cicero may well have exulted that Catiline was no longer at hand to be their guide, and it is not surprising that he should have been tempted to magnify the sagacity of the leader whom they had lost in comparison with the ineptitude of those who remained behind. "Catiline," he exclaims, "would never have fixed for our information the season of the Saturnalia, or announced so long beforehand the day of doom and destruction for the commonwealth; he would never have been so simple as to allow me to lay hands on his own seal, his own letters, or the eye-witnesses of his guilt." "When I drove him from the city, Romans, I had this in my mind that, Catiline once away, I had no reason to fear the sleepy Lentulus or the bloated Cassius or the raving maniac Cethegus." * The conflict was not yet over, but a first great success had been scored, and Cicero was fully justified in addressing his fellow-citizens in a tone of triumph and confidence; † "Night is now upon us; so do you, Romans, offer your thanks to that Jupiter who watches over the city and over you, and then return

---

* Cicero, *Cat.*, iii., 7, 16.
† Cicero, *Cat.*, iii., 12, 29.

to your homes. Though the danger has been averted, yet I would have each one of you keep watch and ward over his own house this night as you did last night. That you shall not be called upon to do so much longer and that you shall enjoy quiet from this time forward, that shall be my care, Romans."

The multitude greeted his words with acclamation, and escorted him back in honour to the house of a friend with whom he was to lodge for the night. The consul could not sleep that night in his own home, for it was in the possession of the Vestal Virgins, who each year celebrated in the house of one of the magistrates certain rites of the "Good Goddess" from which all males were rigorously excluded.

After the interval of one day (Dec. 4th), during which it appears that further evidence was being taken and rewards voted to the informers,* the Senate assembled for the third time on the 5th, the famous Nones of December, and the consul asked its advice on the question what was to be done with Lentulus and his fellows. The place of meeting was the temple of Concord at the foot of the Capitoline Hill. The Forum † was filled with citizens who had armed themselves at the consul's bidding, and the slopes of the Capitol were occupied by bodies of Roman Knights, amongst whom Cicero's friend Atticus was conspicuous.‡

* Cicero, *Cat.*, iv., 5, 10.
† Cicero, *Cat.*, iv., 7, 14.
‡ *Ad Att.*, ii., 1, 7.

FRIEZE OF THE TEMPLE OF CONCORD.
(Duruy.)

The accounts which have been preserved to us of this great debate are strangely conflicting. Plutarch * relates " that the only one of Cato's speeches surviving in his time was that delivered on this occasion ; for Cicero the consul had trained certain writers of special intelligence to use signs which expressed the sense of many letters in a few short marks, and had set them here and there in the Senate-house. For the keeping and employment of what are called shorthand writers had not yet begun, but it is said that this occasion was the first when men struck on the track of any such invention." It might have been hoped that this precaution would have secured us an authentic account of the speeches and motions before the House. Nevertheless we find perplexing discrepancies. Sallust omits Cicero's speech altogether, and Plutarch and Dio Cassius † give accounts of it which are in contradiction of each other, and neither of which agrees very well with the published version. Brutus, who in later years wrote a life of his uncle Cato, went hopelessly astray, believing that Cato was the first to propose the punishment of death. Luckily for us, this blunder caused Cicero to give us in a confidential letter ‡ of criticism, addressed to Atticus, a plain statement of some of the facts, which is our best guide through the labyrinth of contradiction. Lastly as to the nature of Cæsar's proposal, we have two distinct versions ; the one, easy in itself but irreconcilable with what we

---

* Plutarch, *Cato Minor*, 23, 3.

† Plutarch, *Cic.*, 21, 2. Dio Cassius, xxxvii., 35, 4.

‡ *Ad Att.*, xii., 21.

know of the order of debate, is propounded by Appian * and Plutarch; the other, vouched for by Cicero in his published speech and by Sallust, fits in with the other facts as they are known to us but presents serious internal difficulties. This is not the place for a full discussion of these vexed questions: I will only say that I believe that the contemporary authorities, Cicero and Sallust, have preserved the true account of the order of debate and of Cæsar's proposal, and that I shall follow them rather than Appian and Plutarch in the subsequent narrative.

Cicero first put the question to Silanus, the consul elect, who thereupon moved that the five prisoners should be put to death. He was followed by the other senators of consular rank, who all supported the motion. The prætorian benches were next to be consulted. Among the first in this rank came Cæsar, who was prætor-elect and would enter on office at the end of the month. Cæsar, if we may trust Sallust's version † of his speech, while fully agreeing as to the guilt of the accused and acknowledging that no punishment could be too severe for their crimes, urged that the Senate should nevertheless consider not the deserts of the prisoners but its own character as the guardian of the laws and the constitution. He pointed out with much force that it is just by cases like this that bad precedents are set up and the habit of obedience to the law broken through; it was thus that the Thirty at Athens had begun their

* Appian, *Bell. Civ.*, ii., 5 and 6 ; see below pp. 141 and 148.
† Sallust, *Cat.*, 51.

tyranny by putting to death without trial men of
notoriously criminal character. To let the prisoners
go would be manifestly impolitic, but without breaking the law which forbade that any Roman citizen
should be punished with death except by command
of the People, measures might be taken which would
render the conspirators powerless to do harm for the
future. He therefore proposed that the property of
the culprits should be confiscated, and that they
should be confined in chains in corporate towns of
Italy, and that it should be declared illegal for anyone to bring before the Senate or the People any
proposal for their release.

It is obviously very difficult to understand how
such a proposal could follow on such an argument.
Cæsar by proposing an alternative sentence seems to
acknowledge the right of the Senate to try these
men and to condemn them to punishment of some
sort. Why was the Senate better qualified to pronounce a sentence of imprisonment for life, than a
sentence of death? This question, though it seems
to force itself on the notice of the reader, is never
clearly stated, much less solved, by any of our authorities. Appian evades it by making Cæsar propose a mere remand of the prisoners for a legal trial
later on. Sallust and Cicero give us little help in
explanation, though they state the facts correctly.
The most probable answer seems to be that imprisonment in the days of the Roman Republic was not
fully recognised as a species of punishment, but only
as a harsh method of safe-keeping. For this reason it
was not mentioned amongst the punishments against

which a right of appeal was guaranteed to Roman
citizens. All the laws which treat of the right of
appeal speak of death, of scourging and of fine, as
the penalties which are appealed against. The
Senate then, or rather the consul acting under the
advice of the Senate, is justified (so we must suppose
Cæsar to maintain) in punishing dangerous enemies
of the State so long as the punishment inflicted is
not one forbidden *totidem verbis* by the statute.
Thus Cæsar's motion may be * held to " keep on the
windy side of the law," though it seems a strange
subtlety to say that a court, not qualified to pronounce any " capital " sentence (which in this age
commonly meant a sentence of death to be avoided
by voluntary exile and self-deprivation of citizenship), should nevertheless have the right to inflict a
punishment infinitely more severe.

Whatever the reasonableness of Cæsar's proposal,
his speech produced a strong effect, and many of the
senators of prætorian rank signified their assent.
Silanus the consul-elect took alarm, and explained

---

* I assume that the " penal servitude " of later Roman law (by which
a man undoubtedly lost his " caput ") had not yet been invented, and
that the " citizenship " and " liberty " of the prisoners would be
technically intact, just as they were in the case of the insolvent
debtor who was handed over to work in chains for his creditor (see
Ortolan's *Institutes of Justinian*, iii., § 2027, n.). In this case the
sentence would not be technically a " capital " one but might be regarded as detention indefinitely prolonged. Mommsen (*Staats-Recht*,
iii., p. 1250, n. 1) holds on the contrary that perpetual imprisonment
is really a death-sentence indefinitely suspended by way of grace.
If however this is what Cæsar proposed, how could he with any
plausibility afterwards declare his opinion (see below, p. 230), that
the death-sentence had been illegal?

away his own motion by an unworthy quibble. It was worded in the terms "that the extreme penalty be inflicted on the prisoners," and he now interpreted this to mean the same as Cæsar's proposal; "for perpetual imprisonment," he said "is the extreme penalty which can be inflicted on a Roman citizen." * Many of Cicero's friends approved of Cæsar's motion, as it would undoubtedly relieve the consul from the risk and responsibility which he would incur by the actual infliction of death. † His brother Quintus is said to have been among those who wavered. ‡

At this point Cicero intervened in the debate with the speech which he afterwards published as the *Fourth Catilinarian Oration.* As consul, he was not like the rest called upon to deliver his opinion in the order of his place, but might interpose with a magisterial statement at any moment which he deemed expedient. In another respect the consul differs from the ordinary senator. He is present to ask and receive the advice of the Senate, not to give advice himself. He must therefore refrain, much as an English judge charging a jury refrains, from expressing his adhesion to one side or the other, though by his method of summing up and laying the question before the House he may indicate pretty clearly what is his own opinion. In this speech Cicero insists on two points: first he wishes that the Senate shall decide according to what it deems good for the State without regard to what may be the personal

---

* Plutarch, *Cato Minor*, 22, 5.

† Plutarch, *Cic.*, 21, 2.

‡ Suetonius, *Jul.*, 14.

consequences to himself ; these he is ready and proud
to accept : secondly he protests against any delay.
" Now whatever is to be done, whichever way your
minds and your resolutions incline, you must decide
before nightfall. You see what a crime has been
brought before your bar. If you suppose that only
a few are associated in it, you are much mistaken ;
this mischief has spread further than we thought ;
it has not only infected Italy, but it has crossed the
Alps, and working its way in darkness has already
laid hold on several provinces. It cannot be crushed
out by withholding your hand and putting off the
day of reckoning. Whatever the nature of the
punishment which you select, you must inflict it
instantly." *

He next proceeds to explain to the senators the
alternatives presented to them—" I see that there
are two motions before the House, the first that of
Decimus Silanus, who proposes that those who have
attempted to destroy this commonwealth shall be
punished by death, the other that of Caius Cæsar
who, while exempting them from death, provides for
every other punishment in its most aggravated form.
Both these senators have pronounced sentences stern
as their own dignity and the gravity of the crisis demand. The one thinks that men who have attempted
to slaughter the Roman people, to destroy our Empire, to blot out the name of Rome, ought not to be
allowed to enjoy a moment longer the life and breath
which we all draw in common ; and he bears in mind
that this punishment has often been inflicted on

* Cicero, *Cat.*, iv., 3, 6.

wicked citizens in this commonwealth. The other perceives that death has not been established by Heaven as a punishment, but that it is either a debt due to nature, or a haven of rest from toils and troubles; and so wise men never meet it with reluctance, and brave men often seek it of their own will. But chains, and chains to be worn for ever, are truly a device framed for the exemplary punishment of heinous crimes. He adds a heavy penalty on the townships in which they are to be confined, if any of the prisoners escapes from his bonds; he commits them to a dreadful prison, and provides as the crimes of these wretches deserve, that no one shall be allowed to propose to alleviate by decree of Senate or People the penalty to which he condemns them, thus depriving them even of hope, so often the sole consolation of men in trouble: he orders further that their property be confiscated. All that he leaves to these criminals is life, and if he had taken this too, by a single pang he would have relieved them from all the pangs of mind and body and all the expiation of their crime. And for this it was that the men of old, in order to set before the eyes of the wicked some terror in their lifetime, thought it well to teach that pains and penalties not unlike this are reserved for the impious in the world below; they understood, it is clear, that if these were set aside death in itself was nothing to fear. Now, Senators, I see what course is for my own benefit. If you accept the proposal of Caius Cæsar, it is probable, since he has professed those politics which are supposed to be in favour with the many, that having him for the adviser and the voucher for this sentence I shall have less to fear from the attacks of the multitude; if the other proposal be adopted, I do not know but that more of trouble may be in store for me. But let all considerations of my danger give way to the interests of the State. For Cæsar, as his own dignity and the splendour of his ancestry required, has laid this sentence in our hands, as a pledge of his enduring loyalty to the State. The truth is, that Caius Cæsar knows that the Sempronian Law is intended for the benefit of Roman citizens, and that the man who is an enemy to the State cannot by any possibility be a citizen; he knows likewise that the very man * who carried the Sempronian Law paid the penalty of his treason without the command of the People. . . . And so a man of his known kindliness and clemency does not hesitate to commit Publius Lentulus to a life-long dungeon and chains; he provides that for the future no man shall be permitted to gain credit for himself by alleviating the punishment of Lentulus, or to pose as the people's friend, while bringing calamity on the Roman People; he adds that his goods are to be confiscated, so that to all the other torments of mind and body want and beggary are to be added. Therefore, whether you vote with him, you will have given me a coadjutor beloved and acceptable to the commons, to help me to plead my cause to the multitude; or whether you prefer to follow the advice of Silanus, you will have an easy defence both for yourselves and me against

---

* *I. e.*, Caius Gracchus.

any charge of cruelty, and I will maintain that this sentence was far the less severe of the two."

The next feature in the debate was the speech of Cato. He was tribune-elect, and would probably be asked for his opinion immediately after the senators of prætorian rank. Plutarch * tells us that Cato severely rebuked his brother-in-law Silanus for his weakness, and fiercely attacked Cæsar for trying to intimidate the Senate, when he might be thankful if he himself escaped condemnation as an accomplice. Sallust's version of Cato's speech contains nothing about Silanus, and softens down the invective against Cæsar. But the main argument, as Sallust gives it, is so perfectly adapted to the situation, that there can be little doubt that it is the one which Cato actually used. This argument is that the situation calls for administrative action rather than for precise weighing of penalties. † The prisoners are avowedly guilty, so that no injustice can be done; but the really vital question is what effect will the one or the other decision of the House have on the chances of Catiline and his army. ‡

When the question was brought to this point, a sensible man could hardly doubt what answer it was his duty to give. Cæsar's proposal was obviously and notoriously impracticable. What probability was there of such a sentence being carried out? How could the Senate prevent any magistrate from proposing the release of the prisoners? Cicero had

---

* Plutarch, *Cato Minor*, 23, 1.
† Sallust, *Cat.*, 52, 3.
‡ Sallust, *Cat.*, 52, 17.

later on the opportunity of proving in his own person the futility of such restrictive clauses. Clodius in the law which banished him provided that it should be unlawful to propose his recall, but this did not prevent its being both proposed and carried. The same would doubtless have been the case in this instance if Cæsar's motion had been adopted. An agitation would at once have been set on foot to review the sentence. Meanwhile Catiline and his companions in arms would have had no sense of discouragement or terror at the fate of their fellows. They would have regarded Lentulus as simply out of the game for the moment, until they could come and rescue him. His fate would have depended mainly on the issue of the military operations in the field, whereas, as we shall see presently, his immediate execution had a momentous effect on the decision of that issue.

Cato's speech determined the sense of the House, which Cicero had left doubtful. An effort was indeed made at the last moment to put off the decision, in spite of the protest which the consul had uttered against delay. Tiberius Claudius Nero moved to adjourn the question until further measures of defence against Catiline should be provided, and Silanus, tossed to and fro by conflicting anxieties, took refuge at last in this neutral proposal and announced that he should vote with Nero.* But by the rules of

---

* Sallust, *Cat.*, 50, 4. That Nero's proposal came last of all is proved (in contradiction of Appian) by Cicero's statement (*Ad Att.*, xii., 21, 1) that " all who spoke before Cato, excepting Cæsar, had spoken for death."

THE TULLIANUM : ANCIENT PRISON OF THE KINGS.

(*Duruy.*)

the Roman Senate motions for adjournment had no
precedence over those on the main question, and
thus it happened that the proposal of Nero was
never put to the vote.   Cicero first submitted to the
House the proposal of Cato, which was in substance
the same as that of Silanus, but which was more
fully and clearly expressed.*   This was carried by a
great majority and all the other motions before the
House necessarily dropped.

Cicero lost no time in carrying the sentence into
execution.   He at once dismissed the Senate, and
proceeding to the Palatine, where Lentulus was confined, led him along the Sacred Way through the
Forum to the door of the ancient prison of the
Kings close to the Temple of Concord where the debate had been held.   Hither he commanded the other
prisoners to be conveyed, one by one, from their
several places of detention.   The multitude which
thronged the Forum was as yet uncertain for what
purpose they were being brought.   As each arrived
he was handed over to the magistrates charged with
the care of executions, and by them thrust down into the subterranean vault of the prison, where he was
immediately strangled.   When all five had perished
the consul turned to the assembled people and, humouring the superstition which forbade the ill-omened
mention of death, announced their fate in the words,
"They have lived their life."   Night was falling
when Cicero returned homewards amidst the flare
of torches displayed at every door and the shouts of

---

* *Ad Att.*, xii., 21, 1.

the multitude who hailed him as their deliverer and preserver.*

The soundness of Cato's advice and the wisdom of Cicero's action were soon manifested ; the army of Catiline, which had remained unaffected by all the previous decrees of the Senate, began, as soon as the news of Lentulus' execution arrived, to disperse and dwindle until it was reduced to three thousand men. These were soon confronted near Pistoria, some twenty miles from Fæsulæ, by a superior force under Petreius, a brave and experienced officer who was acting as lieutenant to the second consul Antonius. The whole of them were cut to pieces fighting bravely around their leader, whose gallant death atoned in some degree for the criminal stupidity of his attempt against the commonwealth. Scott has recorded for us the plea of the Roman—

> " Who with the gladiators' aid
> For empire enterprised ;
> He stood the cast his rashness played,
> Left not the victims he had made,
> Dug his red grave with his own blade,
> And on the field he lost was laid,
> Abhorred, but not despised."

The defeat and death of Catiline happened on the Nones of January, exactly one month after the execution of Lentulus. There can be no question that the one event was the direct result of the other. Catiline had calculated on having to deal with a weak government, divided by party factions and hampered by constitutional scruples. He was met

* Plutarch, *Cic.*, 22, 3.

by a dramatic revelation of the total collapse of the schemes of his confederates in the city, and by a startling example of the length to which the consul and the Senate were prepared to go in dealing with them. Down to the Nones of December, it was not clear which party had most force on its side. When once this question seemed to be decided, Catiline lost his chief hopes of support. All the outer circle of his followers deserted him, and he was left alone with a handful of desperate men for whom there was no retreat.

No State trial, except that perhaps of Charles I., has ever been the subject of so much controversy as that which consigned Lentulus and his companions to the executioner. The clamour against Cicero's action began a few days later and never ceased until he was driven into banishment by a vote of the People. This condemnation was solemnly reversed, and the exile restored in triumph eighteen months later. But after nineteen centuries the controversy still rages, and the question is eagerly debated whether Cicero's act was that of a bold and public-spirited magistrate, who at a critical moment used his legitimate powers with vigour and discretion, or whether it was a judicial murder,* perpetrated without legal warrant by a timid and self-seeking partisan.

---

* "A brutal judicial murder" is Mommsen's expression in his *Roman History*. In his more recent work, the *Staats-Recht* (vol. iii., p. 1246), Mommsen takes a much more moderate view, holding that the *Senatus consultum ultimum* did really and legally justify the consul in treating all conspiring citizens as enemies caught on Roman territory ; he now seems to blame Cicero only for consulting the Senate, instead of putting the prisoners to death on his own responsibility.

I will attempt to state very shortly the main points at issue.

The Roman constitution, while restricting the capital jurisdiction of the magistrate over citizens, allows him to use any amount of force against enemies of the State. A citizen may commit acts which constitute him an enemy, in which case he by his own deed renounces his civic privileges. The rule for the magistrate by Roman, as by English,* law seems to be that he may not treat any citizen as an enemy on the ground of apprehended or future mischief nor on the ground of past offences, but only in the presence of overt acts implying grave and immediate danger to the State, which can only be repelled by the use of violent methods of self-defence. It follows that the executions must be on a scale not out of proportion to the necessity, and that they must not be continued after the imminent danger has ceased. If the conduct of the magistrate is afterwards called in question, the burden of proof that the forcible act was really necessary lies on him. On the other hand the moment that the necessity is present he is neglecting his duty if he fails to act on it. In extreme cases the private man has the same duty. In the colonies and dependencies of England the exercise of this terrible responsibility has been sometimes preceded by a solemn proclamation of "Martial Law." This proclamation does not, strictly speaking, make any alteration in the rights and duties which each magis-

---

* See Dicey, *Law of the Constitution*, Lecture vii.

trate and each citizen had before,* but it calls attention to the fact that a state of war exists with all the
extraordinary obligations which such condition implies ; it indicates that the magistrate or the officer
expects to be obliged to act on his extreme powers,
and that he intends to do so. In Rome a corresponding proclamation is found in the decree of the Senate
" that the consuls see to it that the State takes no
harm." This decree, on the face of it, does not so
much confer fresh powers, as call upon the magistrates to stir up the powers which they already
possess. Nevertheless it is felt to make a grave
difference in the situation, to bring home to the
magistrate the responsibility for defending the commonwealth, and to justify acts which otherwise would
be held tyrannous and outrageous. It authorises
the consul, as Sallust says, † " to employ every means
of compulsion on aliens and Romans alike and to
exercise extreme authority inside and outside the
city."

As Cicero himself puts the case, the whole dispute
resolves itself into the question, was Lentulus a
citizen or an enemy? About Catiline who was
openly in arms there could be no doubt ; but Lentulus had not actually struck a blow : was he to be
classed in the same category? There was no doubt
on any hand as to the guilt of the accused. They
were taken red-handed in the act of corresponding
with the enemies of the State, and their own public

---

* Stephen, *History of the Criminal Law*, p. 214.
† Sallust, *Cat.*, 29.

confession constituted a plea of " Guilty." But how
were they to be dealt with? The Law of Caius
Gracchus said that no Roman citizen was to be condemned to death without the command of the People.
The democratic exposition of that law was that,
given a citizen, no amount of treason short of physi-
cally appearing in arms against the State could constitute an enemy. The view of the Senate was that
a man who from inside the walls co-operated with
insurgents was really and truly an enemy, and a
more dangerous one because he was posted in
ambush. The common-sense answer to the question seems to be that suggested by Cato's speech as
reported by Sallust (above p. 147). If the peril
from outside had been over, there would have been
no public need for the execution of these men, and
under those circumstances their rights as citizens
would have revived, as they did in fact in the case
of the four criminals * who were included in the sentence of the Senate, and who escaped immediate
seizure; but while Catiline was still threatening the
commonwealth with a dangerous army, his confederates could not justly claim any immunity which
conflicted with the public safety. The determining
factor in the decision was the prospect of the effect
which either course would produce on the operations
in the field.

---

* Sallust, *Cat.*, 50, 4. The fate of these men is not expressly
mentioned, but we should certainly have heard if they had been put
to death. They probably were summoned before the prætor, but
acknowledged their guilt by retiring into exile (as Verres did) without
waiting for the verdict of a jury.

On the ground then of public necessity Cicero
would have been justified in putting the Catilinarians
to death by his own authority or by the advice of
any assessors whom he might select to act with
him. But in view of the fact that no case absolutely
parallel had occurred since* the Law of Caius Gracchus on which his adversaries mainly relied, he
thought it better first to take the advice of the great
public council which the constitution had provided
for him. This was, strictly speaking, an innovation.
The Senate had sometimes condemned rebels by
name as public enemies, thereby directly advising
the consul to put them to death ; but such rebels had
always been persons at large and in arms (as Fulvius),
or supposed to be in arms (as Caius Gracchus), not
prisoners under present detention. The difference
however is one of circumstances, not of principle. In
either case the decree of the Senate could make no
difference in the legal responsibility of the consul.
The legal justification of his act was, not that the
Senate had ordered it, but that it was necessary for
the preservation of the State. He would have been
worthy of blame, if in order to carry out this consultation he had dangerously delayed his action.
But when the advice of the Senate could be asked
without practical inconvenience, it was clearly wise
in the consul to obtain it. It was important for the
sake of the moral impression to be produced, that the

---

* The precedent of the execution of the Bacchanalian conspirators
In 186 B.C. (see Livy, xxxix., 14, *et seq*.), as being previous to the Sempronian Law, probably went for nothing. At any rate Cicero never
refers to it.

execution should appear, not as an act of violence or panic on the part of the magistrate, but as the deliberate judgment of the supreme council of the State, which had seen the proofs of guilt and heard the confessions of the prisoners. By confirming the action of the consul, the Senate, though it could take no legal responsibility off his shoulders, could yet give him moral support to justify his severity from the charge of cruelty and tyranny.*

Cicero's action throughout seems then to have been both righteous and prudent. He never lost his head though pressed by open enemies without and beset with traitors within the city. He refrained from striking prematurely, but allowed time for Catiline to appear in the rebel camp and for Lentulus to commit himself by overt acts of treason. He made the guilt of the conspirators so manifest, that even Cæsar was obliged to concur in the verdict of "Guilty," and to sanction it by proposing an alternative sentence as on convicted criminals. He baffled all attempts within the city by his vigilance, and finally blasted the hopes of Catiline by the exe-

---

* Cicero sometimes does injustice to his own case by yielding (as most orators are liable to yield) to the temptation of proving too much. In the process of refuting the charge of cruelty (as he is fully entitled to do) by alleging the concurrence of the Senate, he is led on to use expressions which seem to evade his own legal responsibility for the decision (*e. g. In Pis.*, 7, 14). That Cicero, nevertheless, really strengthened his cause by this consultation seems to have been recognised by his adversaries; for they found it worth their while to assert that Cicero had forged the *Senatus Consultum*. This absurd invention found a place in the preamble of Clodius' decree of banishment (*Pro Domo*, 19, 50).

cution of his confederates. He acted throughout
with the calmness and indifference to personal danger proper to the chief magistrate of the Imperial
State. He carried the Senate and people with him
at each step, and so when the crisis came he could
adopt the stern measures which led up surely to success, and yet at the same time could avoid any division in the government and enable it to present an
united front to the enemy. There appears not a
single false step to mark from the day when Cicero
detached his fellow-consul from Catiline to the day
when he broke the back of a formidable conspiracy
by the death of five most guilty persons.

Cicero was a man of mild temper and of constitutional timidity, but of honest heart and sincere purpose. On this occasion, in the presence of danger
and under the stimulus of great responsibilities, he
rose above himself and exhibited unexpected resources of strength and courage. Transformed by
the exigencies of his duty into a man of action, he
played his part with coolness, with vigour, and with
marked practical success. His own conscience fully
approved the deed. Nowhere, even in periods of the
darkest depression and suffering, when all the world
seems to have turned against him, do we find the
least hint of a doubt that he has been in very truth
the saviour of his country ; nor do the personal mis-
fortunes which his act entailed upon him ever lead
him to regret the act itself. " For these two mighty
generals," he writes * of Cæsar and Pompey at the
beginning of the Civil War, " so far from setting their

---

* *Ad Att.*, x., 4, 4.

achievements above my own, I would not change my battered fortunes for theirs which seem so glorious. For what man can be happy when his country is enslaved by him or deserted by him? . . . I am sustained by the proud reflection that, when I had the power, I did the State good service, or at any rate never had an intention that was not loyal, and that the Republic has foundered in the very storm which I foresaw fourteen years ago. I take this approving conscience with me as a companion in my flight."

NOTE.—In the present issue pages 121–123 of this chapter have been re-written, so as to correct an error into which I was formerly led as to the date of the consular elections in the year 63 B.C. I had identified the intended massacre on the election-day (Cicero, *Pro Mur.*, 26, 52) with the one fixed for October 28th (Cicero, *Cat.*, i., 3, 7). I am now convinced that those critics are right who maintain that the two passages refer to two separate attempts on Catiline's part. If this be so, there is no reason for putting the elections (as I had done) so late as October, or indeed at any other season than the usual one in the month of July. The events are therefore less crowded than I had supposed. I have to acknowledge the kindness of Prof. A. S. Wilkins in calling my attention to this matter.

CHAPTER VI.

CICERO'S IDEAL PARTY.

63–60 B.C.

HE fortunes of Catiline had been watched with interest from the other side of the Ægean Sea. Pompey saw clearly what a marvellous piece of good fortune the folly of the revolutionaries was preparing for him, and in order to take advantage of it he sent one of his lieutenants, Metellus Nepos, to Rome in time for the tribunician elections in 63 B.C. It was hoped that Catiline might make sufficient head against the government to alarm all classes, and Metellus as tribune was to seize the opportunity to carry by general assent a decree calling upon Pompey to return to Italy with his army and save the State from the anarchists.

Plutarch * tells us that Cato, who had **63 B.C.** just set forth on a journey, met Nepos and his retinue entering the gates of Rome. Cato guessed that

---

* Plutarch, *Cato Minor*, 20.

mischief was afoot, and in order to frustrate it he turned his horse's head and appeared as a rival candidate for the tribunate. Both Cato and Metellus Nepos were elected and entered on office on the 10th of December in the year 63 B.C.

If Catiline had succeeded better, and if the government had shown itself incapable of dealing with the conspiracy, Cato's opposition would have gone for very little, and a prize such as man never won before would have been within Pompey's grasp. Without serious danger, and without breach of duty or loyalty, he would have stepped at once into the position of "saviour of society"; he would have been a Sulla without guilt or bloodshed, claiming from the gratitude of his fellow-citizens that deference which a despot has to extort by force. Neither the jealous Nobles nor the baffled revolutionaries could have refused to recognise his pre-eminence and to accord him that place of acknowledged chief and protector of a free State, to which he aspired.

Such were the prospects of Pompey during the October and November of the year 63 B.C. His hopes were rudely shattered by the Nones of December. The conspiracy in the city was crushed, and Catiline's army had melted away. The "dignus vindice nodus" had been disentangled by other hands, and the "deus ex machina" had missed the opportunity for his appearance. Metellus Nepos proposed indeed that his patron should be given the command against Catiline *; but his tribuneship had

---

* Plutarch, *Cato Minor*, 26, 2.   Schol. Bob. ad Cic. *Pro Sestio* ch. 28 (Orelli, p. 302).

begun five days too late; his arguments had lost their force now that Catiline's power was maimed.

His only resource was to exaggerate, as far as possible, whatever elements of discontent and disorder were still available. Amongst these was the dispute whether the action of Cicero had been legally justified or not. Might not a state of affairs, in which citizens could be put to death without trial, be represented as calling for the intervention of the second Sulla? If Pompey could no longer be summoned to save the State from the anarchy of Catiline, might not the " tyranny of Cicero " * serve, for want of a better, as an available pretext? With this object Nepos took the first opportunity of entering a formal protest against the executions. When Cicero laid down his consulship on the last day of December, he prepared to address, as was the custom, a parting speech to the people. Metellus by virtue of his sacrosanct power as tribune interrupted him, declaring that he who had deprived Roman citizens of their right to plead in their own defence to the people, should not be allowed to speak to the people himself. He forbade him therefore to do more than take the oath prescribed by law. Cicero affected compliance and advanced to take the oath; then lifting up his voice so as to be heard by the assembled multitude, he swore: " This city and commonwealth have been preserved from destruction by me." The unexpected appeal called forth a ready response from his audience. The whole assembly shouted assent and swore along with him.

---

* Plutarch, *Cic.*, 23, 2.

The humiliation which Metellus had intended for
Cicero was thus turned into a triumph, and attacks
which the tribune made on him in the Senate on the
following days were likewise repelled with vigour.
Nevertheless the incident was calculated to cause
him grave uneasiness. The hostility of Metellus
Nepos might, in so far as he alone was concerned,
be viewed with indifference ; but the menace implied
in the action of Pompey's agent was in the highest
degree alarming. The agent at least clearly thought
that the loss of the opportunity of intervening as the
supporter of law and order would make no difference
in Pompey's action, except that he would now come
as the ally of the Revolution instead of as its sup-
pressor.

Pompey's power as the commander of the only
efficient army was so great, that the fortunes of the
commonwealth hinged on his will, and the sole hope
of the constitutionalists lay in his keeping true to his
honour and obedient to the law. Cicero's anxiety
was increased by a letter received somewhat later
from Pompey, which was very cold in tone and
contained no word of congratulation on the achievements of his consulship. Pompey's annoyance may
easily be understood ; and the only strange thing is
that Cicero does not seem to have perceived how inevitable it was that Pompey should feel displeased.
If Catiline had been in Pompey's pay, he could not
have served him better than by the untimely attempt
at revolution. If Cicero had been Pompey's deadliest
enemy, he could not have done more to thwart his
action and frustrate his hopes. If Cicero had made

a false step, if he had not parried Catiline's attempts
to assassinate him, if he had fled from the post of
danger and called for Pompey's assistance, if he had
only allowed matters to drift until riot and massacre
began in Rome, Pompey's course would have been
easy and dignified; duty and interest would have
pointed in the same direction.   But now for the first
time in Pompey's life fortune conspicuously failed
him, and he was called upon to decide between the
sacrifice of his cherished hopes and the sacrifice of
his conscience. The temptation was strong, and
Pompey wavered and waited, hoping that chance
would serve him once more.

Meantime Metellus continued his machinations in
the city.   In spite of the defeat and death of Catiline, he still pressed his proposal that Pompey should
be summoned to restore order * ; and in these efforts
he was encouraged and supported by Cæsar, who
was now prætor.   Cæsar certainly did not wish any
such decree to be really carried ; but he saw that the
proposal could not be forced through, and he wished
by every means to embitter the relations between
Pompey and the Senate, thus averting the one combination which would have been fatal to all revolutionary schemes.   Cato steadily interposed his veto
on the proposals of his colleague, and Metellus and
Cæsar persevered with inflammatory speeches and
riotous assemblies. The disorder grew to such an
extent that the Senate passed decrees which, under
whatever form (for on this point we have conflicting
statements), prohibited both Cæsar and Metellus

* Dio Cassius. xxxvii., 43, 1.

from the exercise of their magisterial functions. Cæsar after a show of resistance submitted and shut himself up in his own house, and the Senate soon afterwards relieved him from his disabilities. Metellus declared that he was under stress of violence, and fled for protection to Pompey's camp.

Cicero's brilliant success as consul had raised him at once to a place amongst the foremost statesmen of Rome. Cato made the first use of his new power as tribune to summon an assembly in which amidst the applause of the multitude he saluted Cicero as "the father of his country." The precedent was followed in later days in favour of the emperors, and the appellation came to be an official title.* When Cicero retired from office and took his seat among the consulars at the beginning of the year 62 B.C., the new consuls asked his opinion first in their consultation of the Senate. His principles and line of policy are to be explained by the changes in the relation of parties which had occurred during the last seven years. The bond between the equestrian order and the democrats, who were equally hostile to the constitution of Sulla, had naturally been loosened by their joint victory. The Knights had now recovered their place in the jury-courts and their seats in the theatre, and had for the present no special grievance against the Senate ; the barrier of aristocratic exclusiveness had been forced by Cicero's election to the consulship, and everything tended towards a reconciliation between the first and the second order in the State.

---

* The contrast is marked by Juvenal (*Sat.*, viii., 244), " Roma patrem patriæ Ciceronem *libera* dixit."

This new union was further cemented by a common fear of the revolutionary designs of Catiline. The Roman Knights could feel no sympathy with the party which had favoured men who conspired to abolish debt and to wage war on capital. Hence it was natural and proper that Cicero and the equestrian party, of which he was one of the acknowledged chiefs, should be on the side of the constitution when the great crisis came. The consul who had risen from the ranks defended the State from revolution as vigorously as the proudest aristocrat could have done, and his success was largely owing to the staunchness with which the equestrian order stood by its leader and by the Senate. To consolidate and perpetuate the "harmony between the orders" thus attained was the dream of Cicero's politics, "the good cause" as he often calls it. His ideal party was to include the moderate men of both orders, and their combination was to present a firm barrier against revolution. As the equestrian order contained not only the great capitalists of Rome but the men of wealth and local importance in the country towns, this "concordia ordinum" implied the "consensio Italiæ," on which the statesman from Arpinum naturally laid great stress.

But no union of parties in Rome could be sufficient unless accompanied by a reconciliation between the civil and the military power. To accomplish this Cicero was anxious to secure Pompey as the leader of his coalition. Seriously as he had crossed the path of his chosen hero, his own loyalty towards him remained unshaken. He marked him out as the man fit to play the part of Scipio, the soldier-chief of a free State, and alongside of him Cicero hoped to fill the place of Lælius, the man of peace, of eloquence, and of learning, who could supplement the qualities of the military leader. This apportionment of functions was suggested in a letter which Cicero wrote to Pompey, in reply to the one which had caused him so much uneasiness early in the year. Cicero's letter * is naturally severe in tone, and he refers not without dignity to his own services to Pompey in the past: " It is my great satisfaction to be conscious that I have not failed in supporting my friends ; and if on any occasion these fail to support me in turn, I am well content that the balance of obligations conferred should rest with me. Of one thing I feel sure, that if the zeal which I have always shown in your service proves an insufficient link to bind us the one to the other, yet nevertheless the interests of the State will draw and unite us together. . . . When you have made yourself acquainted with the truth of the case, you will readily allow me, as scarcely less than Lælius, to be associated both as a political ally and as a friend with you who are so much greater than Africanus."

The failure of Cicero's " good cause " is the story which we have to trace of the politics of the ensuing years ; but it may be well to attempt, once for all, to arrive at a judgment on the practicability of his ideal. The problem presented to Rome was one which had never been solved in the ancient world. Free States there had been and great Empires, but

---

* *Ad Fam.* v., 7.

the two had always proved mutually exclusive. The question then which pressed for solution was this: How can a free State be at the same time a conquering and governing State? How can an Empire be organised without the sacrifice of political liberty? In the absence of representative government, the sole forms of free State known to the ancients were the Confederation, an organisation which common-sense at once discarded as too loose and inefficient for the purpose, and the City-state, as it had been elaborated by Greek politicians and political philosophers. To the mind of all Roman statesmen, excepting perhaps Augustus,* liberty and the City-state were inextricably bound up together, and under these conditions the task of uniting liberty and Empire was in truth an insuperable labour. Cæsar's failure to perform it was at least as conspicuous as that of Cicero and Cato. It is to Cæsar's credit that he saw that the Empire must be maintained and organised at whatever sacrifice; but his plan of organising it was simply to throw up in despair the problem which he was called to solve. He reverted to the method of primitive despotism, that crude and long discredited form of government by which Egypt, Assyria, and Persia had ruled and degraded vast populations. He renounced all the political inheritance of the civilised West, and all the glorious

---

* Suetonius (*Aug.*, 46) tells us that Augustus conceived the project of having the magistrates, and through them the Senate, elected not by a mass-meeting at Rome but by a poll taken in the country-towns. This plan contains the germ of a representative system, but unhappily it was never carried into effect.

hopes and ideals with which Greece and Rome had enriched the world.*   To these hopes and ideals Cicero clung, and unhappily he clung at the same time to the use of the very imperfect machinery which Greece had invented for the fashioning of political liberty and order.

A State great and powerful, as Rome had now become, had really outgrown the forms adapted to the government of a city.   These forms supplied no means by which the collective will of the great body of Roman citizens could find a regular and peaceful expression ; they afforded no effective machinery for making the provincial administration work in due harmony and subordination to the central government, or for bringing home to the central government itself any sense of responsibility whether towards citizens or subjects.   The Senate was too weak when it had to deal with the details of government throughout the empire, or to defend the civilised world by military force and at the same time to keep the soldiers and their commanders in order; it was too strong, whenever for the sake of its own interests it chose to ignore or to defy public opinion at home.   The rectification of abuses, which with better arrangements might have been accomplished by a change of ministry, was possible under this perverse system only at the cost of revolution.

Cicero seems to have been unconscious of these defects.   He never saw that, if the free State was to survive, it must invent a fresh machinery of government.   He looked on the forces which destroyed the

---

* See below, pp. 349 to 352.

Republic as the devices of wicked men breaking into the system, whereas the system was in truth largely responsible for the mischief. He assumed that the traditional powers and methods recognised in the constitution of Rome were absolute and immutable, and that all his combinations must be within the lines thus prescribed for him. These limitations precluded any of those radical reforms which alone could have permanently saved Rome from her fatal revolution. But as a temporary expedient, staving off the evil day for that generation at least, and giving time for the Republic to work out its problems and re-model its institutions, Cicero's policy seems to have been far superior to that of any other statesman of his time. If the great disaster of the military despotism was to be avoided, it was necessary that Senate and Knights should compose their differences once for all and show a united front to the enemy. Still more necessary was it, that Pompey should be attached to the constitution, and diverted from any alliance with the revolutionary party. To accomplish this, Cicero was for frankly conceding to Pompey the exceptional position which he claimed as the first man in the State, and was quite content himself to act as Pompey's lieutenant and coadjutor.

For the success of any such combination, it was needful that all the parties with which he had to work should have shared Cicero's insight into the dangers of the time and his willingness to make sacrifices to meet them. But Cicero failed in his efforts to bring this conviction home to his contemporaries. Nobles alike and men of business preferred authority. Unhappily his capacity for a plain and vigorous policy seems to have been exhausted by this single good action. He fell back on his pitiful habit of silence and reserve, never perceiving that the statesman who tries to refrain from committing himself on the main political issues of the time must of necessity become impotent and ridiculous. The natural and logical sequence to the dispersion of Pompey's army was a frank union with the constitutionalists; and this implied a clear and unmistakable approval of the action of the government in the matter of Catiline. But for this Cicero looked in vain.

During the month of December, 62 B.C., another question had arisen in Rome, petty enough in itself but destined to have serious consequences. A young patrician named Publius Clodius was caught, disguised as a woman, invading the mysteries of the "Good Goddess," whose privacy was polluted by the presence of any male at her worship. The sacrifices were performed in the house of Cæsar, who was prætor for the year, * and in pursuit of an intrigue with Cæsar's wife Clodius thrust himself into the company of Vestals and matrons. Cæsar divorced his wife, and declined to stir further in the business.†

---

* See above p. 138.

† Cicero upbraids him for " lack of gall " in not resenting the affront which Clodius had put upon him (*De Har. Resp.*, 18, 38). But Cæsar had just been engaged in an intrigue of his own which caused Pompey to divorce his wife Mucia; he doubtless felt that his appearance in the character of the injured husband would be somewhat ridiculous. When we recollect that Pompey consoled himself for the loss of Mucia by taking Cæsar's own daughter to fill her place, it must be owned that Roman husbands accepted these mishaps rather calmly.

BONA DEA : THE GODDESS OF FERTILITY
(*Duruy.*)

COIN OF CÆSAR, HEAD OF VENUS.
(*Cohen.*)

But the matter could not rest there. The virgins
performed afresh the ceremonies whose virtue had
been impaired ; the pontiffs declared that sacrilege
had been committed, and it followed that the State
must purge itself from the impiety by the punishment of the offender. After discussions in the
Senate, the consuls were instructed to bring a bill
before the People, constituting a court for his trial.
A tribune, Fufius, proposed in Clodius' interest a
rival scheme, which differed from that of the Senate
by providing that the jury should be chosen by lot,
whereas the consular bill directed the prætor to
select the jurymen.

This was the condition of affairs when Pompey
arrived early in February before the gates of Rome,
and the world eagerly awaited his utterances on all these burning questions. **61 B.C.**
Cicero gives a graphic account * of his first appear-
ances before the people and the Senate. "I have
already told you what Pompey's first speech was
like, with no comfort for the wretched, too un-
substantial to please the disloyal, unsatisfactory
to the comfortable classes, and with not sufficient
firmness for honest men ; and so it fell flat. Not
long after, at the instigation of the consul Piso,
that paltry fellow Fufius the tribune again put
Pompey forward. The scene of this was the Fla-
minian Circus on a market-day with a large attendance. He questioned him as to whether he approved
of a prætor selecting the jurors, who were to sit as that
prætor's court—this being the arrangement proposed

Ad Att., i., 14. 1.

by the Senate in the case of Clodius. Then Pompey replied very much ' en grand seigneur '; he said that the authority of the Senate weighed heavily with him on all occasions and had always done so, and so on at great length. Next the consul Messalla asked Pompey in the Senate, what was his opinion regarding the sacrilege and regarding the bill that had been proposed. He replied by praising in general terms all the decrees of that House ; and as he sat down again beside me, he remarked—' I suppose I have said enough on your business as well.' "

It is not surprising that this hesitation and inability to speak his mind should have produced a bad impression on Pompey's contemporaries. The desire to keep things open and the weak love of silence and reserve could only be indulged in at the expense of his reputation for honesty and straightforwardness. It is of no avail that a man has been seen to make great sacrifices on occasion to the cause of duty, if his daily bearing contradicts the idea of his sincerity. Cicero was strongly provoked with Pompey's conduct and expressed his vexation in no measured language to his friend *—"there is no courtesy, no candour in him, no sense of honour in politics, nothing high-minded or vigorous or straightforward."

On the other hand the leading Optimates were much to blame in not exerting themselves to win Pompey. Whenever he made advances, they were coldly received. Pompey showed what he wished, when he proposed a series of matrimonial alliances

* *Ad Att.*, i., 13, 4.

which would have united him closely with Cato. Cato rejected his overtures, and soon afterwards saw cause to exult in his short-sighted way over his own prudence. Pompey spent money too freely at the elections in 61 B.C. in order to secure the return of his partisan Afranius as consul. " I should have shared in the ill-fame of this," said Cato, " if I had allied myself to Pompey by marriage." Plutarch, who is our authority for the story, very sensibly adds * : " However, if we are to judge by the event, Cato made a fatal error in rejecting the alliance, and leaving Pompey to turn to Cæsar and contract a marriage which, by uniting the forces of the two, nearly ruined Rome and actually destroyed the constitution. None of these things would have happened, if Cato had not taken fright at the small faults of Pompey, and so allowed him to commit the greatest of all in building up the power of another."

Meanwhile the business of Clodius had entered on a fresh phase. Hortensius, who was one of the prominent supporters of the bill, fearing that it would be vetoed at last by Fufius, suggested that it might be well to paralyse his opposition by accepting Fufius' own bill as a substitute. The guilt of Clodius, he thought, was so manifest that no jury, however constituted, could fail to find a true verdict on the question of fact. He would " cut Clodius' throat," he protested " even with a leaden sword." Accordingly, the experiment was tried ; the consuls withdrew their bill, and that of Fufius was carried unopposed. When the jury came to be empanelled, it was manifest

---

* Plutarch, *Cato Minor*, 30, 5.

that the lot had fallen unluckily. The challenges of the accused cleared out the best men, while those of the prosecutor could make little impression on the mass of indifferent characters whose names had come from the ballot-box ; " there never was a more rascally lot collected round a gaming-table." *

Clodius' defence was an *alibi*. He produced witnesses to swear that he was never near Cæsar's house that night, but was fifty miles away at Interamna. Unfortunately Cicero had happened to meet him in Rome only three hours before, and he earned Clodius' deadly hatred by coming forward in disproof of the *alibi*. At first it seemed as if the jury were going to decide according to the facts. When Cicero came forward to give his evidence and the partisans of Clodius hooted and attempted to mob him, the jurors rose as one man, and interposed their persons for his protection. They protested likewise against the coercion of the court by Clodius' rabble, and applied to the Senate for an armed guard, which was immediately granted. Hortensius was triumphant, and all the world believed that a verdict of Guilty was inevitable. But a powerful factor had been left out of consideration. Crassus was the richest man in Rome, and though he loved his money dearly, he loved power and influence still more, and was ready to spend freely when a political object was in view. He had lately become security to Cæsar's creditors for about £200,000,† in order to enable him to get safely out of Rome and to take

* *Ad Att.*, i., 16, 3.
† 830 talents. Plutarch, *Cæsar*, 11, 1.

up his command in Spain. It had doubtless been
settled between the two, that Clodius would be useful to them in the future, and that he must be saved
at all costs. Crassus accordingly paid down an
enormous sum of money, and in the course of two
days bought the votes of a majority of the jury.

The acquittal was a heavy blow to the hopes of
the constitutional party. The scandal was so notorious that it seemed to proclaim the hopelessness of
orderly government and pure justice in Rome.
" That settlement," Cicero writes,* " which you used
to ascribe to my policy, and I to Providence, which
seemed firmly established by the union of all loyal
citizens and by the events of my consulship, has
now, I must tell you, crumbled beneath our feet, unless Heaven takes pity on us, all through this single
verdict—if indeed one can call it a verdict—that
thirty men, as worthless and base as you could find
in our State, should take money to outrage all law
and all right, and that when every man, and, let
alone men, every beast in Rome knows that a thing
was done, Thalna and Plautus and Spongia and
riff-raff of that sort should decide that it was not
done."

The scandal gave rise to some neat epigrams.
" They did not trust you on your oath," Clodius
said, taunting Cicero. " Twenty-five of them," was
the retort, " did trust me, and the other thirty-one
certainly did not trust you, for they got their money
down beforehand." † In the same vein was the re-

---

* *Ad Att.*, i., 16, 6.

† *Ad Att.*, i., 16, 10

12

mark of Catulus to a juror : " What made you ask
us for a guard ? Were you afraid that your pocket
would be lightened as you went home from the
court ? " *

It may be presumed that Pompey was disgusted
with the shameless perversion of justice, for which
the democratic leaders were responsible. At any
rate we find constant evidence in the letters of the
months which follow, that Pompey was now anxious
to be on good terms with the constitutionalists, and
that more especially he was drawing towards Cicero.
He never frankly gives up his clumsy reticence, but
it melts gradually away, and he finds heart at last to
commit himself to a definite approval of the acts of
Cicero's consulship.   In the following December

61 B.C. Cicero writes to Atticus † : " However,
since your friends " (the equestrian order)
" seem unsteady, another road to safety is, as I hope,
being laid.   I cannot speak fully of it by letter, but
I will indicate what I mean.   I am on very intimate
terms with Pompey.   I perceive what you will say ;
yes, I will be cautious, where caution is needed, and
I will write again to you more at length about my

60 B.C. political projects."   On the 1st of February he says ‡ : " Meanwhile you cannot
find a single true statesman, no nor the ghost of one.
One man might be, if he chose, my friend, for I wish
you to understand that he is very much so, Pompey ;
but he only stares in silence on his lap, studying

* *Ad Att.*, i., 16, 5.
† *Ad Att.*, i., 17, 10.
‡ *Ad Att.*, i., 18, 6.

the pattern on that triumphal robe of his. *   Crassus will not say a word to hazard his popularity : for the rest, you know them ; they are so stupid that they think that the State may founder, and yet that their fish-ponds will be safe.   The single man who cares for the public good is Cato ; and he brings to the work principle and honesty, but, as it seems to me, very little judgment or sense."   Next month, Cicero gives to his friend a fuller explanation of the political situation and of his own relations **March, 60, B.C.** to Pompey.   Ever since his consulship he has † " never ceased to act in politics with the same great aims, and worthily to maintain the dignity then achieved."   But the acquittal of Clodius, the weakness of the equestrian order, and the jealousy of the Nobles—" all made me feel that I must look out for some stronger forces and more trustworthy defences.   My first concern was with Pompey.   He had held his tongue far too long ; but I brought him round to a proper state of mind ; so that, speaking in the Senate on several occasions, he ascribed the preservation of the Empire and the peace of the world to my action."   Again **May, 60 B.C.** in May we find ‡ : " In your observations on affairs of State you argue like a true friend and a man of sense, and what you say is really not far away from my own sentiments.   I quite agree with

---

* " Togulam illam pictam silentio tuetur suam."   I venture to give this poetical sense to " tuetur," though it is rare in Cicero.   The sentence might mean " by his silence he keeps his embroidered robe for his own," but this is very flat.

† *Ad Att.*, i., 19, 6.

‡ *Ad Att.*, i., 20, 2.

you that I must not flinch from my post of honour, and that I must not enlist under the banner of any other, but must effect a junction at the head of my own forces. It is true likewise that the person you name has no breadth or greatness of policy and that he is too much inclined to truckle to the mob. But for all that, it is of some use for the quiet of my own life, and of infinitely greater use for the State, that the blows aimed at me by bad citizens should be parried ; and this I accomplished when I strengthened the wavering resolution of a man with such a position, such influence, and such interest, and brought him to frustrate the hopes of the disloyal by recording his approval of my action." Unhappily, though Cicero was so far successful in winning Pompey towards the side of the Senate, he failed, as we shall see just now, in inducing the senatorial party frankly to meet Pompey's advances.

Pompey's position throughout these months was full of anxiety and annoyance. He had pledged his word to his soldiers that their services against Mithridates should be recompensed by grants of land, for the purchase of which ample means were provided by the revenues with which his conquests had enriched the Roman Treasury. But his efforts to get the necessary decrees passed had hitherto been unavailing. Another vexation was, that the Senate refused to confirm the settlement of Asia which Pompey had made before his departure. All the affairs of the provinces of the East with the adjacent free cities and client kingdoms had been regulated and organised by Pompey, and he now wished that his arrangements should be sanctioned *en bloc*. The Senate refused to do this, and insisted that each detail should be reviewed and voted on separately. Thus Pompey was exposed at every point to a galling and wearisome opposition.

His own proceedings showed, as usual, clumsiness and want of tact. By a lavish expenditure of money he succeeded in thrusting in one of his adherents, Afranius, as consul for the year 60 B.C.; but Afranius was disliked by every one and was quite incapable of serving his master effectively. " He is such an absolute nonentity," writes Cicero,* " that he does not know what he has bought "; and again: " He conducts himself in such a way that his office is not so much a consulship as a blot on the reputation of our Great One." †

The other consul was Metellus Celer, the brother of Cicero's old opponent Nepos. Celer has left record of what manner of man he was in a curiously insolent letter which he addressed to Cicero at the time of the dispute with his brother, a letter which Cicero answered with admirable spirit and temper. ‡ If we may trust Cicero's judgment, § Celer was not a bad man at bottom, and meant well by his country; but he must have been a very stupid and wrongheaded politician. He now set himself in violent opposition to Pompey, and thwarted all his efforts to provide for his soldiers. This object had been

---

* *Ad Att.*, i., 19, 4.

† *Ad Att.*, i., 20, 5.

‡ *Ad Fam.*, v., 1 and 2. See also below p. 198.

§ *Ad Att.*, ii., 1, 4.

undertaken by Flavius, one of the tribunes for the year 60 B.C., who proposed in Pompey's interest an Agrarian Law. Cicero acted in a wise and states-manlike manner. He suggested amendments in the proposal to make it more workable, and then gave the measure his support. In the month
60 B.C.
of March he writes * : " The chief po-litical news is that an Agrarian Law is being vigor-ously pushed by the tribune Flavius, backed by Pompey ; nothing in it is popular except its backer. Out of this bill, with full assent of the meeting, I cut all the clauses which infringed on vested inter-ests ; I exempted all the land which had been public property in the tribuneship of Tiberius Gracchus † ; I confirmed Sulla's grantees in their holdings, and left in full possession the people of Volaterra and Arretium, whose lands Sulla had confiscated but never parcelled out. One principle of the bill, however, I accepted, namely, that land for distri-bution should be purchased out of the wind-fall which the Treasury will have in the income to be derived during the next five years from the newly acquired sources of revenue. But the Senate sets itself in opposition to the principle of any Agrarian Law whatever, under the idea that some new power for Pompey is designed. Pompey on his side puts all his energies into carrying the bill."

The struggle over this question was enlivened by a ludicrous episode. ‡ The consul Metellus carried

---

* *Ad Att.*, i., 19, 4.

† This would be mainly the Campanian land. See p. 100.

‡ Dio Cassius, xxxvii., 50.

his obstruction to lengths which Flavius considered unfair. The tribune thereupon by virtue of his sacred and inviolable office personally laid hands on the consul, as on one guilty of contempt, and dragged him off to prison. It would have been easy for Metellus to appeal to another tribune to grant him protection ; but he preferred the cheap martyrdom with which his adversary provided him. Metellus then sat in his prison, but he issued from thence a summons to the Senate to assemble there. Not to be baffled, the tribune placed his bench across the prison door and his own sacrosanct person on the bench, thus setting an insuperable barrier between the senators and the consul within. The Fathers of the State, thus beaten off in front, made an attack on the rear, and began pulling down the back wall of the prison to get at their consul. When the farce had reached this point, Pompey sent word in hot haste to his tribune that he had better let Metellus out.

Under the effect of these ridiculous proceedings "the agrarian project began to fall flat." * The Nobles delighted in the discomfiture of Pompey and gloried in their own outrageous folly. The demands of Pompey were at this time exceedingly moderate ; the loyalty and good faith which he had shown in disbanding his army, might fairly claim liberal and friendly treatment ; and the constitutionalists were bound in honour to see that Pompey did not lose by his respect for the constitution. Common-sense, too, might have shown them that by a little con-

* *Ad Att.*, ii., 1, 6.

ciliatory action on their part they could now win over
the great soldier to the service of the Senate, and
that here lay the only hope of averting the danger
which threatened. A fair chance of respite was now
offered them, and but for their folly in rejecting it,
Horace would not have had to date from this year
the

"" Motum ex Metello consule civicum,""

which destroyed the Roman Republic. Cato, Hortensius, and Lucullus were blind to their own
plainest interests, and their action at this crisis com-
pels us to recognise that they had none of the
instincts of statesmen. A petty jealousy of Pompey
seemed to dominate all their conduct. They strove
to make him feel that in renouncing the rule of the
sword he had laid himself at their mercy. Thus
they drove him to unconstitutional methods which
were destined to ruin himself and them alike.

The Republic had experienced a heavy loss by the
death of Catulus in the latter part of the year 61 B.C.,
and since then Cicero stood alone in recommending
a sane policy. " I am acting," he writes, * " and will
act, so as not to incur the reproach that my old
achievement was only the outcome of chance. My
' honest men,' of whom you speak, and that ' Sparta,' †
in which, as you say, my lot is cast, shall not only
never be deserted by me, but if I am deserted by
them I shall remain firm by my own principles. At
the same time I wish you to understand, that since

---

* *Ad Att.*, i., 20, 3.

† Atticus had quoted a Greek proverb : " Sparta is your lot ;
make the best of Sparta."

the death of Catulus I am holding on this most
excellent way alone, without escort and without
companionship."

Pompey was kept aloof by the obstinacy and ingratitude of the Nobles, and this was in itself sufficient to spoil the hopes which Cicero had entertained
for his "good cause." But in yet another quarter
"the good cause" was perilously shaken. In these
same months the "harmony of the orders," the
union between Senate and Knights, which Cicero
had taken such pains to realise, showed signs of dis-
solution. The scandal of the acquittal of Clodius
had drawn attention to the corruption of the law-
courts, and Cato and others pressed for vigorous
measures against all jurors who had taken bribes.
But as two-thirds of the jurors were now not of
senatorial rank, such measures could not be carried
through without infringing the cherished immunities
of the Roman Knights. * At the same time the
Knights had another quarrel with the Senate, because it refused to give them the consideration
which they held to be their due in the arrangement
of their contracts with the State. In both cases
Cicero would have humoured the equestrian order,
but he pleaded its cause in vain. We first hear of
these jars in a letter of December, 61 B.C. †

"Here we are living in a political condition that
is precarious, pitiful, and unstable. For, as I fancy
you must have heard, our friends the Knights are
all but alienated from the Senate. In the first place

---

* See above, p. 35.

† *Ad Att.*, i., 17, 8.

they are deeply offended that a bill has been introduced on the recommendation of the Senate, providing that all persons who have received bribes as jurors shall be put on their trial. It happened by accident that I was not in the House, when that decree was carried, and I perceived that the equestrian order was offended, though silent; so I took an opportunity to lecture the Senate, and did it, so far as I can judge, with much force. The claim of my clients was hardly a reputable one, but I urged it at length and in a dignified tone. Now we have on our hands another whim of the Knights, which it is hard to put up with; however I have not only put up with it, but made the best of it I could for them. The company, which farmed the province of Asia from the censors, complain that they have been too eager in their bidding, and have contracted to pay too high a figure. They demand therefore that the bargain shall be cancelled. I am the chief among their backers, or rather I should say the second, for Crassus was the man who egged them on to make the demand. It is an awkward business, and such a confession of their own want of caution is discreditable enough. But there is every fear that, if their petition is rejected, they will sever themselves entirely from the Senate. I have risen to the emergency as best I could, and managed that they should have a full House and a friendly hearing, and I made long speeches on the 1st and 2d of December concerning the dignity and union of the orders. . . . The business is not settled, but the feeling of the Senate has been clearly shown. Only one speaker opposed us, Metellus the consul-elect; there was another to come, our hero Cato, but the debate had to be adjourned before his turn was reached. Thus I stand firm by our plans and principles, and maintain so far as I can the union of the orders which was cemented by my exertions."

Cato's opposition proved serious, and it was conducted in a singularly provoking manner. Cato was a master of the art of Parliamentary obstruction, and was able by means of long speeches and irrelevant objections to put off indefinitely the decision of the House. "For two good months," writes Cicero, in a subsequent letter,* Feb., 60 B.C. "he has been harrying the unhappy tax-farmers, who used to be his best friends, and he will not allow the Senate to give an answer to their petition. So we on our side are obliged to obstruct all other business until an answer has been given to the tax-farmers."

Such were the causes of discord which broke up Cicero's ideal party. The precious months, during which it was still possible that a union should be consolidated between Pompey, the Senate, and the equestrian order, were fast passing away. Cicero alone of Roman statesmen saw what was to be aimed at ; but he had preached in vain, and now the man was at hand, who was to take advantage of the confusions of the situation and organise the conflicting forces for his own purposes. In a letter written early in June we find a casual remark that Cæsar is expected in two days' time. For the last year and

* *Ad Att.*, i., 18, 7.

a half he had been away in his Spanish governorship, and his return marks the beginning of the
Revolution. In the same letter* we get a lively
sketch of the situation just before Cæsar's arrival,
and of the hopes and fears which Cicero entertained
at the moment.

"You chide me gently about my intimacy with
Pompey. Now I would not have you think that I
am leagued with him in order to get protection for
myself ; but the position of affairs is such, that if
any difference arose between him and me, it would
inevitably produce serious disturbances in the State.
Against this mischief I have provided, not by swerv-
ing from my own honourable policy, but by inducing
him to amend his ways and renounce some of his
popularity-hunting vagaries. . . . What now if
Cæsar likewise, who has a marvellous fair wind in his
sails just now, can be brought round by me to a
better mind? Shall I have done any great harm to
the State? Why, if no one were envious of me, if
all supported me as they ought to do, even then a
treatment which should restore the unsound members of the commonwealth would be preferable to
heroic surgery. But now, when the Knights, whom
I once posted with you as their chief and standard-
bearer on the slopes of the Capitol, when the
Knights, I say, have deserted the Senate, and when
our chief men think that they are in the seventh
heaven if they have bearded mullets in their fish-
ponds who will come to feed out of their hands, do
you not think that I gain a point, if I bring it about

---

* *Ad Att.*, ii., 1, 6.

that those who could injure me should not wish to
do so? For as for our friend Cato, you cannot be
fonder of him than I am; at the same time, with
the very best intentions and in all good faith he
sometimes does mischief to the State. For he
makes his proposals as if he were speaking in Plato's
Republic instead of in Romulus' gutter. What can
be fairer than that every man should be put on his
trial, who has taken a bribe for his verdict? Such
was Cato's proposal, and the Senate agreed. So the
Knights declare war against the House, not against
me, for I protested. What could be more barefaced
than the tax-farmers repudiating their bargain? For
all that we had better have put up with the loss for
the sake of keeping the good-will of the order. Cato
resisted and gained his point. And so now when we
have a consul shut up in prison and riot continually
afoot, not a finger has been stirred to help by those
who used to throng to the defence of the constitution
whenever I or my immediate successors in the consulship called for their assistance."

With this quotation we leave the politics and parties of Rome for a moment, to turn to other matters
which are wanting to complete the picture of Cicero's
life during the years following his consulship. In
the next chapter we shall find what use Cæsar made
of the political material which lay awaiting his return.

Only two of Cicero's extant speeches belong to
this period. The suppression of Catiline's conspiracy
had been followed up during the year 62 B.C. by prosecutions directed against his accomplices. Cicero mentions the names of several who were condemned by

the juries and driven into exile—Vargunteius, Læca, Servius Sulla, Cornelius, and Autronius. Autronius, along with Publius Sulla, had been unseated for bribery after the consular elections in the year 66 B.C., and he lay under suspicion of having had a hand in the supposed "first conspiracy"* of Catiline in the years 66 and 65 B.C. His companion Publius Sulla was now brought to the bar on charges connected with both conspiracies, and Cicero came forward in his defence. Leaving Hortensius to deal with the first part of the case, he contented himself with rebutting the assertion that Sulla had taken any part in the conspiracy of the year 63 B.C. On this point Cicero was able to speak from his own knowledge, and his exculpation of Sulla was decisive with the jury.

The other speech is of a very different type. The Greek poet Archias, Cicero's earliest tutor, was accused of having improperly usurped the Roman citizenship at the time of the Social War twenty-seven years before, and an inquisition was now held into his title. Cicero appeared, as in duty bound, to speak on behalf of his old friend and teacher. He passed lightly over the technical objections urged against his client's rights, and dwelt by preference on his great fame and merit as a man of letters, whose poems, like those of Ennius, had preserved the record of the martial deeds of Rome; "for, if any one thinks that more glory is reaped when actions are enshrined in Latin poetry than in Greek, he is much mistaken; for the Greek is read in all

---

* See above, p 90.

parts of the world, the Latin is confined to the bounds of its own country which are narrow by comparison."

In pleading this cause Cicero begs to be allowed to deviate from the beaten track of forensic practice, and to speak freely of the glories and delights of literature, and of the benefits which he himself owes it. He expounds here at the bar of a law-court the doctrine which we find so frequently laid down in his treatises on the Art of Rhetoric, that the orator must be not only a "ready man" but a "full man," and that wide reading and deep study are necessary for his perfection. "You ask me, why I take such an extraordinary delight in this man? It is because he supplies me with a refuge where my mind can recruit its powers after the din of the Forum, and where my ears tired out with controversy may take some repose. Do you think, that a man could find the thoughts to express day after day on such a variety of topics, unless he cultivated his mind by study? or that the mind could bear the strain, unless these same studies supplied him with relaxation?" * Cicero was clearly in no great anxiety about the verdict. The jury listened with pleasure to his literary disquisition, and confirmed the citizenship of Archias.

Cicero's own writings at this time were chiefly directed to the history of his consulship. He composed a memoir of it in Latin and another in Greek, and he promises Atticus a poem on the same subject, "that

---

* *Pro Arch.*, 6, 12.

I may not omit any form of self-laudation." * A few very indifferent verses of the poem survive, amongst them the often-quoted

" O fortunatam natam me consule Romam," †

but the treatises in prose have been entirely lost.

We possess, however, in Cicero's speeches and letters ample specimens of his utterances on the achievements of his consulship. He has undoubtedly injured his reputation by the undisguised fashion in which he glories over his own action. His consulship was, as Seneca remarked,‡ "non sine causa, sed sine fine laudatus." He spoiled a good thing by making too much of it, and we get tired, as doubtless did Cicero's contemporaries, of " the great Nones of December," with its " inspirations of Providence," and its " glorious deed," and its " eternal fame."

If it be a deadly sin to be thoroughly pleased with one's own conduct and to express that pleasure unblushingly, Cicero must stand condemned. But two faults, of very different degree of blackness, are liable to be confused under the common name of vanity or self-conceit. There are men into whose souls the poison seems to have eaten deep ; they are pompous,

---

* *Ad Att.*, i., 19, 10.

† Mr. Tyrrell renders the jingle—" O happy fate of Rome to date Her birthday from my consulate." The reference is to his own title of "father of his country." Cicero's enemy, Piso, hit him in a tender place when he said that Cicero was really banished, not for having put Lentulus to death, but for the bad verses he had written on the subject. See *In Pison.*, 29, 72.

‡ Seneca, *De Brevitate Vitæ*, 5.

overweening, repellent ; their power of judgment and
of action is impaired ; they are obstinate because they
are weak ; they would rather perish than allow themselves to be in the wrong, and they delight in rejecting the counsels of common-sense merely to show
their own greatness and independence. Sometimes,
on the other hand, vanity is a mere superficial weakness, the accompaniment of a light heart, a quick,
sensitive temperament, an unsuspicious loquacity,
and an innocent love of display. Carlyle has hit off
the difference very happily in the contrast which he
draws between Boswell and his father—" Old Auchin-
leck had, if not the gay tail-spreading peacock vanity
of his son, no little of the slow-stalking contentious
hissing vanity of the gander, a still more fatal
species."

Now Cicero's vanity is essentially of the innocuous
and peacock-like kind. There is no pompous reticence about him. If he happens to be pleased with
himself he blurts out his satisfaction with an almost
childlike simplicity ; if the laugh turns against him,
he is not wounded or distressed, and on occasion he
can make fun of himself with perfect grace and good
humour. Nothing can be happier than the story, as
told by Cicero, of his own expectations of fame from
his Sicilian quæstorship, and how he was disabused
of them. This has been quoted in its place (above,
p. 23). It is amusing to observe that, when Cicero
finds himself, four-and-twenty years later, again
charged with the administration of a province, he
has just the same admiration for the integrity of his
own conduct, and expresses that admiration with the

13

like *naïveté* and openness.* " In all my life I never experienced so much pleasure as I do in the contemplation of my own incorruptibility. It is not so much the credit I get for it, though that is immense, as the thing itself which delights me. In a word it was worth while coming out here; I did not do myself justice, or recognise what I was capable of in this line. I do well to be puffed up. Nothing is more glorious." Just so with his literary compositions. " The passages from my orations which you commend seemed to me, I assure you, very fine, but I did not venture to say so before; now that they have your approval, I think them picked Attic every word." † He is particularly pleased with his Greek history of his consulship. " I sent my memoir to Posidonius, that he might use it as the foundation of a more eloquent treatise on the same subject; but he writes back to me from Rhodes that, when he read my book, far from being encouraged to write, he felt himself fairly warned off the ground. Now you see! I have discomfited the whole tribe of Greeks, and so the lot of them, who used to press me for material which they might work up, have ceased to pester me." ‡

With the subject-matter of his treatise he is no less delighted, and it never occurs to him for a moment that he ought to conceal his delight. It is true that in requesting the historian Lucceius to take his consulship as the theme for a separate treat-

---

* *Ad Att.*, v., 20, 6.

† *Ad Att.*, i., 13, 5.

‡ *Ad Att.*, ii., 1, 2.

ise, Cicero professes to beg humbly for his en-
comiums, and pretends to hope that he will owe
something to the favour of the writer beyond the
simple requirements of historical truth; but this is
merely an affected modesty, suitable to this studied
and elaborate letter, * which he intended to serve as
the model of the proper way of making such an application. † In his heart of hearts Cicero believed
that neither Lucceius nor any one else could praise
his consulship above its deserts. This comes out
clearly enough when he is writing to Atticus, with
whom he has no disguise. After recounting the various records, in Greek and Latin, in verse and prose,
which he has composed on his conflict with Catiline,
he adds: "Now pray don't object that I am blow-
ing my own trumpet; for if there be any human
action more glorious than mine, I am content that it
should receive the meed of praise, and that I should
incur blame for not having chosen the theme of my
panegyric better—though in truth what I have written is not panegyric but sober history."‡ And a
little later, when Pompey has soiled his good name
by his support of Cæsar's illegalities, though Cicero
grieves over the defection of his old leader, he con-
soles himself with the consideration that the great
rival of his own fame has thus effaced himself.

---

* *Ad Fam.*, v., 12.

† He directs Atticus to get the letter from Lucceius (doubtless with
the intention of having it copied), and describes it as "mighty fine"
(*Ad Att.*, iv., 6, 4). We may compare the letter (*Ad Fam.*, xii., 17),
where he sends his "Orator" to Cornificius with the request, "huic
tu libro maxime velim ex animo ; si minus, gratiæ causa suffragere."

‡ *Ad Att.*, i., 19, 10.

" Nay, that side of my nature which is vainglorious and not indifferent to praise (for it is well to know one's own faults), is affected with a certain satisfaction. For the thought used to vex me that possibly, six hundred years hence, the services of our Great Bashaw to the nation might appear more eminent than my own; now I am relieved from any such anxiety." * Each reader will judge of these utterances according as his own temperament prompts. To me it seems difficult to regard very sternly, or to take as a matter for very serious condemnation, a weakness so frankly and simply displayed. Cicero's vanity and love of praise make him less dignified, but they hardly make him less lovable.

We have still to consider a few points connected with Cicero's private life at this period. In the year after his consulship he bought from Crassus a magnificent house on the Palatine, and borrowed money freely from his friends for the purpose. His burden sat very lightly on him, and it seemed a capital joke that he who had so sternly resisted schemes of national bankruptcy should now be qualified to enlist under another Catiline. "You must know," he says,† "that I am so deep in debt that I should be quite inclined to join in a conspiracy, if any one would have me; but they all fight shy of me."

We hear little of Cicero's wife and children at this time, but much of his brother Quintus. Quintus was prætor in the year 61 B.C., and it was at his bar that Cicero delivered the speech for Archias. Towards

---

* *Ad Att.*, ii., 17, 2.

† *Ad Fam.*, v., 6, 2.

the end of the year he set out to take up the government of the province of Asia. He had wished his
brother-in-law Atticus to accompany him as legate,
but this Atticus declined, as he had always declined
any participation in official life. Quintus considered
himself slighted at the refusal, and he was likewise
deeply offended about other matters of which we
have only obscure hints. It seems probable, however, that his wife Pomponia had stirred up ill-will
between her husband and her brother, for Marcus
Cicero writes * : "Where the blame for this mischief lies, I can guess more easily than I can write
it; for I am afraid lest in excusing my kinsfolk I
should he hard on yours. For I judge that the
breach, if it were not caused by those of his own
household, might at any rate easily have been healed
by them."

Cicero laboured anxiously to reconcile his brother
and his friend, both equally dear to him. "All my
hopes of allaying this irritation," he writes to Atticus,†
"are placed in your kindliness. For if you hold
with me that the tempers of the best men are often
easily excited and again as easily quieted down, and
that this mobility and fluidity, if I may so speak, is
often the characteristic of a kindly nature, and,
which is the main point of all, that we ought to bear
with whatever we find in each other that is inconsid-
erate or faulty or aggressive, I hope and believe that
this unpleasantness may easily be got over. I beseech you to do this; for to me, who love you

---

* *Ad Att.*, i., 17, 3.

† *Ad Att.*, i., 17, 4.

dearly, it is all in all that there should be no one of
mine who dislikes you or is disliked by you. . . .
I have seen, and seen to the bottom, your tender
interest in all my varying fortunes. Often and often
I have found your congratulations on my success
sweet to me, and your support in my hours of anxiety
most cheering. Now when you are absent, it is not
only that I miss your counsel, which none can give
so well, but likewise the interchange of talk which is
sweeter with you than with any one. I feel the void
especially—where shall I say especially? in my calling as a statesman, which does not admit of a
moment's neglect? or in my labours at the bar,
which I once undertook to help me to rise, and which
I must now keep up to win influence for the support
of my position? or lastly in my home circle? In all
these, and the more so since my brother has left, I
long for your presence and conversation. . . .
You and I have hitherto been too delicate to utter
all these feelings; but now their expression seems
to be called for by that part of your letter in which
you strive to clear yourself from all reproaches and
to justify yourself and your conduct."

This letter was written in December, 61 B.C. In the
following February he refers * again to the same
topic. "My chief want at present is a man with
whom to share all my anxieties, one who loves me,
and has sense, and with whom I can talk without
pretence or reserve or concealment. For my brother,
the most open and loving soul in the world, is gone.
Metellus is not a man, but just a desert island—

* *Ad Att.*, i., 18, 1

shore and sky and utter desolation. And you, who
have so often by your talk and your counsel taken
off the burden of my care and disquietude, you who
are used to be my ally in the affairs of State, and
the confidant of my private concerns, and the partner
of all my talk and all my projects, where are you?
I am so lonely that my only solace is the time I
spend with my wife and my girl and my sweet little
Cicero. For as for all these fine friendships of interest and fashion, they have their glitter before the
world, but nothing solid to carry home with me.
And so when my reception rooms are thronged each
morning, and I go down to the Forum marshalled
by troops of friends, out of all the crowd I find no
one to whom I can utter a joke with freedom or
breathe a sigh in confidence. Thus I wait for you
and long for you; nay, more, now I summon you
to my side; for there are many troubles and anxieties
of which I think I could rid my bosom, if I might
only pour them into your ear in the course of a single
walk."

It is pleasant to know that Atticus was not dull to
the affection so heartily lavished on him, and that
no cloud was suffered to come between the friends.
The answer of Atticus was all that Cicero could
desire. "I am glad," Cicero writes in reply,* "that
you understand the value which I set on you, and I
am beyond measure rejoiced that in those matters in
which our family has, as it seems to me, treated you
ungently and inconsiderately, you have acted with
such patience; and I esteem this as the sign of a

* *Ad Att.*, i., 20, 1.

perfect affection and of a large-hearted wisdom. You write about the matter with such gentleness, such reasonableness, such delicacy and such kindliness, that far from having occasion to urge you further, I can only say that I could never have looked for so much placability and tenderness from you or from any one in the world. I think that the most suitable course will be to drop the subject altogether for the present ; when we meet, we can, if desirable, talk the matter over together."

ANCIENT ROMAN AS.

(*Babelon.*)

CHAPTER VII.

THE FIRST TRIUMVIRATE.

60–59 B.C.

ÆSAR had well employed the time of his absence in Spain, and he came back, _{June, 60 B.C.} as Cicero said, "with a marvellous fair wind in his sails." In the first place he had freed himself from the most pressing of his money difficulties ; he " had wanted," so he said, " a million sterling *
to be worth nothing," and now he was able to look his creditors in the face. Notwithstanding his great gains, he brought back the reputation of a good provincial governor. Above all he had served with success his apprenticeship as a general. To himself the secret, that he had a genius for the art of war, was no doubt already revealed, and the consciousness of this power determined the path which he marked out. Even in the eyes of the world his victories over revolted Spanish tribes were such as

---

* Twenty-five million drachmas, Appian, *Bell. Civ.*, ii., 8.

fairly to entitle him to a triumph, and to confirm the inclination of the voters to raise the most popular of the Nobles at once to the consulship.

The triumph he was obliged to forego, owing to the spiteful interposition of Cato, who obstr¹ ted * a dispensation which the Senate would have granted, and compelled Cæsar to forfeit his command by coming within the walls to sue for the consulship. This however was a small matter. Cæsar was duly elected consul for the next year, 59 B.C., having for his colleague Marcus Calpurnius Bibulus, who was the brother-in-law of Cato, and a vehement partisan of the oligarchy.

In anticipation of Cæsar's success the Senate, when assigning provinces for the consuls of 59 B.C., had chosen trivial and obscure spheres of administration. Cæsar did not intend to be thus set aside. He was determined to have a great provincial command, and the control of a powerful army; and to gain this object he set himself to combine all the powers which were at the moment in a state of alienation from the Senate.

He could count on the support of his old ally Crassus; and though Pompey and Crassus were generally on bad terms, he did not despair of uniting them. To Crassus he could point out how necessary it was for the fortunes of the democratic party that Pompey should be estranged once for all from the Senate; and as for Pompey himself, the insults and provocations to which he had been subjected for the last eighteen months, and the embar-

* Plutarch, *Cato Minor*, 31, 3.

rassments of his present position, rendered him very open to the offers which Cæsar was prepared to make. If the three could agree on common action, they might hope to overbear all opposition, and this hope would be almost a certainty if the adherence of Cicero could likewise be secured. His presence in the coalition would disarm the hostility of the middle class and of the country people of Italy, his character would give respectability to the new party, and his eloquence would sway public opinion to its side.

Cæsar's first scheme then was for a quattuorvirate, consisting of himself, Pompey, Crassus, and Cicero. This project was not, of course, openly proclaimed at the time; but four years later Cicero publicly announced the fact. "Cæsar," he says,* "wished me to be one of three consulars most intimately allied with himself. . . . He showed, and I was not insensible to it, how friendly his intentions were, when he offered me a place side by side with the foremost of all the citizens, his own son-in-law." About the same time (56 B.C.) we find Cicero, in a confidential letter to Atticus,† lamenting that he, who had refused to be one of the masters in the coalition, should now be reduced to act as its servant.

Cæsar had probably made some tentative advances even before his arrival in Rome, for, as we saw in the last chapter (p. 188), Cicero expressed so early as the beginning of June the **60 B.C.** hope that he could bring Cæsar to a better mind.

---

* *De Prov. Cons.*, 17, 41.

† See below, p. 269.

Though Cæsar failed in this portion of his scheme, it does not follow that his expectations were irrational or impossible of fulfilment. Cicero had throughout his life acted with the equestrian order, and that order was now estranged from the Senate. He had from the first chosen Pompey as his leader, and after the temporary coolness, caused by the events of his consulship, he and Pompey had again drawn closely together. The Nobles on the other hand had rejected Cicero's latest counsels. It was well worth trying whether he might not be induced to follow Pompey and the Knights in their quest of new allies. Between the time of his election to the consulship and his entry on office Cæsar made serious overtures, which will best be described in Cicero's own words * : " They say that Cæsar looks for my support and has no doubt whatever that he will get it. For Cornelius came to see me just now, Cornelius Balbus I mean, Cæsar's confidential agent. He assures me that Cæsar will in all matters act under the advice of Pompey and myself, and that he will exert himself to unite Pompey and Crassus. To accept this proposal offers many advantages : an intimate alliance with Pompey, and, since it comes to that, with Cæsar too ; reconciliation with my enemies, peace with the multitude, quiet for my old age." On the other side is the conviction that to enter on this new alliance will be to throw up the " good cause " and to derogate from the glories of his consulship. He supports this good resolution by some bad verses from his own poem, and concludes

* *Ad Att.*, ii., 3. 3.

that his duty to his country obliges him to abide fast by his principles. That this resolve was final, is clear from one of the early letters of the next year,* in which he says : " Meantime I pursue my studies with a mind quiet, and even cheerful and contented ; for it never occurs to me to envy Crassus, or to regret that I did not prove false to myself."

It may be doubted, even if Cæsar had gained Cicero's adhesion, whether he could so far have modified his own course of action as to keep the union unimpaired. The presence of an ally who objected to breaking the law would have seriously hampered his proceedings. In seeking Cicero's support, he must either have hoped that this support would enable him to carry out his projects by milder means, or else he must have calculated that Cicero, once committed to his party, would have been unable to shake himself loose, and would have been drawn along wherever it suited Cæsar to carry him.

As it was, Cicero stood aloof ; the coalition was organised as a triumvirate, and Cæsar went on his way unchecked by any scruples. His plan was at once simple and effective. He knew exactly what he wanted, and was prepared to pay the price. Let his confederates give him an extraordinary command for a term of years of a province and an army, and he will undertake to secure for them anything else which they desire. All that they had been vainly striving to obtain for the last two years was to be theirs at once. Pompey was to have his acts in Asia confirmed, and his soldiers were to get their lands ;

---

* *Ad Att.,* ii. 4 ᵹ.

the populace of the capital was likewise to be provided for in an agrarian law; the equestrian order,
the clients of Crassus, were to have their Asiatic contract revised, and were to hear nothing more about
prosecutions for judicial corruption. In case these
objects could not be gained by legal methods, Cæsar
promised to accomplish them in spite of law and constitution. It followed of course that his allies must
not be critical of the means employed; he would
take all the responsibility of carrying his measures,
but they must be prepared to support whatever he
did.

On these terms the great conspiracy, known to
history as the "First Triumvirate" was formed.
Crassus, when once the initial difficulty of reconciliation with Pompey was overcome, was not likely to
find anything objectionable in the conditions; but
the case was different with Pompey. How could
any price tempt Pompey to put another man in
possession of just such a commanding military position as he had himself enjoyed three years before?
Pompey must have recollected afterwards with bitter
repentance that, if he could only have possessed his
integrity in patience for a few months longer, all
would have been well. The migration of the Helvetii and the passage of Ariovistus into Gaul would
have certainly created a situation calling for his
intervention, if he had not already placed Cæsar in a
position to deal with it. The explanation of Pompey's acquiescence doubtless is, that he had no idea
that he was dealing with a man of military genius
equal or superior to his own. Up to the age of forty

Cæsar, though he had shown distinguished bravery
in his youth, had never been in command of troops;
he was famous as a politician and party leader, but
quite unknown as a soldier. Just now indeed he had
supplemented his record by a single year's command
in Spain; but to the veteran warrior this would seem
a very insufficient training, and Cæsar's achievements,
though creditable to him as an officer, were not such
as to undeceive Pompey respecting his powers. There
was then, as yet, little reason to fear a serious rivalry
on this ground; and Cæsar was able to represent his
province and his army merely as a reserve force, on
which his partners at home might fall back in case
of necessity.

Other scruples however must have suggested themselves. Pompey had declined the despotism which
was within his reach, and had refused to violate his
duty to the State in his own interest; and now he
was asked to abandon the character of a loyal republican, and to give his sanction to illegal action and
violent breaches of the constitution. It seems probable that he was too short-sighted to perceive clearly
the treasonable nature of his compact with Cæsar,
and that he salved his conscience by disclaiming
responsibility for whatever he could not approve.
The bargain once struck, Pompey was no longer a
free man. He had reaped the benefit of Cæsar's
illegalities, and could not refuse to support them in
all their consequences; and so we shall find him
during the ensuing years compelled in spite of misgivings to do Cæsar's work for him, and unable to
break with him until Cæsar has made himself too

strong to be safely resisted. Cicero afterwards * remarked with truth that, as the day of the battle of Allia, not that on which the Gauls entered Rome, was marked as the black day in the Roman Calendar, so this compact should be regarded as the fatal epoch, rather than the Civil War which was merely its sequel.

Meantime the temptation of Cæsar's offers was too strong for Pompey. He must have suffered keenly during the months in which he had been worried and thwarted by the senseless and ungrateful opposition of the Nobles, and now his patience was worn out, and, come what might, he was resolved to be even with the pack of them and to carry his measures in their despite. Pompey's surrender dealt a fatal blow to Cicero's ideal party, and indeed to Cicero's position as an independent statesman. For the next eight years we shall find Roman politics dominated by the coalition, and when that coalition breaks up all controversies have to be decided on the battle-field. Cicero becomes almost powerless, and his statesmanship suffers an eclipse, from which it fully emerges only after Cæsar's death.

Cæsar entered on his consulship on the 1st of January, 59, and at once proceeded to carry out the engagements into which he had entered.

59 B.C.
January.

Of the bills which he announced only one was of the nature of a legislative reform. This was the " Lex Julia Repetundarum " which consolidated and amended the laws against extortion in the provinces. His other proposals were

---
* *Ad Att.,* ix., 5. 2.

strictly party measures. He brought in a bill for the purchase of lands, alike for Pompey's veterans and for the fathers of large families among the poorer citizens. He proposed another bill for the confirmation of Pompey's acts in Asia, and a third remitting part of the sum which the tax-farmers had agreed to pay to the Treasury. At the same time he contrived an ingenious scheme to provide himself and his confederates with money. It will be remembered that the title of the present ruler of Egypt was defective, and that Rome had claims on the country under the Will of the late king (see page 102). For twenty-two years Roman statesmen had failed to make up their minds whether they should annex Egypt or not. Cæsar and Crassus, who had been for annexation six years before, now looked to the North rather than to the East for their provincial base of operations, and were disposed to utilise Egypt in another way. It was therefore resolved to procure a decree of the people, recognising Ptolemy Auletes as king, and for this service Ptolemy paid the triumvirs a bribe of 6000 talents, about a million and a half sterling.* The prize which Cæsar had marked for himself, the command for five years in Cisalpine Gaul and Illyricum, was to be bestowed not by a law of his own proposing but by one brought in by the tribune Vatinius.

Cæsar at first affected to act with moderation. He submitted all his bills to the Senate, and in the case of the Agrarian Law in particular he declared himself ready and willing to listen to argument and to accept

---

* Suetonius, *Jul.*, 54.

amendments. It was not likely, however, that the Senate would, except under compulsion, grant to Cæsar what they had refused the year before to Pompey and Cicero. Accordingly a bitter opposition was raised to the measure in the Senate. Cato in particular spoke at such length and with such virulence, that Cæsar ordered him to be arrested for contempt. Like Metellus the year before, Cato would not appeal for protection to a tribune, and he was marched off by the lictors continuing his speech as he walked towards the prison, while the senators rose from their places to accompany him to his confinement. This did not suit the plans of the consul, and he sent word to one of his own tribunes to interpose and release the prisoner.

The obstinate opposition to Cæsar's measures gave him, however, an excuse for declaring that no fair treatment could be got from the Senate, and that he should therefore cease to consult it and should bring his bills direct before the People. It has been explained in the second chapter (p. 27) how such an action on the part of a magistrate was a breach of constitutional order, and how it could not be carried through to the end without an actual violation of the law. Cæsar had complete command of the streets, and could easily provide an assembly to say " aye " to his proposals, if only his power of initiating them were unimpeded. But this power of initiative was subject to the veto of his colleague and of the tribunes. Of the tribunes some were little more than his own servants, but there were also some ready to obey with equal promptitude the orders of the Senate. Bibulus accompanied by two tribunes appeared in the Forum on the day appointed for the voting on the Agrarian Law, and in due order vetoed the bill. This rendered all further proceedings un- lawful. But Cæsar set law at defiance ; his mob drove Bibulus and the tribunes with blows from the spot,* and he then submitted his proposal to the assembly and declared it to be carried. A bill so passed was, of course, invalid, and could only be sustained, even as it had been enacted, by the strong hand.

It was now clear that the personal interposition of the veto could be made only at the peril of the life of the intervening magistrate, and Bibulus was not inclined to face the risk again. But the constitution allowed the exercise of the veto in a more convenient form, namely by the allegation of religious obstacles to the business. At this period the religious, no less than the civil, veto was an essential part of the constitu- tion, and the conditions under which it might be ap- plied were strictly regulated by the law.

The antiquarian history of this religious veto is curious and interesting.† The desire to ascertain be- forehand what is the pleasure of the gods, forms only a secondary motive in Roman augury ; the primary object is to win the luck to your side, to avoid anything unchancy, to catch up and appro- priate any word or sight which may have a happy significance. The Romans were full of contrivances for manufacturing good luck. Like Balak, if the

* Dio Cassius, xxxviii., 6.

† See Mommsen *Staats-recht*, i., p. 77 *et seq.*

first sacrifice turned out unpropitious, they tried another, and continued the process until they found what they wanted. They starved the sacred chickens to make sure of their feeding, and then gave them porridge to eat, so that some of the food should drop from their beaks, which was esteemed a particularly happy augury. An omen again was held to be significant, not as it occurred in nature, but as it caught the attention of the person concerned, and this doctrine admitted of many developments. If anything happened which it was inconvenient for the magistrate to see, he might refuse to notice it; much as Nelson put the telescope to his blind eye to look for the signal ordering him to retreat. The Marcellus of the Second Punic War, an excellent augur, as Cicero tells us,* always went in a closed litter when he meant to give battle, and so escaped the chance of seeing anything unlucky. Again, if an attendant falsely reported an omen to the magistrate, the magistrate might accept it as reported. The attendant indeed took the curse of the falsehood on his own head †; but it was not difficult to find persons willing thus to purchase to themselves damnation in the way of their calling.

Now the Roman magistrate, entering on any official business, was accustomed to consecrate that business by the previous consultation of the auspices. The omen which was most desired was a flash of lightning on the left hand, and this was at once ob-

---

* *De Divin.*, ii., 36, 77.

† Those who wish to see this doctrine illustrated by an amusing story may look at Livy. x.. 40.

tained by asking the attendant if he saw such a flash
and receiving his answer in the affirmative. This
was technically termed *servare de cœlo* " to observe
something (*i. e.* lightning) coming from the sky."
But this omen, so good in itself, might be used as an
obstruction to other business. A thunderstorm occurring during a meeting of the People was unlucky
and broke up the assembly; and accordingly the
flash of lightning, which the magistrate was supposed
to have seen, arrested all legislation for the day. To
avoid this inconvenience the consul, when he fixed a
day for the assembly of the People, used to issue an
edict forbidding any inferior magistrate to look for
lightning for any purpose of his own on that day.
Such a prohibition was, however, of no avail against
the consul's colleague or against the tribunes of the
plebs, who were not bound to obey his orders. The
duties and powers of the magistrates in this matter
were accurately fixed for them by the Law of Ælius
and Fufius (*circ.* 150 B.C.). By this law every magistrate holding an assembly of the People was forbidden to ignore any omen officially reported to him
by his colleague, and every magistrate who had the
right to " observe lightning " for his own purposes,
might cause the same to be reported as a deterrent
omen for his colleague who was proposing a bill to
the People. Such a report rendered all proceedings
by the assembly null and void. It is manifest that
any sincere religious feeling on the subject, which
may once have existed, must have died out before
this cut-and-dried procedure was ordained. The
regulation must be regarded not as a piece of super-

stition, but as a portion of constitutional law. It was a machinery contrived to extend the power of veto (for under this form it might be used by the consul even against a tribune), and to make its application more easy and convenient.

Driven by armed force from the Forum, Bibulus now resorted to this method. He shut himself up in his house, and on every day when the people assembled he "saw lightning" and caused an official intimation of it to be sent to Cæsar.* Cæsar systematically ignored the prohibition and passed his measures one by one. He thereby broke the law, and usurped powers which were not his. As consul he had the legal right to propose measures to the people, but only provided that his initiative was not lawfully impeded. His colleague had an absolute right to forbid him. The whole business of the lightning was indeed a constitutional fiction, and absurd enough in itself ; but it was not more absurd than the other fiction,† that by reading a bill to the handful of partisans whom he could collect in the Forum, Cæsar had obtained the sanction of the nine hundred thousand Roman citizens who were scattered through Italy. Bibulus effected his purpose, so far as this, that he established abundant and valid grounds for hereafter setting aside the laws of Cæsar, if ever the constitutional party should again become strong enough to insist on its rights.

The moment that Cæsar received his governorship of Cisalpine Gaul, which legally commenced on

* Dio Cassius, xxxviii., 6, 5.
† See above, p. 26.

the 1st of March of his consulship, he hurried on
the enlistment of troops, so that he soon had an
armed force collected at the gates of Rome. Many
of Pompey's veterans were likewise invited to the
city to support the measures in which their general was interested. Cæsar, under the pretence that
violence was likely to be used against him, had publicly appealed to Pompey for assistance, and Pompey
had solemnly replied that, if the opponents of the
consul ventured to draw the sword, he would provide
both shield and sword in his defence.* Meanwhile
he indulged himself in his favourite weakness of
disclaiming responsibility. Every one knew that
Cæsar's measures were carried in the interest of
Pompey, and that Cæsar would have been powerless
without Pompey's support. Nevertheless, "he takes
refuge in quibbles of this sort. He approves the
substance of Cæsar's laws, but Cæsar himself is to
answer for his procedure. The Agrarian Law was
quite to his mind ; whether or no it could be vetoed
is no business of his. He was glad that the Egyptian question should be settled at last; whether or
not Bibulus observed lightning on that occasion, it
was not for him to inquire. As for the tax-farmers,
he was willing to oblige that order; what would be
the result of Bibulus coming down to the Forum he
could not have predicted." †

Cicero had declined any partnership with Cæsar,
but it was not yet clear whether he would venture
on active opposition. Cæsar was resolved to hold

---

* Plutarch, *Pomp.*, 47, 5.

† *Ad Att.*, ii., 16, 2.

him in check, and to accomplish this he possessed an
effective instrument.   We have seen that Clodius
had an old grudge against Cicero, and an old debt of
gratitude to Cæsar and Crassus.   He would be delighted to wipe off both scores at once, and to inflict
punishment on Cicero, nominally for having put the
Catilinarian conspirators to death, really for not being
sufficiently submissive to the triumvirs.   To deliver
this attack it was necessary that Clodius should become tribune of the plebs, but he was debarred from
the office by his patrician birth.   The obstacle might
be removed by his adoption into a plebeian family,
and such adoptions were in the control of Cæsar as
Pontifex Maximus.   Cæsar was prepared to use this
control according as Cicero behaved.

This question was decided early in the year,
probably during the month of March.
March, 59 B.C.
Caius Antonius, Cicero's colleague in
his consulship, who had since grossly misconducted
himself in his province of Macedonia, was put on his
trial, not only, as was reasonable, for extortion, but
on the charge of complicity in the Catilinarian conspiracy.   Cicero was counsel for the defence, and, as
he himself tells us,* "uttered in the course of my
speech some complaints regarding the present state
of the nation, which seemed to me to bear on the
case of my unfortunate client."   This was at noon,
and Cicero's remarks were forthwith reported (in an
exaggerated form, he says) to the consul.   Cæsar
accepted the words as evidence that Cicero meant
to throw in his lot with the opposition, and he in-

* *Pro Domo.* 16. 41.

stantly took up the challenge. At three o'clock the same afternoon Clodius was transferred to the plebs. Pompey officiated as augur on the occasion. He took the precaution indeed of exacting from Clodius and his brother Appius a solemn engagement that they would make no attack on Cicero; but Clodius' promises were notoriously worthless, and Clodius was ready to make any number of them that might be desired, if only Pompey would put him in a position in which he would have the power to break them.

Soon after receiving this significant warning Cicero retired into the country, where he spent the months of April and May. The tone of his letters to Atticus is at first more careless and cheerful than might have been expected. He was convinced, and not without reason, that the high-handed proceedings of the triumvirs must set public opinion against them,* and that dissensions must arise even amongst their own followers. He forgot for the moment that the triumvirs were resolved to rule by force, and that with force on their side they could afford to ignore public opinion. The country-people, as was natural, were disgusted with the doings in the capital. "You write that at Rome there is dead silence; so I supposed; but here in the fields men are by no means silent; the very fields themselves rebel against your tyranny. If you come to this 'far Læstrygonia'—to Formiæ, I mean—you will see how men chafe under it, how indignant they grow, how they detest our friend the Great One. His surname will soon be as

---

* *Ad Att.,* ii., 9, 2.

much out of date as that of Crassus the Rich. *
Trust me, I have not met a single man who takes
these things so quietly as I do myself." †

After the rejection of his own policy, Cicero had
good reason to be sick of public life, and he seems
to have contemplated with satisfaction a complete
retirement. " I was weary of piloting the State,
even while I was allowed to do so; and now that I
have been turned out of the boat, and have not
abandoned the helm but have had it wrenched out
of my hand, I had rather watch their ship-wreck
from the shore, and as your friend Sophocles says—

> ' Beneath my roof-tree list with drowsy sense
> The plashing of the rain.'" ‡

At one time Cicero fancied that the triumvirs
would offer him a mission to Egypt, but though he
liked the prospect, he felt that he could
not accept the offer at their hands. In
the same letter he inquires, § who is to have the
vacant augurship, and adds, " that is the only bait
with which they could catch me. Observe my
venality. But why do I talk of these things, when all
I want is to get rid of them and to devote my whole
mind to philosophy? That, I say, is my intention,
and I only wish I had done so from the first." Of
course this hankering after the augurship is only a
momentary whim, which goes down, as does every

April, 59 B.C.

---

* This is not the triumvir, but another person of the name who had
fallen from great wealth to bankruptcy.

† *Ad Att.*, ii., 13, 2.

‡ *Ad Att.*, ii., 7, 4.

§ *Ad Att.*, ii., 5.

passing thought, on paper to his friend. If Cicero
had been seriously willing to sell his services for any
such price, Cæsar would gladly have paid it twenty
times over.*

In the month of May, Cicero began to be more
anxious. He was alarmed by Pompey's marriage
with Cæsar's daughter Julia, and by a fresh agrarian
proposal, under which the Campanian land, expressly
exempted from the former law, was destined for
distribution. "These things," he writes,† "are
bad enough in themselves, but they cannot be
meant to stop here. For what have these people
gained by them as yet? They would never have
gone so far, except to pave the way for further
abominations."

From the month of June onwards Cicero is again
in Rome, and his letters to Atticus (who has now
retired to his estate in Epirus) give a lively picture
of the situation. The triumvirs are absolute masters,
but they are likewise the objects of universal hatred.
"Speech is a little freer than it was, at least when
people converse together in public places, or at dinner.
Indignation begins to overpower fear."‡ Things are
really much worse than before, because men have
lost patience. "The poison administered at first was
so slow in working that I thought we might have a
painless extinction; now I fear that the hisses of
the Commons, the plain-speaking of decent folk, and

---

* Cicero afterwards tells Cato (*Ad Fam.*, xv., 4, 13), with apparent
reference to this time, that he could have had the augurship if he had
pressed for it.

† *Ad Att.*, ii., 17, 1.   ‡ *Ad Att.*, ii., 18, 2.

the indignation of Italy will stir them up to violence."*
Bibulus' edicts, full of invective against Pompey and
Cæsar were eagerly welcomed; "there is a block in
the street, where they are posted up, from the numbers who stand to read them. They cut Pompey to
the heart, so that he is vilely fallen away with fretting;
and to myself they are, I confess, unpleasing, both
because they give too much pain to one for whom I
have always had a regard, and because I fear lest a
man of his stubborn nature, who is so used to wear
his hand on his sword-hilt and so unaccustomed to
listen to abuse, should abandon himself to the dic-
tates of vexation and displeasure."† Cicero tells us
in the same letter that he could not restrain his tears
at sight of the abject figure which Pompey made,
when in face of a hostile audience he tried to defend
himself against these attacks at a public meeting.
"It was a sight to please Crassus . . . for myself I felt as Apelles or Protogenes might feel if they
saw their masterpieces dragged in the dirt."

At the games the young Curio, who had been
bolder than others in his opposition, was heartily
cheered alike by the equestrian benches and by
the people, while Cæsar himself was received in dead
silence. The audience caught up every line in the
play which could be applied against their masters.

" The time shall come when thou shalt rue his valour,"

and

" If neither law nor duty can restrain you,"

---

* *Ad Att.*, ii., 21, 1.
† *Ad Att.*, ii., 21, 4.

were received with rounds of applause, and the actor
Diphilus was rapturously encored, when he turned on
Pompey with the words—

> " By our misery thou art Great." *

To Cæsar all this signified little ; indeed it was so
far to his advantage that the unpopularity of Pompey
made him the less able to dispense with his allies.
Cæsar had now ample force at his command, and all
else was indifferent to him ; think what they might,
Cæsar could rig an assembly to vote whatever he
should please. This was indeed so evident that the
Senate at his request added Transalpine Gaul to his
province in order to prevent that too being given
away over their heads by decree of the People.†
When his year of office was over, Cæsar ventured to
give a yet more striking proof of the lengths to which
he could go with the Senate. Two of the new
prætors foolishly brought the question of the validity
of Cæsar's acts before the House. Law and right
were absolutely on their side ; but force was not.
Cæsar accepted the challenge, and with a feigned
courtesy begged the Senate to decide the question
once for all under the eyes of his soldiers. The
Senate was, of course, helpless, and could only evade
a formal surrender by ignominiously declining to
entertain the question.‡ While he could thus
trample the Senate under foot, it was not likely that
Cæsar should trouble himself about any other un-

---

* *Ad Att.*, ii., 19, 3.

† Dio Cassius, xxxviii., 8, 4, confirmed by Cicero, *De Prov. Cons.*,
15, 36.

‡ Suetonius, *Jul.*, 23.

armed members of the commonwealth. The only
notice which he took of the demonstrations in the
theatre was to hint to the Knights that, unless they
behaved themselves, he would take away their reserved seats, and to the populace that, if they hissed
the wrong men, he would cut off the distribution of
corn.* Pompey on the other hand felt his conscience
uneasy and his position awkward. " I must inform
you," † Cicero writes to Atticus about the month of
August, " that our friend, the Great
Bashaw, is heartily sick of the state of
affairs and is anxious to recover the position from
which he has fallen ; he confides his distress to me
and openly begs me to suggest a remedy, which for
my part I am wholly unable to do."

Aug., 59 B.C.

Meanwhile the triumvirs made their arrangements
for the magistracies of the next year. They put
into the consulship Pompey's old adherent Gabinius,
and along with him Piso, whose daughter Calpurnia
was lately married to Cæsar. At the same time
Clodius was elected tribune. Since his adoption he
had been playing strange pranks. In the month of
April we find him announcing that he will stand for
the tribuneship as an opponent of the triumvirs and
with the intention of cancelling Cæsar's laws. "In
that case," retorted the chief pontiff and the officiat-
ing augur, "we shall deny that we ever made a plebeian of you." ‡ His sister Clodia, the terrible
beauty of Rome, with whom Atticus was on very

---

* *Ad Att.*, ii., 19, 3.
† *Ad Att.*, ii., 23, 2.
‡ *Ad Att.*, ii., 12, 1.

intimate terms, assured Cicero's friend that she was
urging her brother on this new course,* but it is not
clear that she told Atticus the truth. In any case this
quarrel was soon patched up, and before Clodius was
elected tribune he and Cæsar were again fast friends.
He now openly announced that he intended to attack
Cicero, and Pompey as vehemently protested that
he would allow no such thing. " He declares that
there is no danger; he takes his oath to it; he adds
that Clodius will have to pass over his dead body
before he shall do me any harm." † And again :
" It would be an everlasting disgrace to him, he says,
if any mischief came to me, through the man into
whose hands he placed a weapon of offence, when he
allowed him to become a plebeian." ‡

Cæsar however had otherwise determined. From
the time when he returned from Spain to the end of
his life, it was a principle of Cæsar's policy that
Cicero must be brought over to his side. Sometimes
he tries to attract him by friendly offers and delicate
acts of kindness, sometimes to drive him by well-
directed strokes of chastisement. The means employed might differ, but in pursuit of the end Cæsar
never wearied ; he knew full well that the great orator
must be either a useful ally or a dangerous enemy,
and that he could not afford to neglect him. In the
present crisis he was prepared to employ either
method as occasion might serve. For the moment
he held Clodius in leash, but he made it clear that

---

* *Ad Att.*, ii., 9, 1.

‡ *Ad Att.*, ii., 20, 2.

‡ *Ad Att.*, ii., 22, 2.

he was to be slipped on his prey, unless Cicero gave sufficient guarantees that he had abandoned his opposition to the triumvirs. That Cicero should now have a voice in the counsels of the confederates, was of course out of the question; but he might still, if he pleased, receive protection from them as the price of his silence. So far as outward position went, Cæsar's offers were meant to be honourable and complimentary to Cicero; and in after times Cæsar unhesitatingly appealed to them as evidence of his good-will. Ten years later Cicero writes*: "When he is justifying his conduct, he always throws on me the blame for the occurrences of that time; I was so bitter against him, he says, that I would not accept even honours from his hand." But these honours would effectually have closed Cicero's mouth. He was offered either a vacant place on the board of commissioners for executing Cæsar's Agrarian Law, or else the post of Cæsar's lieutenant in Gaul. Finally he was allowed the option of simple retirement by the acceptance of an honorary commission, which would have removed him for a year from Italy.

All these offers Cicero declined. He claimed complete freedom of action, and thought himself strong enough to face the attack of Clodius unaided. "I am now bearing myself," he writes in the autumn,† "so that every day increases my forces and the good-will with which I am supported. I let politics alone, and work with all my might in my old field of labour, the law-courts. I find that this is favourably re-

* *Ad Att.*, ix., 2, b. 1.
† *Ad Att.*, ii., 22, 3.

garded not only by my clients but by the public. My house is thronged, crowds come to greet me, the memory of my consulship is revived ; I am promised support, and I have raised my hopes, till I sometimes think that the struggle which lies before me is a thing to be welcomed."

Cicero's efforts to fortify his position by speeches at the bar may receive illustration from his successful defence of Lucius Flaccus, the only oration of this year which has been preserved to us. Flaccus, now accused of extortion in his province of Asia, had been prætor in 63 B.C., and was one of the two who arrested the Allobroges on the Mulvian Bridge. Cicero speaks in his behalf, as if the prosecution were directed against himself and all his coadjutors in the suppression of the conspiracy.

59 B.C.

"Caius Antonius has been overwhelmed. Be it so; he had his faults ; yet even he would never, if I may be allowed to say as much, have been found guilty by such a jury as that to which I speak to-day. On his condemnation the tomb of Lucius Catilina was wreathed with flowers ; abandoned men and traitors to the State thronged to the spot and feasted there ; Catiline's ghost had its due. Now you are asked to wreak on Flaccus vengeance for Lentulus. How can you find a victim more sweet for Publius Lentulus, that Lentulus who tried to slaughter you in the arms of your wives and children and to bury you beneath the ashes of our country, than by sating with the blood of Lucius Flaccus that bitter hatred which he had for all of us. Let us perform then an expiatory sacrifice for Lentulus, let us appease the shade of Cethegus, let us call back their associates from banishment. Let us, if so it must be, in our turn bear the punishment due to too exact a loyalty and to an excessive love of our country. For it is we who are now named by informers, against us charges are invented, for us perils are afoot. . . . Well, we see now clearly enough the mind and will of the Roman People. In every way which is open to it the Roman People makes it clear what it thinks; there is no difference of opinion or of wish or of utterance. So if any man summons me to that bar, here I am. I do not refuse the Roman People for judge in this quarrel, nay I claim its decision. Only let force be absent, let swords and stones be kept out of the way, let the hired gangs depart, let the slaves be silent. No one who hears me, if he be but a citizen and a freeman, will be so unfair as not to judge that the question is not of punishment for me, but of reward." *

Cicero's demands for a free decision of the people were of course absurd. Cæsar's object was, not to give the Roman People an opportunity of expressing its opinion about the execution of Lentulus, but merely to coerce or to muzzle a dangerous political opponent. Cicero had rejected his offers, and though Cæsar had no wish to hurt Cicero unnecessarily, he had decided that the blow should fall. To this most practical of statesmen it would have appeared the extreme of simplicity to allow his victim a chance of escape. He intended to effect Cicero's

---

* *Pro Flacco*, ch. 38.

banishment, as he had effected the measures of his consulship, by the exercise of sheer force.

To the latter part of this year belongs a strange story, for which a brief allusion must suffice. A creature named Vettius, who had acted as a spy on the Catilinarians for Cicero **59 B.C.** during his consulship, proposed to young Curio a plot to kill Pompey. Curio reported the matter to his father; the two gave information to Pompey, and Vettius was promptly arrested. He now disclosed a tale about a great conspiracy of the Nobles in which Bibulus and Cicero were implicated. The triumvirs at first tried to make political capital out of the story, to damage the character of their opponents and rouse some popular feeling in favour of themselves. But Vettius proved to be a clumsy liar, and the contradictions and absurdities of his evidence were too glaring for him to be of any service. He was found strangled in prison, and the matter was hushed up. Whether the whole business was contrived by the triumvirs and their adherents (as Cicero himself undoubtedly believed), * or whether some mad partisans of the oligarchy really had formed a plan of assassination, which served Vettius as the foundation of his lies about the senatorial leaders, it is impossible at this distance of time to determine.

For us the chief interest of the transaction lies in the fact that the alarm brought Atticus back in hot haste from Epirus to his friend's side. Cicero had just before pressed him to return—"As you love me, if you are asleep, wake up; if you are on your

Ad Att. ii. 24.

and effected certain constitutional changes with respect to the auspices and the censorship.

Having thus prepared the way, he brought in a bill "that any one who had put citizens to death without trial should be outlawed." Cicero was afterwards of opinion that he committed a fatal blunder in not expressing his approval of this decree, and taking his stand absolutely on the ground that Lentulus was not a citizen but an enemy. At the moment, however, he publicly recognised Clodius' proposal as directed against himself. He and his friends put on mourning and commended themselves to the people. The Roman Knights, always friendly to Cicero, stood by him on this occasion, and the Senate proclaimed its sympathies by a decree enjoining every member to lay aside the dress of his order as in times of public calamity. The consuls nullified this proceeding by an edict forbidding any senator to appear except in his proper robes. In the prevailing violence and disorder the tribunician protection, the proper remedy in such a case, was not available and the senators were obliged to submit. The Roman Knights were roughly handled by Clodius' mobs, and were insulted by the consul Gabinius, who further arbitrarily ordered out of the city one of their number, Ælius Lamia, because he had made himself conspicuous among Cicero's defenders.

Clodius commanded the streets with gangs of roughs whom he had enrolled under the pretence of founding "collegia," or street-guilds; these were only the advanced guard of his force; behind them

were the triumvirs and Cæsar's army. After Cicero
had been restored from exile by aid of the Three, he
was obliged to speak with reserve of the part they
had taken in banishing him. Nevertheless he indicates pretty clearly that Clodius was little more than
their instrument. What disturbed him, he says, was
Clodius' declaration " that his measures had the approval of these three and that he could command
their help in carrying them through. Now one of
these three had a powerful army in Italy ; the other
two, though private men, could raise an army if they
chose; and this he said that they would do. He
threatened me, not with the judgment of the People,
not with any prosecution or trial or answer to the
law, but with violence, with arms, with troops and
generals and camps."*

Cicero constantly complains of the " silence " of the
Three when Clodius maintained that he was their
agent, and indeed both their silence and their utterances left him no doubt that for once Clodius was
telling the truth. Clodius held a meeting outside
the gates that Cæsar might be present, and he publicly questioned the proconsul as to his opinion on
the execution of Lentulus. Cæsar replied, " that in
his judgment Cicero had acted illegally, but that he
should prefer to let by-gones be by-gones and advised them not to persecute Cicero further." † This
reply, as it stood, was certainly hypocritical, for
Cæsar could have stopped Clodius' action by raising
his finger ; but we may perhaps find a better excuse

---

* *Pro Sestio,* 17, 40.

† Dio Cassius, xxxviii., 17 ; Plutarch *Cic.,* 30, 4.

for him than that he merely wished to shirk responsibility. It is probable that now, as all along, Cæsar's
action was determined solely by his desire to force
Cicero to his side, that he looked on his exile as a
mere temporary measure of policy, and was resolved
to recall him so soon as he had humbled and fright-
ened him sufficiently. In that case, he was wise in
not committing himself to any public participation
in his banishment, which would have made it more
awkward for him to consent to his restoration.
Meantime Clodius reaped all the fruits of Cæsar's
support, and openly boasted that he would march
Cæsar's army down on the Senate-house.

From Crassus Cicero expected no help ; the two
had never been friends. Young Publius indeed, the
son of Crassus, was one of Cicero's warmest admir-
ers and had put on mourning along with him ; but
he could not influence his father. Pompey shows
very badly on this occasion. Almost to the last he
had encouraged Cicero by his promises, and now in
the hour of peril " suddenly he fell away from him."*
He studiously kept out of Cicero's way, and referred
him to the consuls, whose help he pretended to desire ; he would be only too glad to oppose force to
the violence of Clodius, but he was a private man,
and must really wait till he was summoned by the
consuls.†   To the consuls accordingly Cicero turned.
Gabinius rudely repulsed him. Piso affected some
concern ; " but," said he, " Gabinius is in difficulties ;
he is quite out at elbows ; he is a ruined man unless

---

* " Subita defectio Pompeii," *Ad Q. F.*, i., 4, 4.
† *Pro Sestio*, 18, 41.

THE THREE COLUMNS OF THE TEMPLE OF CASTOR.

(*Duruy.*)

he gets a province, and if I stand by him he has good hopes of one from the tribune, for it is hopeless to look for anything from the Senate. I must oblige him, just as you did your colleague Antonius. It is of no use your applying to the consuls; every one must look after himself." * Shortly afterwards when publicly questioned by Clodius what he thought of Cicero's consulship, Piso delivered himself of the oracular response, that " he did not approve of cruelty."

Meanwhile the day for the passing of Clodius' bill drew on. His new law about the auspices seems to have barred any attempt to invalidate the proceedings as those of Cæsar had been invalidated by Bibulus. The veto of Clodius' colleagues in the tribuneship could only be exercised personally, and if they interposed except under the protection of an armed force they were certain to be killed on the spot. Clodius did not content himself with the bludgeons of his newly formed guilds, but occupied the temple of Castor in the Forum with armed men, removing the steps which led up to the temple, so as to make it a veritable fortress. It became every day more clear that Cicero must either fly or else fight a pitched battle. He had on his side the Senate, the equestrian order, and the whole country population of Italy; but it would require time to collect and marshal these forces, whereas the gangs of Clodius were ready armed and organised. Even if the tribune were disposed of, Cicero would have still to deal with the consuls and with Cæsar, so that,

---

* *In Pisonem*, 6, 12.

as Clodius maliciously pointed out to him, he would either be knocked on the head once for all, or else have to win a battle twice over.* Lucullus notwithstanding gave his voice for fighting, and Cato probably was of the same mind.† Hortensius, on the other hand, strongly advised that Cicero should bow to the storm, and retire voluntarily from the city. The majority of the Nobles agreed with him, protesting that it would only be a matter of a few days, and that Cicero would soon be brought home in triumph.

Cicero made a final appeal to Pompey. In his despair he flung himself at his feet and begged him to redeem his promise; but Pompey did not even raise him from the ground and coldly replied that he could do nothing against Cæsar's wishes.‡ Thus baulked of his last hope, Cicero removed from his house a consecrated image of Minerva bearing the inscription " The Guardian of the City," and deposited it as a pledge and memorial in the temple of Jupiter on the Capitol; then with a heavy heart he departed from Rome.

58 B.C., End of March.

The same day Clodius carried his bill. The opposition to his measures had now collapsed, and he might do what he pleased. After first paying the consuls their hire, he next carried a resolution

---

* *Pro Sestio*, 19, 43.

† Dio Cassius (xxxviii., 17, 4) and Plutarch (*Cato Minor*, 35, 1) assert the contrary, but their authority is not sufficient to outweigh Cicero's words (*Ad Att.*, iii., 15, 2) expressly exonerating Cato from the blame which he heaps on Hortensius. See also *Ad. Fam.*, xv., 4, 12.

‡ *Ad Att.*, x., 4, 3.

directed against Cicero by name. This decree set
forth, not that Cicero should be outlawed, but that
he "had been outlawed" already by the terms of
the general law. * It further fixed a limit of space,
400 miles, within which this outlawry was to be
operative ; anyone who received or comforted the
banished man within these limits was himself liable
to proscription. By the same decree Cicero's goods
were confiscated, and his house ordered to be razed
to the ground. No time was lost in carrying out
these last provisions; Clodius with his mob sacked
and burned the house on the Palatine, seized all the
property of Cicero on which he could lay hands, and
threatened Terentia with legal proceedings on the
charge that she was concealing some of her husband's
goods.

Cæsar, who had remained at the gates until Cicero
was driven from Rome, now swept northwards. In
eight days he was on the banks of the Rhone ; before the summer was out, he had annihilated the
armed nation of the Helvetii and had driven the
mighty hosts of the Germans back across the Rhine.
After these two splendid victories, Cæsar withdrew
his army, as he tells us, into winter-quarters "some
what earlier than the usual season."

Before departing for his province, he had made

---

* Cicero, (*Pro Domo*, 18, 47) speaks of the perfect tense as a
monstrous blunder, but it was probably correct. The second decree
is a declaratory act, which proceeds on the assumption that Cicero
was hit by the terms of the first law and that he has acknowledged
his guilt by retiring into exile. There is a close parallel in Livy,
xxvi., 3, 12. " Postquam dies comitiorum aderat, Cn. Fulvius
exulatum Tarquinios abiit. Id ei justum exilium esse scivit plebs."

arrangements for expelling from Rome the other statesman who shared with Cicero the honour of being feared by Cæsar as a leader of opposition. Cato was to be removed more gently than his comrade had been, but quite as effectually. Clodius had passed a law for the annexation of the kingdom of Cyprus, and the deposition of the Ptolemy who reigned there. This king was the brother of that Ptolemy Auletes who had purchased his recognition as King of Egypt from Cæsar (above p. 209), and it was an act of cynical injustice thus to ruin the Cypriot ruler, whose title was just the same, as a punishment for not having bribed the triumvirs. Clodius had undertaken the business with all the more zest because the King of Cyprus had once refused to ransom him from the pirates. Clodius now passed a supplementary decree, commanding Cato by name to execute the deposition of Ptolemy. This order he did not venture to disobey. He wrote to Ptolemy promising to treat him with all consideration; but the unfortunate king put an end to his own life, and Cato was obliged to content himself with an ostentatious incorruptibility in administering his effects and paying the money realised into the Treasury. Meantime Cæsar's object was accomplished, and he wrote a letter * to Clodius, congratulating him that he had got Cato out of the way for the rest of his tribunate, and had likewise shut his mouth for the future about extraordinary commissions. Cato did not come back to Rome for more than two years.

We must now turn to accompany Cicero on his

---

* *Pro Domo*, 9, 22.

melancholy journey. After wandering for a while in
southern Italy, always in dread lest he should bring
ruin on his hosts, he crossed over into Epirus from
Brundisium on the last day of April.

58 B.C.

He would have preferred Athens for
his place of residence, but was afraid of Autronius
and other exiled Catilinarians who infested Greece.
Finally he resolved to avoid Greece altogether, and
proceeded by the great northern road across Macedonia to Thessalonica, where he arrived on the 22d
of May. Here he was received with great kindness
by Plancius the quæstor of the province, who afforded
him ample protection and such consolation as was
possible under the circumstances.

But consolation was the last thing of which Cicero
would accept at this time. He was crushed in spirit
by the blow which had fallen on him, and his letters
are full of nothing but lamentation and self-reproach
and upbraidings of his friends. His retirement, for
which he could find abundance of excellent reasons
a few months later, now appears to him an act of incredible folly and perverseness. Why had he not
stayed and fought it out as Lucullus recommended?
Why had Hortensius and the rest given him such
treacherous advice? Why had they said that his
absence would be an affair of a few days? Why
had Atticus contented himself with tears for his
misfortune, when he might have averted it by sager
counsel? Why, when all was lost, had his friend re-
strained him from falling on his own sword, the only
honourable resource? It will come to that in the
end, he thinks, but the opportunity for dying with

credit has been lost. He is convinced that never
has there been such a fall as his; he measures it by
all the height of his former position of honour and
influence. He has brought ruin not only on himself
but on his dear ones at home; he does not trust
himself to meet his brother Quintus, now returning
home from his province; they would both be too
much unmanned. Throughout he despairs of any
improvement in the situation, and turns a deaf ear to
the hopes which his friends hold out to him.

Lessing in his famous treatise on the *Laocoön*
has drawn an interesting contrast between the con-
ventions of ancient and modern life with regard to
the manifestations of pain and grief. The northern
peoples of Europe have inherited notions of the
dignity of stoical endurance, which, though far less
thorough than those of some barbaric races, lead us
to consider tears and lamentations as unworthy of
a man. The Greeks and, to a certain extent, the
Romans were more natural in their utterance of their
feelings. Philoctetes can howl from the pain of his
wound, and Achilles roll on the sand in the agony
of his bereavement, without degradation or loss of
sympathy. It is said * that the modern Italians
show something of the same unconventionality and
absence of self-restraint.

In Cicero we find these characteristics carried to
an extreme. Stoical reserve is sadly wanting in him.
The versatile intelligence, the susceptibility to im-
pressions, the quick wit and the genial receptiveness,

---

* See Adolphus Trollope's *Beppo the Conscript*, ch. 7 (the Bad
Number).

which give their charm to his writings as they doubtless did to his conversation, are compensated in the
economy of nature by an equal sensitiveness to pain.
There never was a man of less equable temperament
than Cicero, nor one born more completely under the
influence of the planet Mercury. In the stir of life
and action he is alert and sanguine ; when he is struck
down by misfortune he becomes nerveless and de-
pressed, and all that remains of his ingenuity is
employed in devising fresh reasons for torturing
himself. During times of prosperity he suns himself
in the society of his friends, in the affection of his
children, in the applause of his fellows, in the approval of his own judgment and conscience ; whenever these fail him, the gloom of anxiety and
disappointment closes around him, and he sets forth
his grief and despair as frankly as he had set forth
his self-satisfaction. Happiness and misery affect
him with equal keenness, and his unrivalled powers
of expression are employed in both cases to display
to his friends, and, as fortune would have it, through
them to future centuries, feelings which had better
have been buried in his own breast. If we are inclined to think hardly of him, let us remember that
these are, as the French say, "the defects of his
qualities."

About the end of the year Cicero left Thessalonica
for Epirus. He could hardly remain in Macedon ;
his friend Plancius' term of office was
out, and his enemy Piso was expected   Dec., 58 B.C.
as the new governor. Besides the horizon had already
begun to clear ; Cicero could now afford to disregard

the limits to which Clodius' law confined him, and was at liberty to approach close to Italy and await the restoration which was drawing nigh.

Clodius had become intolerable in Rome. "Like Cæsar himself," writes Mommsen, "Cæsar's ape kept governorships and other posts great and small on sale for the benefit of his fellow-citizens, and sold the sovereign rights of the State for the benefit of subject kings and cities." "What region," asks * Cicero, "what district of any extent was there on the face of the earth, in which some principality was not set up? What king was there who did not recognise that it was time for him to buy what was another's right, or to pay black-mail for what was his own?"

Grown bold with impunity, Clodius at length ventured to cross the path of Pompey himself. He

May, 58 B.C.

accepted money from the King of Armenia to procure the release of his son, who had been brought to Rome as a hostage, and in pursuance of his bargain carried off the young prince from the custody in which Pompey had placed him. When Pompey tried to oppose force by force, Clodius not only defeated him in the streets, but attempted his life by means of an assassin. Pompey was obliged to barricade himself in his own house for the remainder of Clodius' year of office.

The departure of Cæsar's army and the estrangement of Pompey left the Romans more free to ex-

June, 58 B.C.

press their real feelings as to Cicero's banishment. Though not one of Clodius' colleagues had dared to interpose his veto

* *Pro Sestio*, 30, 66,

at the critical moment, Ninnius, as early as the 1st
of June brought the question of Cicero's recall before the Senate, and elicited an unanimous resolution
in favour of it; in October, eight of the tribunes not
only consulted the Senate but proposed a bill to the
People.* These measures were inoperative except
as a demonstration, for they were vetoed by Clodius
and his single adherent among the tribunes. The
consular elections in the summer resulted in favour
of Lentulus Spinther and Metellus Nepos, the same
who, as tribune, had forbidden Cicero to speak to the
people when he went out of office at the end of the
year 63 (see above p. 161). He now announced that
he would forget his old feud, and not oppose any
measures in Cicero's favour. His colleague declared
himself from the first Cicero's friend, and almost all
the tribunes-elect were on the same side. Amongst
them were Titus Annius Milo, and Publius Sestius.
Sestius before the end of the year undertook a journey into Gaul to beg the Autumn, 58 B.C.
acquiescence of Cæsar. † As early as August Cicero
had mentioned in a letter ‡ some information received from Varro which seemed to indicate that
Cæsar showed signs of relenting. Nevertheless
Sestius' overtures were at first unsuccessful, and
some delay was thus caused; for Pompey could
hardly permit Cicero to return without first gaining
Cæsar's consent. At length his objections were removed, apparently by negotiations with Quintus

---

* *Pro Sestio*, 31, 68 ; and 32, 69.

† *Pro Sestio*, 33, 71.

‡ *Ad Att.*, iii. 15, 3.

16

Cicero, who gave certain pledges on his brother's account to the triumvirs, and Cæsar now expressed his approval of the measures which Pompey wished to adopt (see below p. 266).

The proceedings of Clodius in the last months of his tribuneship were like the tricks of a mischievous monkey. His quarrel with Pompey implied a breach in his alliance with Gabinius; accordingly he set his gangs upon him, wounded his attendants, and broke up his consular fasces. Then he put up an altar of incense and, standing before it with veiled head, consecrated all the goods of the consul to the temple of Ceres; as at a solemn sacrifice, a flute-player piped the accompaniment to the traditional words of banning. One of his colleagues mimicked the ceremony and consecrated Clodius' goods under the same form. Clodius next turned upon Cæsar. He convened an assembly in the Forum and summoned Bibulus and the college of augurs to attend. He put the question to Bibulus, whether he had not observed lightning on each occasion when Cæsar carried his laws? He elicited a response from the augurs that such an observation invalidated the proceedings. " In that case," summed up this impartial judge, " it appears that Cæsar's official acts, including my adoption, are null and void. Let them all be set aside by a decree of the Senate. Cicero is the preserver of Rome, and I will bring him home again on my own shoulders." *

The first act of Lentulus Spinther as consul was to bring the question of Cicero's recall again before

---

* *Pro Domo*, 15, 40.

the Senate, and the matter was fully discussed on
the first of January, 57 B.C.* Lucius Aurelius
Cotta, the first senator who was asked his opinion,
protested that no legislation was required; the whole
of the proceedings against Cicero, he argued, were
null and void; he had merely yielded to violence,
and now he should be simply invited to resume his
place in the State. Pompey, who came next, while
agreeing with much that Cotta said, recommended
that for the avoidance of all scruples a bill should be
proposed annulling the former decree and expressly
restoring all Cicero's rights. This view (which was
Cicero's own) met with the approval of the Senate.
Though some delays occurred through
the opposition of a single tribune, a Jan., 57 B.C.
decree was actually brought before the people on
the 24th of January.

But Clodius, though no longer tribune, was still
master of the streets. His gangs were reinforced by
some gladiators whom he was training, and with
these he made an armed attack on the supporters of
the bill. A regular battle was fought †; the Forum
had to be swabbed with sponges to clear away the
blood, and corpses were tossed into the river or
choked the sewers; Quintus Cicero barely escaped
with his life; the day ended with the victory of
Clodius and the bill was not carried. On another
day the tribune Sestius was assailed with equal
violence; he was left for dead on the ground, but
none of his wounds proved mortal. Milo attempted

---

* *Pro Sestio*, 34.

† *Pro Sestio*, 35, 75, *seq.*

to bring Clodius to justice, but found his family connections too powerful. He then resolved to meet
Clodius with his own weapons and himself hired
a band of gladiators ; many of Cicero's friends seem
to have contributed to bear the expense. The two
champions fought out their quarrel much in the
fashion of the Montagues and Capulets, and neither
could drive his adversary from the field. It was
sufficient however for Milo to hold Clodius in check,
and so soon as he accomplished this, the public feeling in favor of Cicero's recall bore down all other
obstacles. Meanwhile the Senate refused to transact
any other business until this measure was carried
through, and it passed decrees commending Cicero's
safety to the protection of all magistrates in the
provinces, and giving thanks to those communities
which had sheltered and comforted him.*

At length after months of obstruction the bill was
again introduced. The Senate, combining the advice of Cotta and of Pompey, now issued a proclamation that all who desired the salvation of the State †
should come to Rome to vote in Cicero's cause, and
at the same time they decreed that, in case the vote
should be delayed for more than five lawful days,
they invited Cicero to return as a citizen under no
legal condemnation or disability. On the strength
of this invitation Cicero crossed over into Italy and
landed at Brundisium on the 5th of
Aug., 57 B.C.   August. Here the whole population
of the town went forth to greet his landing, and

---

* *Pro Sestio*, 60, 128, and *Pro Domo*, 32, 85.

† *Pro Domo*, 28, 73.

with them his daughter Tullia, who had come thus far to meet her father. By a happy coincidence* the day was the anniversary of the foundation of the town and was likewise Tullia's birthday.

Three days later Cicero received the news that the bill had actually passed on the 4th of August. Every circumstance served to heighten his triumph. The immense crowds of citizens from the country, who had flocked to Rome† and now assembled on the Campus Martius to proclaim their good-will to Cicero, afforded a striking contrast to the handful of roughs and slaves whose assent had given the form of law to his banishment. The assembly was by centuries, the most solemn and august fashion for the utterance of the popular voice; the bill was introduced by both the consuls; Pompey himself urged its acceptance and delivered a panegyric on Cicero; men of rank and position not only appeared to give their votes, but were proud to discharge in person the subordinate functions of distributing the ballots and counting the votes. Clodius was present and was permitted to say what he had to say against the proposal; but the feeling of the assembled multitude was practically unanimous, and every century voted in the affirmative. So far as the unwieldy forms of a mass-meeting permit a real expression of the will of the majority, this was a truly representative assembly, and this decree stands almost alone in the latter

---

* *Ad Att.*, iv., 1, 4.

† Clodius accused Cicero (*Ad Att.*, iv., 1, 6, and *Pro Domo*, 6, 14) of having made corn dear, apparently on the ground that the number of strangers who had come to vote for him had eaten up the supplies.

days of the Republic, as having received not only
the formal but the real assent of the Roman people.

Cicero's journey homeward was a triumphal progress. Along the way he was stopped by deputations
sent from all parts of Italy to congratulate him.
When he reached the gates he found that every one
with the least pretence to be a notable person in
Rome had come forth to greet him; even Crassus
was there, and none stayed behind except those
whose hostility had been too notorious for them to
be able to pretend to join in the welcome. As
Cicero advanced he found the steps of the temples
occupied from top to bottom by enthusiastic crowds,
whose plaudits accompanied him through the densely
thronged Forum and up to the Capitol, whither
he went to offer thanks to the gods for his safe
return.*

One thing was wanting to complete Cicero's restoration. The site of his house on the Palatine had
been consecrated by Clodius, and a shrine of Liberty
erected thereon. It was doubtful therefore whether
it could again be applied to secular uses. The
question was referred to the college of pontiffs, and
their unanimous vote† declared the consecration to
be null and void. Cicero's house was rebuilt on the
old site at the public expense.

Cicero was pleased to find that he was still regarded as the unquestioned leader of the bar. The
applications of clients the instant he returned to
Rome sufficiently convinced him of this. The devo-

* *Ad Att.*, iv., 1, 5.
† *De Har. Resp.*, 6, 12.

tion of all loyal citizens in his cause seems even to have alarmed him, as likely to rekindle the jealousy from which he had suffered so much. He now shakes off all the despondency of his exile, and can look forward with a light heart. " I feel," he writes to Atticus,* " as if I was starting at the commencement of a new life."

The enthusiasm displayed by the Romans was partly due to sympathy with Cicero himself, partly it was a manifestation of disgust at the reign of lawlessness and rascality which had been the first-fruits of Cæsar's attack on the constitution. With the return of Cicero, men began to hope that this most discreditable page in the national history was turned down once for all. They did not perceive how seriously the fabric of the constitution had been shaken, nor how imminent was the danger to those republican institutions which they still cherished as their most precious birthright. In real truth it would have taxed the utmost resources of statesmanship now to find a solution. Whether the triumvirate held together, or whether it dissolved, the issue was likely to be equally disastrous to the survival of the free State. Cicero's " new life " began in a world which admitted only of counsels of despair.

Three days after his return we find Cicero once more handling affairs of State. The Senate was called to suggest remedies for a dearth, which caused much discontent, and Cicero moved that Pompey should be invested with proconsular power for five years, and should exercise control over the corn-supply of

* *Ad Att.*, iv., 1, 8.

the whole world.* The motion was carried, and the consuls immediately embodied the resolution in a bill which received the assent of the people. The proposal of this honorable charge for Pompey was in accordance with the general policy which Cicero had pursued since his first entry on public life ; it was likewise a graceful act of recognition of Pompey's services in procuring his recall from exile. It seems however, to have given offence to the leaders of the optimate party—"The consulars," Cicero writes, "take their cue from Favonius and express dissatisfaction." Clodius availed himself of their resentment when Cicero pleaded before the pontiffs for the restoration of his house, and Cicero found himself obliged to defend his action at length, and to deprecate any prejudice which it might occasion in the minds of his judges.†

But that which the Optimates thought too much for Pompey was much less than what Pompey himself desired. His real wishes were revealed by a counter-proposal of the tribune Messius, which would have given to the Commissioner of the corn-supply the disposal of the Treasury, an army, a fleet, and a power in every province superior to that of the actual governor. Public opinion was not yet ripe for so thorough a measure. Even if the Republicans had accepted it, we may doubt whether Cæsar would have acquiesced, and whether the effect would not rather have been to hurry on the civil war. This risk, however, might well have been faced. Cæsar's army was not as yet fashioned to that perfect ef-

* *Ad Att.*, iv., 1, 7.   † *Pro Domo*, ch. 2–9.

ficiency which it afterwards attained, and though even now the Republicans would have found it difficult to hold Italy, they might have made a fight for it in the East with far better chances than when they tried the fortune of war six years later. At this eleventh hour the sole chance for the Republic was to place itself unreservedly in Pompey's hands, and to trust that the loyalty which he had shown at the end of the Mithridatic war would still be the guiding principle of his conduct.

This was the more to be hoped, because Pompey's subsequent defection from honour and duty had borne him bitter fruits. He had expected to use Cæsar as his instrument, and now his eyes were opened to the fact that Cæsar was fast becoming his master. Two years of splendid victories had half revealed to the world the supreme military genius. Cæsar's army was devoted, not to any party or principle, but solely to its incomparable chief. He had made himself a position independent of his confederate and could conquer and govern at will throughout his vast province, while a tribune or two in his pay at home served to secure his interests in the central government. Pompey meanwhile was sorely perplexed in his new position. He had little capacity and little inclination for guiding the turbulent politics of the capital. His main object now was to secure himself some military force and some base of operations independent of Cæsar. But here he was met by constant difficulties; he was checked alike by his own best feelings, and by the memory of his past defection. On the one hand the Optimates

wished that he should divorce Julia * ; but Pompey
steadily refused to sacrifice the tender and beautiful
woman, whose love both for her husband and for her
father bound them together by a tie more honourable
than that of political expediency. On the other
hand, Pompey bore, and not unjustly, the odium
which resulted from the lawless acts of Cæsar's consulship, and he was still compelled to play the part
of figure-head in a Cabinet in which the decisive word
lay no longer with him. The constitutional party
had now some excuse for refusing to trust him.

Pompey was still further hampered by his own reserve and mystery and dread of committing himself.
These bad habits had by long indulgence now completely gained the mastery over him. It is pitiful to
see how a man, honest and well-meaning at bottom,
earned the reputation of insincerity and double-deal-
ing, merely because he was afraid to speak his mind.
No one now relied on him. Cicero expresses this
distrust in an amusing way to Atticus a few months
later.† "He had a long conversation with me on
politics, and was by no means satisfied with his position—*so he said* (for that is as much as one can vouch
for in case of Pompey) : he did not care for Syria, and
thought nothing of Spain—add, if you please, '*so he
said.*' I think indeed that whenever we speak of him
we may append the tag, '*so he said,*' like the refrain
of 'thus saith Phocylides' in the epigrams." ‡

---

* Plutarch, *Pomp.*, 49, 3.   † *Ad Att.*, iv., 9, 1.

‡ This tag was used both by Phocylides and Demodocus. The following epigram (it is doubtful to which of the two it belongs) will
serve as an example :

Καὶ τόδε Φωκυλίδου· Μιλήσιοι ἀξύνετοι μὲν
Οὐκ εἰσίν· δρῶσιν δ᾽ οἱάπερ ἀξύνετοι.

On this question of the corn-supply, while pressing the more thorough-going proposal of Messius by means of his friends and adherents, he affected to prefer that of Cicero. This hesitancy destroyed the last chance of Messius' success. "The bill," writes Cicero,* "which the consuls brought forward on my recommendation, now appears moderate, and this of Messius not to be borne." Pompey accepted the commission with its restricted powers, and this opportunity was lost to the Republic.

Pompey's hopes were next directed towards Egypt. King Ptolemy, "the Piper," had been forcibly expelled by his subjects not long after Cæsar had obtained his recognition by Rome. As the triumvirs had sold him his throne for a great sum, he naturally expected them to guarantee him quiet possession of his purchase. He sent envoys to Rome, requesting that he might be restored and that Pompey might be authorised to re-instate him. This commission would have given Pompey just what he wanted—a fleet, an army, and a base of operations. It will be recollected that some years before (in 65 and again in 63) Cæsar and Crassus had looked to Egypt as the place where they might build up a power against that of Pompey. Now the positions are reversed; Cæsar is the man in possession of military force, and Pompey would fain counterbalance that force by establishing himself in Egypt.

But here again the Nobles could not recognise the fact, which seems to us so obvious, that Cæsar was the really dangerous man, and that the only chance of resisting him was to make Pompey strong enough

---

* *Ad Att.,* iv., 1, 7.

to be independent of him. Their alarms were still directed to Pompey; he was to them still what a "scatterbrained young man" * had nick-named him during Cæsar's consulship, "The Dictator without office." The majority then of the Senate resolved in their wisdom that Pompey was not to be trusted with an army, and accordingly, on the pretext of a Sibylline oracle, unearthed for the occasion, they passed a decree that the King of Egypt must not be restored by military force. Even with this restriction they were unwilling that Pompey should be allowed to meddle with Egypt; and, indeed, there were numerous rival candidates for so lucrative a commission. While Pompey's adherents urged his claims, Pompey himself affected to approve of Cicero's exertions on behalf of his benefactor Lentulus Spinther, who after his consulship had become governor of Cilicia and Cyprus. Cicero writes to Lentulus that "when he hears Pompey speak, he acquits him of any hankering after the job," but that his action is so inconsistent that he cannot penetrate his real wishes. "You know," he adds, "how slow the man is, and how incapable of speaking out." † The time was wasted in endless wrangles, and nothing could be settled in the Senate. Ptolemy remained an exile till the next year (55 B.C.) when Gabinius, the governor of Syria, without any authorisation from the home government, restored him to his throne.

---

* This "adolescens nullius consilii," as Cicero (*Ad Q. F.*, i., 2, 15) called him, was Caius Cato, a person whom we must take care not to confuse with his great namesake Marcus.

† *Ad Fam.*, i., 5, b. 2.

So far then the Nobles had thwarted all Pompey's efforts. Their dislike to him was curiously evinced by their attitude towards Clodius at this period. Clodius had indeed done much to outrage the feelings of the Optimates; but, after all, he was one of themselves, a Noble of the bluest blood, and they were disposed to put up with many eccentricities from such a one. The principal sufferer had been Cicero, and the wrongs of a "new man" did not rouse much sympathy in their minds. Besides, Cicero had been restored, and what more did he want? True, Clodius had appeared with his mob, and driven off the masons who were rebuilding Cicero's house; he had attacked Cicero himself with stones and swords, as he was proceeding (happily with a sufficient escort) along the Sacred Way, and he had succeeded in setting fire to the house of Quintus. But the Ciceros might look after themselves; men who had risen from the middle class had no business to stand on their dignity. The Nobles then petted and encouraged Clodius, who was always ready to show sport by insulting and annoying Pompey. They had baffled all Milo's efforts, as tribune, to bring him to trial, and now (in the year 56) Clodius was ædile, and could in turn arraign Milo before the People. When a namesake and creature of their favourite, Sextus Clodius, was tried before a jury for complicity in his patron's lawless proceedings, a majority among the non-senatorial jurors was for a verdict of "Guilty," but the senators' votes turned the scale, and procured an acquittal.

Cicero was naturally indignant at all this. In a
speech, delivered in the Senate early in this year,
56 B.C.   he upbraids the Nobles with the folly
and indecency of their conduct. "I
am not surprised at Clodius; he does after his kind.
But I am astonished at those men of sense and
character, first, that they listen so readily when they
hear a great citizen and a noble servant of the commonwealth traduced by the tongue of a scoundrel;
next, that they hold a doctrine most contrary to
their own interests, that the glory and dignity of
any man are at the mercy of the insults of a rascal,
bankrupt in fortune and reputation; lastly, that
they do not appreciate, though I fancy they must
have some suspicion of it, that these same wild and
whirling words may one day be directed against
themselves. . . . Can we believe it that worthy
citizens have brooked to gather to their bosoms and
hold as their darling this fanged and deadly adder?
With what bait did he catch them? 'We wish,'
they say, 'that there should be some one to speak
against Pompey, and to cast reproach on Pompey.'
What! does Clodius cast reproach on Pompey by
abusing him? I hope that great man, to whom I
owe so much, will take what I say in the spirit in
which it is meant; at any rate, I will speak my mind.
To me, I protest, it seems that some reproach was
cast on his noble and honoured name; but it was
on the occasion when Clodius praised him to the
skies." *

The situation was yet further complicated by

* *De Har. Resp.*, 24, 50.

dissensions between Pompey and Crassus. There
never was much love lost between the two, and
though Cæsar had brought them together, their true
feelings manifested themselves now that Cæsar's
presence was withdrawn. We find Pompey complaining to Cicero in February, 56, "that plots were
being laid against his life; that money was being
supplied by Crassus to Clodius and to Clodius' associate, Caius Cato, and that Curio, Bibulus, and
others of his old opponents were likewise backing
up the pair." * In order to protect himself, Pompey
was obliged to enroll a band of roughs, whom he
imported from his native Picenum.

Meanwhile Clodius did not have it all his own
way in the streets. Cicero's escort showed fight on
the occasion when Clodius set upon him in the
"Via Sacra." They retired into a friend's portico,
and beat back their assailants from thence. At one
moment Clodius' life was at their mercy, but Cicero
would not give the word. " I am weary," he writes,†
" of heroic surgery, and am trying to starve out the
disease." Milo was less scrupulous. " I
think," says Cicero in the same letter,‡ Nov., 57 B.C.
"that Publius will be brought to trial by Milo,
unless he is killed first. If he puts himself in
Milo's road during a riot, Milo will certainly do it;
he is quite resolved and announces it openly; he
has no fear of falling as I did, for he puts his trust
in no one but himself."

* *Ad Q. F.*, ii., 3, 4.
† *Ad Att.*, iv., 3, 3.
‡ *Ad Att.*, iv., 3, 5.

Clodius had no luck when he tried to carry the war of prosecutions at law into the enemy's camp. His accusation of Milo before the people came to nothing, and a charge of rioting which he brought before a jury against Sestius, whom we have seen as tribune exerting himself to procure Cicero's restoration, led to a signal triumph for Clodius' opponents.

Feb. 14, 56 B.C. The occasion brought Cicero at once to the front. "Sestius was unwell," he writes to his brother*; "I went straight to his house, and placed myself, as I was bound to do, entirely at his disposal. This, however, was more than people expected of me, for they thought that I had good reasons for being vexed with Sestius. So both he and the public consider that I have behaved like a kind friend and a grateful man, and I mean to act up to the character."

Cicero nobly redeemed this pledge, and his speech for Sestius remains as an admirable specimen of forensic oratory applied to a State trial. The story of Sestius' tribunate, of his labours crowned at last with success in Cicero's cause, and of the desperate lawlessness, with which he had to contend, is set **Mar. 11, 56 B.C.** forth with every grace of language and every force of argument. The jury responded readily to Cicero's appeal, and Sestius was acquitted by an absolutely unanimous vote.

Among the witnesses for the prosecution in this case was Publius Vatinius, the same who as tribune, in 59 B.C., had passed the law which gave Cæsar his command in Gaul. Cicero availed himself of the

---

* *Ad Q. F.*, ii., 3, 5.

curious practice of the Roman law-courts, to direct against Vatinius a speech of fierce invective under the form of questions in his cross-examination. "In defending our surly-tempered friend," he writes immediately afterwards, * "I gave him his due, full measure and running over; and, as he particularly wished it, I turned upon Vatinius who was an avowedly hostile witness. I cut into him at my leisure to the satisfaction of heaven and earth. . . . The end of it was that Vatinius, impudent and reckless as he is, retired quite baffled and crest-fallen."

Cicero's speech against Vatinius is not pleasant reading. The invective, which rises to dignity when aimed at great antagonists, like Catiline and Antony, sinks to vulgar abuse when directed against underlings, such as Vatinius, Piso, and Gabinius. The account which Cicero, in his confidential letter to his brother, gives of the effectiveness of the speech is undoubtedly true; but we can only wonder at the fact. It must be remembered, however, that the Romans tolerated and expected a roundness of invective, which is much at variance with the greater decorum of modern habits of speech. One reason for the difference probably is, that our notions of what is proper and gentlemanlike are an inheritance from days when the practice of duelling compelled every one to be punctilious both about the language he used and the language of which he must take notice. Now, nothing like the duel had existed in the civic communities of the ancient world, and so

* *Ad Q. F.*, ii., 4, 1.
17

the point of honour was not liable to be touched in the controversies of society or of politics. To a Roman, abuse was mere words and wind, carrying no responsibility with it ; neither did the man who uttered it suffer from loss of dignity, nor was the object of it under any obligation to clear his character.

Notwithstanding its sins against good taste, the speech against Vatinius has an interest of its own as illustrating Cicero's attitude towards Cæsar. He could hardly attack Cæsar's jackal without approaching dangerously near to the proconsul himself. When he inveighs against Vatinius for carrying laws in defiance of the auspices, do not his words reflect on Vatinius' master? Cicero will not allow his victim to associate his cause with that of Cæsar—"and that not only for the sake of the commonwealth, but for the sake of Cæsar, lest a stain from your despicable vileness should seem to rest on his worthy name. . . . Suppose that Cæsar did break out into some excesses ; that the strain of conflict, his ambitious aspirations, his pre-eminent genius, his exalted birth, did hurry him into acts, to which we could submit at the time from such a man, and which should now be blotted from our minds by his glorious services meanwhile ; do you, rascal, dare to presume on the same forbearance? and shall we give ear to the voice of Vatinius, the pirate and the temple-robber, when he demands that the same privilege shall be extended to him as to Cæsar?" *

This argument was really sound, as regarded the past. Cæsar as consul had done fearful mischief to

---

* *In Vat.*, 6, 15.

Rome, but the Romans might well condone it in consideration of the splendid deeds of the proconsul. The doubt arose when men looked to the future. Cæsar had shown himself utterly unscrupulous; he had trampled on all law and constitution. Could such a man be trusted with power? Would not the acquiescence in Cæsar's supremacy mean the servitude of the commonwealth? These anxieties, though but dimly felt, certainly affected the minds both of Cicero and Pompey at this time. Both of them were uneasy, and inclined to enter on lines of policy, likely to bring them into collision with Cæsar.

The relations of political parties were unsettled, and the position of Pompey in particular was doubtful and anxious. Towards the end of March Cicero writes to his brother: **March, 56 B.C.** "Pompey is not what he was; the mob are cool towards him on Milo's account, and the loyalists find much wanting and much to blame. My only objection to Marcellinus" (consul for the year) "is that he handles Pompey too severely. The Senate however is pleased to see it, and this makes me the more inclined to absent myself from the House, and maintain an attitude of reserve. In the law-courts I am all that I ever was, and my levée is as thronged as in my best days." *

In spite of all drawbacks, Cicero was at this time very confident in his own strength. He writes to Quintus †: "In other respects my position is what

---

* *Ad Q. F.*, ii., 4, 5. The reference to the letters to Quintus is always to the corrected arrangement as given in Wesenberg's Teubner Edition.   † *Ad Q. F.*, ii., 3, 7.

you used to declare it would be, though I could never
believe it, full of honour and influence; these have
been restored to me, my dear brother, and with me
to yourself, by your patience, your courage, your devotion, and your affection." The acquittal of Sestius
confirmed him in this opinion. The tide of public
feeling, which had borne him in triumph home,
seemed still to be setting steadily in his favour. He
thought himself able to take a stronger line in politics; and now, as before his exile, his main object
was to draw Pompey over to the side of the constitution. He had marked Pompey's distrust of Cæsar,
and he seems to have believed that the confederacy
between them was fast breaking up. At any rate
he was satisfied that Pompey would see without displeasure an assault on the Julian legislation, and
Cicero resolved to deliver that assault in person.

The point selected for attack was the vexed question of the public lands in Campania.* It seems that
Pompey's veterans had been provided for elsewhere,
on lands acquired by purchase, and that this Campanian land was destined for distribution among the
poor citizens.† Thus Pompey's interests were not
directly involved in upholding Cæsar's law. At
the end of the year 57, one of the tribunes, a supporter of Pompey, had mentioned the matter in a
tentative way,‡ and now on the 5th of
April Cicero brought it again to the
notice of the Senate "which was as uproarious," he
says, § "as if it had been a public meeting." On

April 5, 56 B.C.

---

* See above p. 219.   ‡ *Ad Q. F.*, ii., 1, 1.

† Suetonius, *Jul.*, 20.   § *Ad Q. F.*, ii., 5, 1.

Cicero's motion, it was resolved that the question should be submitted formally to the House by the consuls on the Ides of May. This was, as he after-wards said to Lentulus,* "to attack the enemy in the very heart of his position."

Pompey showed no displeasure. On the 8th of April Cicero writes to his brother,† then acting as Pompey's legate in Sardinia : "Yesterday I dined with Crassipes, and after dinner was carried in a lit-ter to Pompey's garden. I had failed to catch him earlier in the day, as he was from home, and I wished to see him, because I was leaving Rome the next day, and he was bound for Sardinia. I found him at home, and begged him to let you come back as soon as possible. 'You shall have him immediately,' he replied. He was leaving, as he said, on the 11th to embark either from Labro or from Pisa." Evidently Cicero told the truth to Lentulus two years later, when he said that Pompey left Rome without giving him a hint that he was offended by his line of action.‡ But a bitter disappointment was in store. The events of the next few days completely altered the situation, and left Cicero in a painful and humiliating position.

* *Ad Fam.*, i., 9, 8.
† *Ad Q. F.*, ii., 5, 3.
‡ *Ad Fam.*, i., 9, 9.

CHAPTER IX.

ROME AFTER THE CONFERENCE OF LUCA.

56–52 B.C.

CÆSAR had spent the winter of 57–56 B.C. in his southern provinces, Illyricum and Cisalpine Gaul. A crisis was evidently at hand, and it was needful for him to be as near as possible to the capital "to set a form upon that indigest."

Towards the end of March he summoned Crassus to meet him at Ravenna. While they were consulting on the political situation the news arrived of Cicero's action in the matter of the Campanian land. The importance of this move was instantly manifest to Cæsar. An offensive and defensive alliance between Pompey and Cicero seemed imminent, and the two, once united, would secure the adherence of the equestrian order and of the country-people of Italy. If Pompey should support Cicero

April 5, 56 B.C.

in this first assault, the Nobles would probably attack the grant of a province to Cæsar by the law of Vatinius. Domitius Ahenobarbus, whose candidature for next year's consulship seemed certain of success, openly declared his intention to propose Cæsar's recall.* If then Cæsar held his hand and allowed things to drift, they were likely to drift towards civil war, and for civil war he was not yet ready. Even at this moment news had arrived of fresh trouble in Gaul. The maritime people of the Veneti on the shores of the Bay of Biscay had massacred his commissariat officers and had risen in arms. He must have time to complete and consolidate his conquests, and to obtain time he was willing to pay a heavy price. Considerations, other than those of ambition and expediency doubtless co-operated in making him anxious to find terms of agreement. "It is probable," as Mommsen remarks, "that Cæsar hesitated to break the heart of his beloved daughter, who was sincerely attached to her husband ; in his soul there was room for much besides the statesman."

The conference was adjourned to Luca, the southernmost point in Cæsar's dominion, and thither Pompey was invited to come to meet his confederates. This must have been about the middle of April. The assembly of these great potentates was like a congress of sovereign princes. Cæsar was attended by a great retinue of his officers. Roman politicians and place-hunters flocked to Luca, and provincial governors found the little town on the way to or from

April, 56 B.C.

---

* Suetonius, *Jul.*, 24.

their posts. It is said that 120 lictors could be counted and 200 senators.* But no state or pageantry could adequately express the importance of this meeting between the three chiefs. If they could come to an agreement, their power was sufficient to dispose of an Empire which was the civilised world.

The terms which Cæsar offered were so liberal that Pompey at once assented to them, and the bonds of the coalition were drawn closer than ever. As on the occasion of the first formation of the triumvirate, all that Pompey had been in vain endeavouring by painful intrigues to extract from his natural allies the constitutionalists, was granted to him in a word by his magnificent rival. It was arranged that Pompey and Crassus should forget their differences, and be consuls together for the next year (55 B.C.). After their consulship, Crassus was to lead an expedition against Parthia, and Pompey was to have for five years the governorship of Spain, which, however, he might administer by means of lieutenants, while he remained at the head of affairs in Rome. In return, Cæsar stipulated for an extension of five years in his command of the Gallic provinces, and for the defence at home of all the Acts of his consulship.

To secure this last condition, it was necessary that Cicero should either be persuaded to renounce his opposition, or that he should again be driven into exile. Pompey, who had for his own purposes encouraged Cicero to put himself in the fore-front of the battle, accepted the ungracious task of checking and humiliating him. Now, as two years before,

---

* Plutarch, *Pomp.*, 51, 2.

LUGA.
(Durky.)

Cicero found that the support of Pompey was not to be relied on. Pompey was far more scrupulous than Cæsar, when it was a question of committing criminal acts, but he had none of Cæsar's delicacy where personal honour was concerned. He wanted the partisan loyalty, which made Cæsar aver, "that if he had been obliged to use the help of cut-throats and foot-pads in maintaining his cause, even to them he would not fail in awarding a due recompense."* Cicero had all along served Pompey faithfully, but Pompey seems to have felt no remorse in using him and then dropping him, whenever it suited his own convenience.

After the conference of Luca, Cæsar once more turned his back on the intrigues of the capital, and hurried to meet his foes on the shores of the Atlantic. The details of the arrangement between the Three were kept a profound secret for the moment; but that they had come to an arrangement was soon manifest. Pompey sent to Cicero a request, which was equivalent to an order, that he should suspend all action on the question of the Campanian land until he himself should return to Rome.† To Quintus Cicero whom he met immediately afterwards in Sardinia he expressed himself for once with an almost brutal frankness: "'You are the very man I want,' he said, 'nothing could be luckier; unless you take pains to keep your brother Marcus straight, I shall hold you responsible for your pledges on his account.' To make a long story short, he com-

---

* Suetonius, *Jul.*, 72.
† *Ad Fam.*, i., 9, 10.

plained bitterly; recounted the obligations under which he had laid us and his own stipulations and my brother's engagements as to Cæsar's Acts, and appealed to my brother's own knowledge that all which he had done for my restoration had been done with Cæsar's consent. By way of recommending Cæsar's cause and dignity to me, he begged that I would not assail them, if I could not or would not defend them." *

These announcements came as a crushing blow to Cicero. The ground on which he was taking his stand had shifted under his feet. On the Ides of May he absented himself from the Senate, and the discussion fell through. "As for the previous arrangement," he writes,† "that the question of the Campanian land was to be dealt with on the 15th and 16th, it was not dealt with. In this matter there is a stoppage in the current of my action."

So far Cicero had no choice but to submit. But he had still to decide how to shape his general policy in view of the altered circumstances. The union, which he had been encouraged to attempt, of Pompey with the Nobles in defence of the constitution against Cæsar was now obviously impossible. Pompey was committed to an entirely different line of action. Lucullus was dead, and the Republic had no general but Pompey, so that it would have been madness to persist in words which could not be supported by deeds. Cicero then must either continue to follow his old leader in this new departure, or else

---

* *Ad Fam.*, i., 9, 9.

† *Ad Q. F.*, ii., 6, 2.

efface himself completely and sit down in silence and inactivity in company with the more obstinate of the Nobles. He would be obliged even to renounce his great position as leader of the Roman bar, for politics were ever intruding themselves into forensic contests. Such a sacrifice, had Cicero been prepared to make it, would perhaps have been the most honourable, certainly it would have been the most dignified course.

But it was doubtful whether he could count on a cordial reception from the Nobles, and still more doubtful whether they could or would afford him effective protection from Clodius and his other enemies. Cicero had been convinced all along that the Nobles had deserted him in his hour of peril, and now he was equally sure that they were jealous of him and would be glad to see him reduced to a nonentity; as he had written to his friend soon after his return: " Those same men, my dear Atticus, who clipped my wings, are displeased to see them growing again, for growing I hope they are."* Even during the last month, some of them had not been able to conceal their delight † that Cicero, who had so often supported Pompey against what they considered the interests of the party, should now have incurred his displeasure and that of Cæsar. Further the Nobles continued to abet Clodius, and by this conduct they forfeited, as Cicero thought, their claim to be considered the party of order‡; Pompey was

* *Ad Att.*, iv., 2, 5.
† *Ad Fam.*, i., 9, 10.
‡ *Ad Fam.*, i., 7, 7, and 9, 17.

at least the enemy of his enemy.* Cicero feared likewise to compromise his brother's fortunes. Quintus had pledged himself for Cicero's good behaviour to Pompey, and Pompey had pledged himself to Cæsar.† Should these pledges go unredeemed? It was soon made clear to him that more was expected from him than a passive acquiescence in the supremacy of the triumvirs, and that his active support would be welcomed, and recompensed with ample protection from his enemies and with at least outward deference and consideration. Cicero had now, as frequently before, grave reason to resent Pompey's conduct; but after all it was Pompey more than any one else who had restored him from his exile, and he dreaded the reproach of ingratitude. His instincts of personal loyalty bound him to his old chief, and on the whole he resolved to abide by him, even though his adherence involved the acceptance of the mild but inexorable yoke of Cæsar.

It was not without many misgivings and much upbraiding from his own conscience, that he came to this conclusion. He expresses these feelings very frankly soon after in a letter to Atticus ‡ : "What is more degraded than the life which we are living—I especially; for you, though you are a statesman by nature, yet have no bondage of your own to serve and have only your share in the national servitude. But I, who, if I speak as I ought, am reckoned for a

---

* *Ad Fam.*, i., 9, 11, "meumque inimicum unum in civitate habuit inimicum."

† *Ad Fam.*, i., 9. 12.

‡ *Ad Att.*, iv., 6, 2.

madman; if as I must, for a slave; if I hold my peace,
am accounted as crushed and baffled, how bitter
should be my grief? So indeed it is, and all the
more bitter because I cannot even grieve without
seeming ungrateful. Well, can I rest on my oars, and
take refuge in a haven of peace? Nay, the only
haven that waits for us is a camp and a battle-field.
Well, then I must submit to be a servant, I who refused to be one of the masters.* So it must be; for
this, I see, is your decision, and would that I had
always hearkened to your advice."

Cicero's first action in the Senate on these new
lines related to certain votes in favour of Cæsar,
which, though fully justified by the
work which Cæsar was now doing for _{June, 56 B.C.}
Rome, were awkwardly inconsistent with the attack
which had been contemplated on his position.
Cicero describes these measures in very reserved
language to Lentulus Spinther†: "You ask me
about the political situation; there is much contention, but no struggle on equal terms. For those
who have the advantage in resources, in arms and in
power, seem to me through the folly and inconsistency of their opponents to have been given the advantage in argument as well. So with very faint
opposition they have obtained through the Senate
what they never expected to obtain even through
the People without revolution. With little or no
trouble pay has been voted for Cæsar's troops, ten
lieutenants have been granted him, and in assigning

---

* See above, p. 203.

† *Ad Fam.*, i., 7, 10.

provinces under Gracchus' law,* it has been resolved
that he shall not be susperseded. I tell my story
briefly, for I take no pleasure in the present state
of things."

Cicero had himself given his voice in favour of a
Thanksgiving of fifteen days for Cæsar's victories,
and for the other measures in his interest, which he
recounted to Lentulus. The controversy whether
the consuls of 55 B.C. were to succeed Cæsar in his
Gallic provinces was, if the combatants had known
it, a mere beating of the air. The consulships for
55 had been settled on Pompey and Crassus, and
their future provinces determined for them at the
conference of Luca, and Gaul had been entailed for
years to come on Cæsar. But all this was as yet a
secret; and Cicero argued the question in June, 56,
as if the Senate really had the disposal of the
provinces. He urged that the provinces named
should be Syria and Macedonia, in order that his
enemies, Gabinius and Piso, might be recalled from
their posts, and he protested against any scheme
which should cut short Cæsar's career of conquest.

Cicero's speech has been preserved to us under
the title *De Provinciis Consularibus.* The orator
cannot avoid some reference to Cæsar's Acts in his
consulship, but he touches the painful subject as
lightly as possible, taking refuge in a somewhat
weak *argumentum ad hominem.* Those who wished
to set them aside were the same men who now
acknowledged as valid the laws of Clodius' tribunate.

---

* By this law the Senate was obliged *before* the election of next
year's consuls to decide what provinces should be assigned to them.

Yet the adoption of Clodius was one of Cæsar's
Acts, and if they were cancelled then Clodius was a
patrician and therefore no tribune. "You must
permit me to decline an inquisition into the title of
useful measures, when you refuse such an inquisition
in the case of most mischievous ones." * Cicero is
more successful when he tells the story of his personal relations with Cæsar, and justifies his full reconciliation. Their early friendship, Cæsar's flattering
offers of alliance when consul, his co-operation with
Pompey in Cicero's restoration,—all authorise him to
forget and forgive, even if he has some grievances
to complain of in the matter of his exile.† Above
all, is he not bound to lay aside private resentments
when recommending what is for the good of the
State? Cæsar is no longer the turbulent demagogue
of the capital, but the champion of the Roman
State; he is now bound to the Senate by the extraordinary honours which it has conferred on him, and
it is folly to alienate him by petty attacks. "I do
not pretend to penetrate into any man's intentions
in the future; but I know what I hope. It is my
duty as a senator to secure to the best of my
power that no eminent or powerful man shall have
just ground for complaint against this House;
and this, even if I were Cæsar's bitterest enemy,
I should maintain for the good of the commonwealth."‡

---

* *De Prov. Cons.*, 19, 46.
† *De Prov. Cons.*, 17 and 18.
‡ *De Prov. Cons.*, 16, 39.

In setting forth the recent services, on which
Cæsar rests his claims to the consideration of the
Senate, Cicero has a theme worthy of his eloquence.
Here there is no need for hesitation or apology.
" He has striven on glorious battle-fields with the
fierce tribes and mighty hosts of Germania and
Helvetia; the rest he has terrified, checked, and
tamed, and taught them to obey the commands of
the Roman People. Over regions and nations which
no book, no traveller, no report had made known to
us, our general, our soldiers, and the arms of the
Roman People have found a way. It was but a
strip of Gaul that we held before, Senators; the rest
was occupied by tribes, enemies of our rule or rebels
against it, or by men unknown to us, or known only
as dangerous, savage, and warlike. Every one
desired that these tribes should be broken and subdued ; from the first days of our empire there never
has been a prudent statesman who did not recognise
that Gaul was the great danger to our State. But
owing to the might and multitude of those races we
never before ventured to try conclusions with them
as a nation. It was always we that were the challenged, and we fought only on the defensive. Now
at length we have reached the consummation that
our empire extends to the utmost limits of that
land. Not without the Providence of Heaven
nature piled the Alps to be a rampart to Italy. For
if that approach had lain open to the fierce hordes
of Gaul, never would this city have survived to be
the seat and home of sovereignty. Now let them
sink in the earth! for beyond those mountain peaks

as far as the extremest verge of ocean there is nothing left for Italy to fear." *

Cicero forthwith published this splendid oration. As a master-piece of his art, he might well be proud of it; but as marking definitely his submission to the Triumvirate, the "recantation," as he called it, caused him shame and self-reproach. "What is this you say," he writes to Atticus,† "do you think that there is any one by whom I wish my works to be read and approved rather than by yourself? Why then did I send it to any one else first? Well, I was pressed by the person to whom I sent it, and I had not another copy; and besides—I keep nibbling round what I have got to swallow—this recantation seemed to me to be somewhat discreditable. But a long good night to the thorough downright honest policy. It is incredible what treachery I find in these noble chiefs,‡ as they wish to be, and as they might be if they had any loyalty. I felt and knew how I had been led on by them and then deserted and tossed aside; still my hope was that I might work together with them in politics. But no, they were the same as ever, and by the aid of your monitions I have at last come to my senses. . . . Let us finish with them. Since those, who have no power, will none of my love, let me take care that those who have the power § shall love me. You will

* *De Prov. Cons.*, 13, 33 *seq.*

† *Ad. Att.*, iv., 5.

‡ *I. e.*, Hortensius, Bibulus, Domitius and other leaders of the optimate party.

§ *I. e.*, The triumvirs.

18

say, ' I only wish you had thought of this before ' ; I know that you wished it, and that I have been a downright ass."

The reconstitution of the triumvirate was followed by a period of quiet at Rome, and the State moved along the lines which the Three had traced for it. Pompey and Crassus were consuls in 55 B.C., and each of the confederates received the provincial command for which he had stipulated. The union between them seemed now absolutely re-established, and Cicero did not at this time appreciate how hollow the alliance necessarily was. In this settlement, which left Pompey for the moment the acknowledged head of the State, Cicero believed that he was obliged to acquiesce. Early in the year 55 he writes to Lentulus * : " The State lies beyond question in the power of our friends, and that so absolutely that it is unlikely that this generation will see any change in the situation. I subordinate my action to the wishes of the man whom I am bound in honour not to oppose; and I am not playing the hypocrite in this, as some fancy ; for such is my earnestness in Pompey's cause, and such my devotion to him, that they have power to make his interests and wishes seem to me all that is right. To my mind, even his opponents would not do wrong if, feeling themselves to be no match for him, they were now to desist from contending. . . . Peace is the best we can hope for now, and that the present rulers seem likely to secure us, if men will submit patiently to their domination. As for my

55 B.C.

* *Ad. Fam.*, i., 8, 1-4.

old consular dignity of a brave and consistent senator, there is no use thinking of that; it has been lost,
all through the fault of those who estranged from
the Senate that order which would have been their
best friend, and that man who would have been their
most glorious champion." *

We hear little of Clodius at this time; probably
he had received notice from Cæsar that he must not
disturb the peace. At any rate we find that Cicero
was able to be reconciled with two of Clodius' chief
backers, his brother Appius and Crassus, the third
member of the triumvirate. In the latter case a
renunciation of their long-standing feud was pressed
upon both of them by Pompey and Cæsar, and was
rendered the easier by the mediation of young
Publius Crassus,† then as always a devoted friend of
Cicero. With all his violence of expression Cicero
was of a very placable nature, and found it almost
impossible to refuse a hand which was held out to
him. In the matter of Crassus, he says to Lentulus,‡
"I obeyed the call not only of expediency, but of
my own disposition." Immediately Nov., 55 B.C.
before his departure for the East Crassus accepted an invitation to dinner from Cicero in
the gardens of his son-in-law Crassipes, " so that he
started for his province almost from my hearth-
stone."

During the year 54, no great change occurred in

---

* *I. e.,* The Knights and Pompey.

† *Ad. Q. F.,* ii., 7, 2.

‡ *Ad. Fam.,* i., 9, 20. The reconciliation did not alter Cicero's
opinion of Crassus' character, " What a rascal it is ! " he exclaims in
a confidential letter (*Ad. Att.,* iv., 13, 2) immediately afterwards.

the situation.   Cæsar was still fighting hard in Gaul,
Pompey ruling, as best he could, at home.   Throughout a long letter of explanation to
54 B.C.   Lentulus, written in this year, Cicero
refers to the supremacy of Pompey in the State as
the central fact in the situation, and he seems entirely
to have forgotten that this supremacy might come
to be challenged by Cæsar.

To maintain for any length of time good order in
Rome was beyond Pompey's power.   The elections
were not only scandalously corrupt,* but so turbulent
that year after year had to begin with an "interregnum," because no consuls could be chosen at the
proper time.   A painful accident occurring at one of
these scenes of tumult had serious consequences in
the future.   Some one standing near to Pompey was
struck by a stone or a bludgeon, and Pompey's gown
was bespattered with blood.   The gown was carried
home, and unhappily met the eye of his young wife.
The shock of the sight occasioned a miscarriage, from
the effect of which Julia never recovered, and her
death some months later severed one of the main
bonds which united Cæsar and Pompey.

The glimpses which we get of the law-courts at this
time do not give a high idea of the administration of
justice.   "Now for the news of Rome.
54 B.C.   On the 5th of July Sufenas and Caius
Cato were acquitted, and Procilius convicted ; from

---

* In the year 54 B.C. the rate of interest rose from four to eight per
cent., owing to the demand for ready money to be spent in bribery ;
£100,000 was promised for the vote of the first century ; Scaurus,
who came rather late into the field, is reported "to have satisfied the
electors tribe by tribe at his house," and so forth.

which we may gather that our potent, grave, and reverend signors do not care a straw for bribery, for the elections, for the interregnum, for treason, nor for the safety of the whole commonwealth, but that we must draw the line at killing householders in their own homes; they do not appear to be very sure about that either, for 22 voted not-guilty against 29. Clodius, who prosecuted, roused the feelings of the jury by a peroration which was certainly fine. Hortensius was for the defence in his usual style. I did not open my lips; for my little girl, who is now near her time, was nervous about me, and would not have me cross Clodius' path." *

Whatever may have been the alarms in which Tullia was privileged to indulge, her father had not much to fear from Clodius, so long as he kept on good terms with the triumvirs. Shortly before this, he had written in answer to his brother's inquiries † : "Your question comes to this; what sort of year is before me? Well I think that it will be one of complete peace, or at least that I have ample protection. My levée, the Forum, and the expressions of feeling in the theatre give daily evidence of this; my friends are free from anxiety knowing the forces I have at command in the support of Cæsar and Pompey. All this makes me confident; but if any outburst of that mad fellow should occur, everything is prepared to crush him."

July, 54 B.C.

As an advocate Cicero reigned pre-eminent. He

---

* *Ad Att.*, iv., 15, 4.

† *Ad Q. F.*, ii., 14, 2.

was in urgent request for every important case, and
he tells his brother that he was never before so
pressed with business. "In your last letter," he
adds,* "as frequently before, you cheer me on to
fresh exertions and fresh ambitions. I will do as you
wish; but O when shall I find time to live?"

Of the cases in which Cicero was engaged at this
time, one must have given him great satisfaction.
His old friend Plancius, the same who had sheltered
him in his exile, was elected ædile and then, almost
as a matter of course, put on his trial for his proceedings during the election. Cicero delivered in his
behalf an admirable speech (from which I have had
occasion to quote freely †) and procured an acquittal.

Other briefs Cicero was obliged to undertake, not
because he wished them, but because he could not
refuse his powerful friends. The most notable cases
were those of two objects of his former vituperations,
Vatinius and Gabinius. Of the first he says ‡ that
it was an easy business. Pompey had patched up a
reconciliation between them, and Cæsar had earnestly
pressed him to undertake the defence. Vatinius was
an unscrupulous but amusing and good-humoured
rascal, who disarmed hostility § by making fun of his
own physical deformities and moral obliquities. He
was acquitted, and lived to show Cicero much kind-
ness‖ after the battle of Pharsalia, and to beg the

* *Ad Q. F.*, iii., 1, 12.
† See pp. 7, 22, 94, 108.
‡ *Ad Q. F.*, ii., 15, 3.
§ Seneca *de Const. Sap.*, 17, 3, and Cicero *in Vat.*, 17, 41.
‖ *Ad Att.*, xi., 5, 4.

favour of Cicero's advocacy of his interests again
later on.*

It was much more painful to Cicero to have to defend Gabinius, the man who had sold him to Clodius,
and who had shared with his colleague Piso and with
Clodius himself Cicero's extremest hatred. There
were several accusations against Gabinius, but the
most serious was for treason in having quitted his
province without leave to restore the King of Egypt
(see p. 252).   Cicero was one of the witnesses against
him at the first trial, but he declined to prosecute out
of regard for Pompey. Gabinius was very humble
now to Cicero; he refused to cross-examine him at
the trial, professed gratitude for his forbearance, and
said that, if he were permitted to retain his place in
the State, he would one day make amends for the
injuries he had done him.† Pompey, while begging
Cicero to undertake the defence at a second trial for
extortion, acknowledged that he could ask the favour
only supposing that Gabinius made atonement for
his conduct.‡ What Gabinius said or did to satisfy
him, we are not informed: but Cicero after holding
out for some time longer yielded at last. This second
trial took place before the stern bar of Cato,§ and all
the exertions of Cicero and all the influence of Pompey were unable to procure a verdict. The result
was very damaging to Pompey, especially following

---

* *Ad Fam.*, v., 9.

† *Ad Q. F.*, iii., 4, 3.

‡ *Ad Att.*, iv., 18, 1. The references in the fourth book of the
Letters to Atticus are to Wesenberg's Teubner edition.

§ *Ad Q. F.*, iii., 1, 15.

as it did on the acquittal of Vatinius. Pompey had failed, where Cæsar had succeeded, in saving from ruin a partisan, whose sole virtue was that he had been a zealous and useful servant to his chief. Gabinius judged that so ineffective a master had best be deserted, and when the Civil War came, he no less than Vatinius was to be found on the side of Cæsar. Cicero never really forgave himself for his pliancy on this occasion. "Why," he writes in the bitterness of his heart five years later—"why should I take account of my enemies? there are friends of mine, men whom I have defended at the bar, whom I cannot see in the Senate-house without pain, nor associate with them without disgrace." *

During the years following the conference of Luca, Cæsar was untiring in his efforts to win the regard of Cicero, and to unite him to himself by every bond of personal and political friendship. There was no fear lest Cicero should forget that Cæsar could deal heavy blows, if he were so minded ; and now no opportunity was lost to impress him with the conviction, that Cæsar had been driven to strike against his will, and that his earnest desire was for cordial and intimate alliance. Cæsar never failed where good breeding was required, and he courted the restored exile with a delicacy and a geniality which strongly affected him. "Never does the slightest word of mine pass in Cæsar's cause, to say nothing of acts, without his acknowledging it with such a distinguished courtesy that I cannot but feel myself bound to him." † Cæsar

---

* *Ad Att.*, x., 8, 3.

† *Ad Fam.*, i., 9, 21.

pressed him to recommend to his care any friends who wished for an opening in his province, and these he always treated with such marked favour as to make them feel that Cicero's request was all-powerful with him. He would not hear a word of thanks: "As for Mescinius Rufus, whom you mentioned to me, I will make him King of Gaul if you please, or else you may hand him over to Lepta, and send me some one else to make much of." * When Clodius wrote to Cæsar with some calumnies against Cicero, Cæsar showed his contempt by not answering the letter,† and he took care that this should come to Cicero's ears. In the embarrassments which resulted from Cicero's building operations, Cæsar freely accommodated him with loans of money. To Cicero likewise in conjunction with his own confidential agent Oppius he entrusted the spending of great sums on the erection of public buildings and the adornment of the city. We find that they put up a town-hall ‡ on the Campus Martius and marble polling-places on the same spot. The Forum was also enlarged at a cost of £600,000. Cicero was much pleased at the compliment conveyed by this honourable commission. It was entrusted, as he writes to Atticus,§ "to Cæsar's friends, Oppius and myself— yes, you may fret and fume—I say, to Cæsar's friends."

---

* *Ad Fam.*, vii., 5, 2.

† *Ad Q. F.*, iii., 1, 11.

‡ This *villa publica* seems to have been used chiefly for the business of the census.

§ *Ad Att.*, iv., 16, 8.

Above all Cæsar approached Cicero on his most sensitive side by constant kindness and attention to his brother Quintus, who was now serving as lieutenant-general in Gaul. The two were together in Britain during the summer of 54 B.C., and when the troops went into winter camps, the choice of quarters was allowed to Quintus, who selected the territory of the Nervii, one of the Belgic tribes. The younger Cicero was a brave and skilful officer. By a sudden rising the Gauls overwhelmed one division of the Roman army, and they next made a furious attack on the isolated station of Quintus. The whole country was in arms, and it was long before a messenger could get through to Cæsar. Quintus Cicero defended his post with unwearied though almost desperate valour. It was like the stand made at Lucknow after the disaster of Cawnpore in the Indian mutiny. When the relieving force, led by Cæsar in person, at length appeared, the Roman eagle still crowned the camp of Cicero's legion, but of those who had kept it so well nine out of ten were either killed or wounded.

Cæsar's reception of the first proposal that Quintus should serve under him, gives a characteristic picture both of the man and of the situation.* Marcus Cicero had, it appears, written to Cæsar to make the offer of his brother's services. The mail in which this offer was conveyed got soaked on the road and Cicero's letter was reduced to such a state of pulp, that it could not even be recognised for his. Fortunately a letter of Balbus in the same packet had

* *Ad Q. F.*, ii., 10, 4.

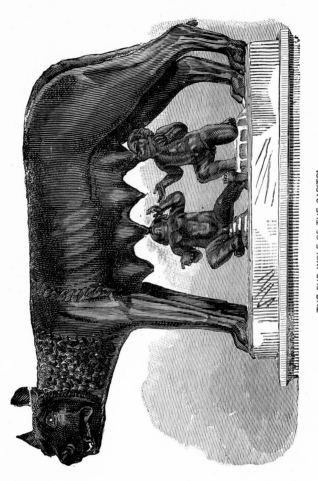

THE SHE-WOLF OF THE CAPITOL.

(Duruy.)

not fared quite so badly. Cæsar was able to read a
few words of it, and wrote in reply as follows : " I
see that you have written something about Cicero ;
I could not make it all out, but so far as I can
decipher the meaning it was something so good that
I could wish for it, but hardly hope for it." On receiving another copy, Cæsar joyfully accepted the
proposal, modestly, however, warning Cicero that
he feared his brother would be disappointed if he
expected he was coming to a rich province.

Cicero was not the man to resist such constant
and flattering attentions. He was completely dazzled
alike by the splendour of Cæsar's exploits, and by
the friendship which he displayed towards himself.
To his brother in Cæsar's camp he expresses himself
very warmly. " I have taken Cæsar to my bosom
and will never let him slip." * " Like a belated
traveller, I must make up for lost time. I have
been too much behindhand in availing myself of
his friendship ; now I will put my best foot forward." † " I can have no reserve when I deal with
Cæsar. He comes next to you and to our children
in my affection, and not far behind." ‡ Perhaps it is
not safe to take these letters, which were to travel
in Cæsar's despatch-boxes, as absolutely confidential. § But even in the letters to Atticus, " in which

* *Ad Q. F.*, ii., 11, 1.

† *Ad Q. F.*, ii., 13, 2.

‡ *Ad Q. F.*, iii., 1, 18.

§ Cicero believed that his letters might be opened and read on the
road (*Ad Q. F.*, iii., 1, 21, and 8, 2, and 9, 3). The Romans were
not very exact in their code of honour in this matter. Cicero several
times opened letters of members of his family under circumstances
which would not to our notions justify the action.

there are so many confidences, that we do not trust
even our secretaries for fear anything should get
wind," * there is not a hint that any distrust of
Cæsar survives. "One thing," he writes, "at any
rate I have gained, that I have full evidence of
Cæsar's esteem and affection" †; and again : " The
delightful friendship with Cæsar is the one plank
saved from my shipwreck, which gives me real
pleasure. Just see with what honour, consideration,
and favour he treats our dear Quintus! Good
Heavens! I could do no more, if I were commander.
in-chief myself." ‡

Though he is thus appreciative of Cæsar's personal
charm, which blinds him for the moment to the
dangers which the commonwealth has to fear from
him, it must not be supposed that Cicero does not
feel keenly the destruction of his old
Oct., 54 B.C.   ideals. "We have lost, my dear Atticus, not only the blood and substance but the very
outward hue and complexion of the State as it
used to be. There is no Republic left which can
give me any pleasure or on which my eye can rest
with satisfaction. 'And do you take that so easily?'
you will say. Well yes, even that. . . . The
place in my heart, where resentment used to dwell,
has grown callous." §

In the year 53 B.C. occurred the destruction of

---

* *Ad Att.*, iv., 17, 1.
† *Ad Att.*, iv., 15, 10.
‡ *Ad Att.*, iv., 19, 2.
§ *Ad Att.*, iv., 18, 2.

Crassus and his army in Mesopotamia. This disaster
entailed on the Romans much anxiety
for the safety of the eastern portion of   53 B.C.
their empire. But the external danger passed away
without serious consequences, and the death of
Crassus was important chiefly as it affected the
situation of Roman leaders and Roman parties.
For Cæsar it was a most untoward event; it deprived him of a reserved force on whose co-operation he might rely in case of a civil war with Pompey.
To such an issue the Roman factions were now
slowly but surely drifting. Pompey was becoming
thoroughly alarmed at the growing power and great
position of Cæsar, and the leaders of the optimate
party now, when it was too late, began to open their
eyes to the true state of the case. They recognised
that they had taken fright in the wrong direction,
and that the only chance for the Republic was
staked on the sword of the man whom they had
opposed and distrusted for the last twenty years.
Pompey on his side was glad to draw towards that
party to which his nature and aspirations would
always have attached him, if he had not been kept
aloof by the folly of its leaders. He marked his new
departure by declining Cæsar's offer of the hand of
his niece Octavia, and by arranging a marriage with
Cornelia, daughter of Scipio Metellus, one of the
chief men of the optimate party.

A gap of two years and a half occurs at this
period in the correspondence between Cicero and
Atticus. From the end of the year 54 B.C. onwards
the two appear to have been constantly together in

Rome. We cannot, therefore, trace the opinions of Cicero on the altered situation, and do not even know how far he was admitted to share the counsels of the Optimates or of Pompey.

Milo was candidate for the consulship during the year 53 B.C., and Clodius for the prætorship, and the two heartily renewed their old faction-fights. Pompey's destined father-in-law, Scipio Metellus, was in competition with Milo, and this circumstance now inclined Pompey to favour Clodius. Bribery and intimidation were carried on to a reckless extent on both sides. No election could be held, and the next year began as usual with an interregnum. Milo and Clodius roamed the streets, each with his armed gang, and leaders and followers alike carried their lives in their hands.

52 B.C.

On the evening of the 17th of January, 52 B.C., the two came into collision on the Appian Way, some ten miles from Rome. The victory in this "Battle of Bovillæ" remained with Milo, and Clodius was left dead on the road. The body was found the same night and conveyed to the city. The death of Clodius caused intense excitement amongst the lowest classes in Rome. The corpse was seized upon and burned by a tumultuous mob in the Forum. By accident or design the flames spread and destroyed the Curia Hostilia, the ordinary meeting-place of the Senate. Stormy discussions ensued in the House; Milo was fiercely attacked by the kinsmen of Clodius, and was defended with equal vigour by Cicero, Cato, and Marcus

RUINS OF THE CIRCUS OF BOVILLÆ.

(*Durny.*)

Marcellus. The tribunes were divided between the one party and the other.

Rome now looked to Pompey as the only man capable of restoring order. The Senate issued its proclamation of martial law, and as there were no consuls to whom it could be addressed, the mandate ran "that the interrex and the tribunes of the plebs and the proconsul Cnæus Pompeius should see to it that the State took no harm." Finally the reconciliation of Pompey with the Optimates was sealed by a decree, proposed by Bibulus and assented to by Cato, that Pompey should be elected sole consul. This recommendation was carried out by the interrex and the assembly of the People, and Pompey assumed a position resembling that of the dictator in the Old Republic. His first care was to enlist a strong body of troops. He next passed severe and retrospective laws against rioting and electoral corruption, and provided a machinery for trials under them, by which the bribing of a jury was made almost impossible.

Milo was speedily arraigned. The most damning charge against him was that, after Clodius had been wounded and carried into a house, Milo had caused him to be dragged forth and despatched.* This accusation is not noticed in Cicero's speech, but the verdict of the jury makes it highly probable that it was true.† The Forum was occupied during the trial by armed guards, and the consul himself took

---

* Asconius *In Milonianam.*

† " For more than two years Milo had been ' looking for Clodius,' as they say in Texas" (Tyrrell). See above p. 255.

his station with a strong reserve force at the door of the treasury of Saturn which overlooked the court. These precautions seem to have been absolutely necessary to preserve order, and we cannot fairly accuse Pompey, though his own wishes were against the prisoner, of attempting to coerce the jury. Cicero, who had throughout been unremitting in his exertions, and who owed Milo a debt of gratitude for many deeds of faithful partisanship, was sole counsel for the defence. It must have been a bitter disappointment to him that this speech was a failure. His nerve broke down in the presence of the drawn swords of the soldiers, and of the intense excitement of the by-standers. Perhaps likewise his great anxiety for success on this supreme occasion defeated its own object. Asconius tells us that the speech which he actually delivered was taken down by shorthand writers, and that it differed widely from the magnificent oration which he afterwards wrote out and published. When Cicero sent a copy to Milo in his exile, Milo is reported * to have said: "It is just as well that Cicero did not succeed in delivering this speech, or I should never have known the taste of these excellent mullets of Massilia."

Milo's name lives in those splendid pages; but probably Rome was well rid of him, as well as of Clodius. Cicero, to prove that Milo had no interest in killing Clodius, urges that while he lived Milo was a necessary man. Now he is dead, Milo's importance is diminished. "The killing was unin-tentional," he says, "and we can only thank the

* Dio Cassius, xl., 54.

Providence which made Clodius lay an ambush to attack so brave a man as Milo; but every one of you must breathe more freely now that this ruffian is removed from your path; will you then bless the deed and yet punish the doer?" The jurors appear to have argued differently. The two had held each other in check, but the survivor would be intolerable; Milo's occupation was gone, and they judged that he had better go too.

Cicero could not save Milo, but he procured the acquittal of Saufeius, Milo's comrade in the fight, and when he brought to the bar Munatius Bursa, who had taken a leading part in the riotous proceedings after Clodius' death, the jury convicted in spite of the efforts of Pompey on his behalf. "They were brave citizens," writes Cicero to his friend Marius,* "who dared convict him against all the influence of the man who had selected them as jurors. They would not have done it, if they had not made my indignation their own."

Throughout the year 52, though still professedly acting as Cæsar's associate, Pompey was passing laws which were in reality framed to work against Cæsar's interests. It was **52 B.C.** of vital importance to Cæsar that he should be able to hold on to his province and army until he should enter on a second consulship. Pompey and the Optimates, while granting all his specific demands, proceeded so to arrange the order of succession to the provincial governorships as to deprive him of his legitimate expectations. Thus the ground

---

* *Ad Fam.*, vii., **2, 3.**
10

was prepared for a dispute, which was destined to end in civil war. Meantime the new arrangements about the provinces necessitated the acceptance by Cicero of the governorship of Cilicia, for which he set out in the spring of the year 51 B.C.

The death of the younger Crassus, who fell fighting bravely by his father's side against the Parthians, occasioned a vacancy in a plebeian stall of the college of augurs, and Cicero was elected to fill the place. The augurship always had an attraction for him,* and in his political writings of this time, the power and dignity of his new office are dwelt on with evident satisfaction.

In his private affairs we find Cicero at one time much embarrassed, owing to the plunder and destruction of his houses by Clodius. He had to borrow freely to meet the expenses of building and furnishing. As early as the year 54 B.C. he seems to be pretty free from these difficulties. " Very little is now wanting," he writes to Quintus, † " for my habits of life are simple, and I shall have no difficulty in meeting what calls remain if only I keep my health." His debt to Cæsar however was still owing, and his letters to Atticus in 51 B.C. are full of instructions as to its discharge. In view of the political complications which were likely to arise between Cæsar and the Senate, Cicero felt it necessary for his own freedom of action that he should no longer be Cæsar's debtor.

Cicero's son and nephew were passing through

---

* See above p. 218.

† *Ad Q. F.*, ii., 14, 3.

their boyhood during these years, and he was much
interested in their education. Tullia, whose first
husband, Piso, had died during Cicero's banishment,
was again married in the year 56 B.C. to Furius Crassipes, but divorced before Cicero left Rome for his
province in 51 B.C. About the same time Atticus
married a lady named Pilia. She and Tullia were
warm friends, and kind messages to and fro occur
frequently in the letters. We hear not a word of
Terentia in these five years. " Other matters are
vexing me," writes Cicero on one occasion,* " but
they are too private for a letter. My brother and my
daughter are full of affection for me." The ominous
silence as to his wife in this sentence seems to point
to the beginning of the estrangement which led at
last to a divorce.

Before finishing the story of Cicero's residence in
Rome since his banishment, we must look back at
his literary labours during this period. In the year
55 B.C. he was engaged on one of the most delightful of his creations, the dialogue *De Oratore*. The
scene is laid during the last days (91 B.C.) of the life
of Lucius Crassus, the foremost orator of the generation before Cicero. The second person of the
dialogue is Antonius, the great rival of Crassus, and
the minor parts are taken by the younger statesmen
of the day ; Cicero's old master, Scævola the augur,
appears in the opening scene, but like the aged Ceph-
alus in Plato's *Republic*,† he soon retires. The
technical discussions in this book are admirably in-

---

* *Ad Att.*, iv., 2, 7.

† *Ad Att.*, iv., 16, 3.

terwoven with anecdote and conversation, and in charm and interest the work is only inferior to a dialogue of Plato.

The distraction of literary composition gave Cicero some relief from his drudgery in the law-courts, and some consolation in his disgust at the political situation. During a holiday at Puteoli, where probably the greater part of the *De Oratore* was planned, we find him writing to Atticus * : " Here I am feasting in Faustus Sulla's library. Don't suppose I mean on the oysters of the Lucrine—not that they are wanting. But the truth is that in proportion as my taste for all other pleasures is spoiled by grief for the commonwealth, I find myself more and more dependent on literature for support and comfort."

Cicero's next effort was in the direction of political philosophy. In May 54 B.C., he begs Atticus to give him the run of his library during his absence. He wishes particularly to consult some writings of Varro, " for the purpose of the work which I have in hand and which I think will give you pleasure." †
This work was that which afterwards developed into the two treatises on *The Commonwealth*, and on *The Laws*. We gather ‡ that Cicero had at first written nine books of the dialogues of Scipio and his friends. Afterwards he cut off the last three books and made them the nucleus of the separate treatise entitled *The Laws*, in which he drops his historical personages and makes Atticus, Quintus, and

---

* *Ad Att.*, iv., 10, 1.

† *Ad Att.*, iv., 14, 1.

‡ *Ad Q. F.*, iii., 5, 1.

himself the speakers. In this latter dialogue he repeatedly refers to the outlines of the State laid down by Scipio in the former treatise as supplying the principles on which he is working, and the two must undoubtedly be taken together as portions of the same task. Only fragments of the later and more important books of *The Commonwealth* survive; but it is clear that after describing the unmixed forms of government, which he considers to be all unsatisfactory, monarchy being the best of them, Scipio is made to decide in favour of a mixed constitution, such as he conceives that of Rome to be. In *The Laws*, accordingly, we find even the most perverse details of the Roman constitution preserved. Cicero has much to say of the duties of a statesman, but he seems blind to the faults in the machinery of government. His methods of reasoning are those of the Greek philosophers, his conclusions those of a Roman statesman with all a Roman's limitations. The experience of the world has silently worked out the problem which the greatest men of antiquity could not solve. Cæsar and Cicero were the " least mortal minds " of Republican Rome, yet neither of them conceived it as possible, that not only a free city could be organised but a free nation.

We can gather little from these treatises regarding Cicero's opinion on the questions before the world at the moment when he wrote. It has been supposed indeed that in the fragments of the fifth book of *The Commonwealth*, the picture of the " princeps," " the guide of the State," " the director of the Commonwealth," is meant to indicate that a place might be found in Rome for a kind of monarchical power, to be exercised by Pompey. It is clear, however, from the account of the magistracies in the third book of *The Laws*, that no extraordinary authority, like that established by Augustus in the next generation, was contemplated in Cicero's Republic. The character drawn, so far as we can judge from the few lines that remain, seems to be only that of the " best citizen," the ideal statesman,* who guides a free commonwealth by his advice and influence. It was a part which might have been played by Pompey or by Cæsar or by Cicero himself, or even by all three at once.

---

* When St. Augustine (*de Civ. Dic.*, v., 13) applies to this passage of Cicero the words " ubi loquitur de instituendo principe civitatis," it is clear from the context that " instituere" is to be taken not in the sense of "set up," "institute," but in the sense of "form," "train," "educate." Cicero must have been describing how the ideal statesman is to be reared.

CHAPTER X.

CICERO AS PROVINCIAL GOVERNOR. TIRO. CÆLIUS.
ROME ON THE EVE OF THE CIVIL WAR.

51–50 B.C.

ICERO accepted the governorship of a province unwillingly,
and was most
desirous that his   51 B.C.
command should not be prolonged beyond a single year.
He felt that this was not the
work for which he was best
fitted. "They have clapped
a saddle on the ox," * he says.
The political situation at home was fearfully critical,
and it distressed him to be away from the centre of
events at such a time. Cilicia and its concerns
seemed petty, as lying outside of the main current
of grave interests and anxious counsels at Rome.
" I cannot tell you," he writes to Atticus,† " how I
burn with desire for the city, and how hard I find it
to put up with all this paltry insipid business."

---

* *Ad Att.*, v., 15, 3.

† *Ad Att.*, v., 11, 1.

Cicero feels, however, that his character is at stake; "the principles which I have professed for so many years will now be put to the test of practice."* He is most anxious about the behaviour of his lieutenants, the insolence of whose manners to the provincials disgusts him.† He is able, however, to give them a good character, so far as actions are concerned. "Thus far," he writes on his journey,‡ "I have no reason to find fault with any of my suite. They seem to recognise what ground I have taken and on what terms I allow them to come with me. They really regulate their conduct, as my reputation demands. For the future, if it be true that 'like master, like man,' they will certainly persevere; for I mean them to see no act of mine which can give them an excuse for misbehaving. If that proves insufficient, I must try stronger measures."

One of the worst features of the rule of Republican Rome in her provinces was the want of continuity. The power of the governor was so arbitrary that all depended on the accident of his personal character.

July 31, 51 B.C. Cicero entered on a province "simply wrecked and ruined for good and all"§ by his predecessor. The wounds which Appius Claudius had inflicted "stared him in the face and could not be concealed."‖ Cicero at once set about reversing many of his iniquitous measures, but was

---

* *Ad Att.*, v., 13, 1.
† *Ad Att.*, v., 10, 3.
‡ *Ad Att.*, v., 11, 5.
§ *Ad Att.*, v., 16, 2.
‖ *Ad Att.*, v., 15, 2.

careful to screen his reputation as much as possible.*
This did not save him from many bitter reproaches
from his predecessor, which he answered with good-
tempered but spirited vindications of his action. It
was like a change of doctors, he remarks to Atticus †;
Appius had adopted a lowering treatment, and was
vexed to see Cicero feeding the patient up again.

A Roman province was a unity, merely as the
Persian Empire was a unity, in the sense that it all
had one master. If we look at its internal organisation, a province is rather an aggregate of isolated
commonwealths. Every acre of ground is part of
the territory of some State, and each State has its
own laws, its own courts of justice, its own treasury,
and its own power of self-taxation. Super-imposed
on these, but not substituted for them, comes the
Roman administration of public order and defence,
of justice, and of imperial finance.

The first thing which Cicero did for his subjects
was to allow them to settle all their own controversies in their own courts. In Sicily, as we learn from
the speech against Verres, this was a right guaranteed
by the constitution of the province ; but in Cilicia the
extent of interference by the Roman authority appears to have been at the discretion of the governor.
Cicero seemed to be giving away a profitable privilege and the Greeks hailed his indulgence " as if he
had restored them independence."‡ In cases where
Roman citizens were concerned, the native courts

---

* *Ad Att.*, v., 17, 6.
† *Ad Att.*, vi., 1, 2.
‡ *Ad Att.*, vi., 2, 4.

had no jurisdiction, and these still came before the
governor or his deputy.   Cicero in his edict,* while
adopting the ordinances which his old instructor
Scævola had instituted in his governorship of Asia,
forty-three years before, for the regulation of inherit.
ance and debt, and for suits between the tax-farmers
and the subjects, announced that in other matters he
should follow the rules laid down in the edict of the
prætor at Rome.   This observance helps us to see
how Roman law and Roman methods of procedure
were gradually extended among the subject peoples.

We are not informed what was the nature of the
imperial taxes in Cilicia.   It appears, however, that
the tax-farmers had to deal, not with individuals, but
with the communities; for these communities were
deeply in debt to them, and had to stave off the
evil day by entering into special agreements, by
which exorbitant interest was often charged on the
arrears.   Cicero found that from the first foundation
of the province such agreements had been held to be
exempt from the general rule, which limited the rate
of interest to 12 per cent.   He hit upon a happy
compromise †; naming a tolerably easy term for
payment, he ordained that for all debts discharged
before that day he would allow only the legal rate
of interest; if the term were exceeded, then the
letter of the bond was to be exacted.   But this
method would be fruitless, unless some means were
found of replenishing the exhausted treasuries of the
subject States.   Cicero adopted a twofold means

---

* *Ad Att.*, vi., I, 15.

† *Ad Att.*, vi., I, 16.

of relief. In the first place he stopped absolutely
the drain on the yearly income which had been occasioned by the illegal exactions of his predecessors.
The burden of these may be guessed from the fact*
that the island of Cyprus alone had been compelled
to pay Appius two hundred Attic talents (£50,000)
under the threat that otherwise he would billet his
troops upon them. Secondly † Cicero looked into
the local budgets of the States, and found that the
Greek magistrates had been in the habit of systematically robbing the exchequers. The proconsul
does not seem to have felt much scruple in com-
pounding the felony. He made the defaulters dis-
gorge all that they had embezzled for the last ten
years, under promise that no further proceedings
should be taken against them. By these means
enough was realised to pay off all the arrears due to
the tax-farmers, who were beginning to be seriously
alarmed about their money. " For this," he says,
"I have become as dear to them as the apple of their
eye." With Cicero's views as to the "harmony of
the orders," it was very necessary that he should be
on good terms with the tax-farmers. They submitted, we find, with a good grace to the cutting off
of their usurious interest, and Cicero repaid them,
"full measure and running over with complimentary
speeches and invitations to dinner." He sums up
his relations with them in answer to Atticus' inquiries
—"I pet them, and show them attentions, I make
much of them in the way of praise and compliments;

* *Ad Att.*, v., 21, 7.
† *Ad Att.*, vi., 2, 5.

I take good care that they do not oppress any
one."*

The revenue of the local exchequers came partly
from lands which were the property of the subject
republics. We find an impudent request from Cælius (to which of course Cicero did not listen for a
moment) on behalf of a friend who farmed some such
land, and who wished not to be obliged to pay his
rent.† This source of revenue, however, seems barely
to have sufficed for the ordinary local expenses. The
sums which the communities had to pay in bribes to
the Roman governor were raised by a direct tax on
land and income, called "tributum." Sometimes
they were obliged to anticipate their revenue, by
selling the right to collect these rates for a lump sum
to a tax-farmer, and then they were driven to impose
on themselves a fresh contribution, which Cicero
characterises to Appius ‡ as "that most oppressive
burden, which you know full well, of the poll-tax
and the door-tax." All such taxes were levied by
the authority of the local senates and magistrates,
though of course the Roman governor could practically compel their imposition.§

To avoid these extremities, Cicero was anxious
that his subjects should not involve themselves in
unnecessary expenses, and on this ground he ordered
that they should not without his permission vote
sums for complimentary embassies to Rome in laud-

---

* *Ad Att.*, vi., 1, 16.
† *Ad Fam.*, viii., 9, 4.
‡ *Ad Fam.*, iii., 8, 5.
§ *In Verrem*, iii., 42, 100.

ation of his predecessor. He would "praise any,'
he said,* "who undertook such a mission at his own
cost ; he would allow the expenses if modest, but
would disallow them if excessive." Appius wrote
very angrily about this, and Cicero permitted the
embassies in some cases where a majority of the local
senate was in favour of the vote.†   He appears likewise to have withdrawn an objection which he had
raised on grounds of economy to the erection of
some sort of public building in honour of Appius.‡
Cicero felt himself bound to prove the sincerity of
his reconciliation with the brother of Publius Clodius
by doing all that he reasonably could for him ; and
he was further stimulated by the knowledge that,
before the trial of Appius for his misdoing was over,
he would very likely hear that Dolabella, Appius'
accuser at Rome, had become his own son-in-law.
Cicero had left the choice of Tullia's new husband to
herself and her mother, and Dolabella was in fact
the man whom they chose.   Cicero, notwithstanding
his full knowledge of the enormities of his predecessor, publicly complimented and favoured him, " not
so as to offend against my own good name, but still
with all good-will towards him." §   Apart from personal reasons this conduct was necessary in the interests of his subjects. Pompey was expected to take
command against the Parthians, and Pompey's son
was lately married to Appius Claudius' daughter.

* *Ad Fam.*, iii., 8, 3.
† *Ad Fam.*, iii., 10, 6.
‡ *Ad Fam.*, iii., 7, 2.
§ *Ad Att.*, vi., 2, 10.

Cicero would have done the Cilicians an ill turn by embroiling them with Appius, and of this they were fully conscious. They were anxious to stand well with their late oppressor, and eager to render him thanks for having harried them. Thus the corrupt judge was tenderly treated while his decrees were reversed, a process which we find going on as late as March in the year 50 B.C. "If Appius, as Brutus' letters indicate, is grateful to me, I am glad to hear it. For all that, this very day, which is dawning as I write, will be largely spent in cancelling unjust arrangements and decisions of his." * Such were the necessities of Roman politics.

It would have been well if the demands on a proconsul had been limited to the salving over of past iniquities. It required no little firmness to resist the appeals of friends at home to perpetrate all manner of fresh injustice on their behalf. "When any one applies to you," Cicero writes † to Atticus, "unless you feel quite sure that it is something which I can grant, pray give an absolute denial." One specimen of such applications will be sufficient. A certain Scaptius, armed with strong letters of introduction from Marcus Brutus, applied to Cicero for an appointment as prefect in Cyprus, where he was owed money by the State of Salamis. Cicero refused absolutely on two grounds : in the first place he would never give such an office to any one who was trading in his province ; secondly, Scaptius had already shown how he understood the functions of prefect.

* *Ad Att.*, vi., 1, 2.
† *Ad Att.*, v., 21, 5.

tion ; but it was well managed and successful.
Quintus was acting as his brother's lieutenant, and
he was, as we have seen, a skilful and experienced
officer.

Cicero's troops gave him the greeting with which
a victorious army used to salute its general. A
Roman commander-in-chief was always addressed
by his own soldiers as " Imperator," * but custom
forbade him to use the title himself or to accept it
from civilians, unless it had been first stamped on
him by such a public and universal acclamation from
the troops. From the moment of this greeting,
Cicero was justified in wreathing the fasces of his
lictors with laurel, and in signing " Imperator " after
his name in all formal letters. The next step in the
recognition of his success would be for the Senate
to decree a Thanksgiving on account of it, and this
again would naturally lead up to a triumph. The
Thanksgiving was voted in spite of the opposition
of Cato, who, however, proposed an alternative
motion, giving thanks not to the gods but to Cicero
for the wisdom and purity of his administration as
governor. He likewise wrote to Cicero an elaborate
explanation and apology for the line he had taken.†
Cæsar wrote with warm congratulations, and exulted
over Cato's untimely scrupulosity, which he hoped
would cause ill-will between him and Cicero. Cicero
seems at first to have been quite satisfied with Cato.
" His amendment," he writes to Atticus,‡ " was more

---

* See Smith's *Dict. Ant.* (2d edition) *ad voc.*

† *Ad Fam.*, xv., 5.

‡ *Ad Att.*, vii., 1, 7.

honourable to me than if he had voted me all the triumphs in the world. . . . Then he was one of the witnesses who registered the decree, and he has written me a most gratifying letter about his own amendment." Later on, when Cato had supported the claims of Bibulus to a Thanksgiving, because his lieutenant had driven the Parthians from his province, Cicero's tone changed. " Cato," he says,* " was disgustingly ill-natured to me ; he bore testimony to my purity, justice, kindliness, and good faith, which I did not require, and refused that which I asked for."

On his journey homeward from his province Cicero was obliged to leave behind him at Patræ his freedman Tiro, who was attacked by a dangerous illness. Cicero was always a kind and generous master to his dependents, and for Tiro in particular he had a sincere and tender affection. " I beseech you, my dear Tiro," he writes on this occasion, † " spare no expense in all that relates to your health. I have written to Curius to let you have any sum you may mention. I think it will be well to make a present to the physician to render him the more attentive. The obligations which you have conferred on me are countless, in my home and in the Forum, at Rome and in my province ; they extend alike to my public and my private concerns, to my studies and to my writings. But I shall esteem it the greatest of all if you let me see you again, as I trust I shall, in good health. I think that your best plan,

---

* *Ad Att.*, vii., 2, 7.

† *Ad Fam.*, xvi., 4, 2.

if you are sufficiently recovered, will be to come home with Mescinius the quæstor. He is a kindly man, and seemed to have a liking for you. But then, my dear Tiro, I wish you to be careful not only about your health but about the dangers of the passage. I would not have you hurry on any account. My sole anxiety is to have you safe and sound."

The society of the ancient world was founded on slavery, and in attempting to reconstruct the picture we cannot afford to neglect the background. At this epoch we already find traces of that secret power exercised by the slaves and freedmen of the leading statesmen, which grew to so scandalous a height under the Empire. We have seen in the first chapter the odious domination of Sulla's freedman, Chrysogonus. The first Cæsar was too strong a man to allow himself to be governed by his servants, but of the dependents of Pompey we hear only too much. Plutarch tells us * an entertaining story of Cato's experiences in Syria during the Mithridatic War. On approaching the city of Antioch Cato found that the population had turned out in festal attire with white robes and crowns and music. He naturally supposed that this greeting was intended for the Roman officer, and he scolded those of his escort who had been sent before to make preparations, because they had not stopped the display. But at this moment a venerable man, bearing a wand and appearing to be the marshal of the procession, advanced, and, without so much as saluting Cato, inquired

* Plutarch, *Cato Minor,* 13.

whether he had seen Demetrius on the road, and at what hour he might be expected. The procession had indeed been organised to do honour to Pompey's freedman.

Quintus Cicero had a confidential servant named Statius, and Pomponia, Quintus' wife, who was something of a domestic tyrant, was very jealous of this Statius. Cicero gives an amusing picture of the family to Pomponia's brother Atticus.[*] "When we arrived, Quintus said in the kindest way in the world, 'Pomponia, do you invite the women, and I will see after the lads'; nothing could be more pleasant, to my judgment, and that not only in the words but in the tone and manner. But she, in my presence, replied: 'I am a stranger in this house'; and all because Statius had been sent beforehand to get ready some breakfast for us. 'See,' says Quintus to me, 'what I have to submit to every day.'" Quintus Cicero was a man of choleric and blustering temper in the outside world, but he was meek as a lamb at home. The poor husband rebelled at last and divorced Pomponia, but even here he could not act on his own account, but must needs make Statius the confidant of his plans. A letter of his freedman on this matter fell into the hands of his son and caused some unpleasantness. Quintus would never marry again; he had learnt, he declared, to appreciate the blessing of going to sleep without a curtain lecture.[†] When Quintus Cicero was governor of Asia, Statius appears to have acted as his vicegerent.

[*] *Ad Att.*, v., 1, 3.
[†] *Ad Att.*, xiv., 13, 5.

but the letter which Acastus has just brought has made them look up a little. Rufus is here very brisk and cheerful. He wanted to hear something of my composition, but I told him that my books were dumb in your absence." It is pleasant to read of the master's concern when his postman arrives with only a message from Tiro who is too weak to put pen to paper, and to learn from a postscript that a second carrier has come while Cicero is writing, and that the invalid has summoned up strength to scrawl a few lines nevertheless, "with the letters all tottering" *; and that Cicero is sending a nurse and a cook to aid in his convalescence.

Tiro had, during his master's lifetime, formed a plan of making a collection of his letters. Cicero jokes with him about it, and says that he believes Tiro wants to have his own included in the collection. † He seems, however, seriously to have approved the notion, for in the year before his death he writes to Atticus ‡ : " There is no collection of my letters, but Tiro has about seventy, besides a few still to come from you. Before they are published, I must read them through and correct them." We may be thankful indeed that this plan was never carried out. Tiro, notwithstanding his feeble health, lived to a good old age, and devoted the rest of his life to the pious task of collecting and publishing the works of his beloved master and friend. Instead of the seventy and odd letters, carefully edited

---

* *Ad Fam.*, xvi., 15, 2.
† *Ad Fam.*, xvi., 17.
‡ *Ad Att.*, xvi., 5, 5.

and altered, which Cicero would have allowed to posterity, Tiro has preserved over eight hundred and
fifty, and these he has treated as a sacred trust, and
has kept them absolutely untampered with, so that
we read them to-day just as they came from his
master's pen.

Cicero landed at Brundisium on the twenty-third
of November, 50 B.C., having been absent from Italy
50 B.C. not quite a year and a half. The interval had been occupied with a long
series of intrigues and proposals for compromise
regarding Cæsar's claim to retain his province and
army, until he should enter on his second consulship
at the beginning of the year 48 B.C. Cæsar's opponents wished that there should be an interval between his proconsulship and his consulship, and it is
pretty certain that they meant to use the interval,
during which he would be unshielded by office, to
bring him to trial for his illegal acts, when consul ten
years before.* Of this controversy it will be sufficient
to say that Cæsar appears to have had no legal ground
for resisting supersession at any time after March 1, 49
B.C., when his ten years' governorship would expire;
but that a successor could not have been sent out to
take his place until the end of that year, had not the
rules for the appointment of provincial governors
been purposely altered by Pompey during his sole
consulship in 52 B.C. (see above, p. 289). Thus Cæsar
was practically cheated of an expectation, which
under the old rules of succession he had a full right

* Suetonius, *Jul.*, 30,

to entertain. * The true cause of quarrel of course lay deeper. Cæsar had acquired so strong a position that, if he were again consul, he would be practically master of the State, and he had given such abundant evidence of his unscrupulousness that the constitutionalists had good grounds for supposing that he would use his power to destroy the Republic. With the help of Pompey, they now thought themselves strong enough to prevent this; Cæsar with a juster appreciation believed that the chances of war were in his favour. Thus both sides were strongly inclined to fight, and the proposals for compromise were not so much serious attempts at a tolerable settlement, as contrivances of each party to put the other in the wrong and to toss to and fro the responsibility for breaking the peace.

When Cicero left Italy for his province in June, 51, he seems to have recognised that the Republic ran some danger from Cæsar, but not that there was the prospect of actual armed attack. He pictures Cæsar as consul in Rome and attempting all sorts of revolutionary measures, but believes that the presence of Pompey will be sufficient to hold him in check. Thus he strongly objects to a notion which Pompey was entertaining at the time, that he should retire to his Spanish province. † On his outward journey (May, 51 B.C.) Cicero visited Pompey, and at his request passed some days at his Tarentine

---

* The whole question is admirably discussed by Mommsen in a monograph, entitled *Rechts-frage zwischen Cæsar und den Senat.*

† *Ad Att.,* v., 11, 3.

villa. "I consented willingly," he writes to Atticus,*
"for I shall hear much excellent discourse on affairs
of State, and likewise get valuable hints
for my provincial business." A few
days later he writes,† "I am just leaving that admirable man, who is fully prepared for resistance to
all that we have to fear." In contrast to this grave
and sententious approval, it is worth while to note
the observations of the irreverent Cælius‡: "If you
have come across Pompey, as you hoped you would,
pray write me what impression he made on you,
what he said to you, and what sort of intentions he
manifested ; for his habit is to say one thing and
mean another, and yet not to have wit enough to
conceal what his real purpose is."

May, 51 B.C.

Cicero, during the whole of his year in Cilicia, seems
to have remained under the same illusion as to the
nature of the danger that was to be apprehended,
and his Roman correspondents did little to enlighten
him. Atticus with strange self-deception writes to
him § about the end of the year 51, that all his hopes
of peace and quiet are placed on Pompey, and Cicero
in answer expresses his full agreement. Even as late
as June, 50, on the news of the desertion of the cause
by Curio and the consul Paullus, who were both
bought by Cæsar, Cicero writes to Atticus, ‖ "not
that I fear any danger, while Pompey stands firm,

---

* *Ad Att.*, v., 6, 1.
† *Ad Att.*, v., 7.
‡ *Ad Fam.*, viii., 1, 3.
§ *Ad Att.*, vi., 1, 11.
‖ *Ad Att.*, vi., 3, 4

or even while he sits quiet, if only his health be spared." The first clear statement that Civil War is impending comes in the month of September from Cicero's keen-witted correspondent Cælius. "Unless," he writes,* " one or other of them is shipped off to the Parthian war, I see that a mighty conflict is at hand, which must be decided by cold steel. Both the champions are full of determination and amply equipped. If we were not the stake which is being played for, this would be a grand and delicious spectacle that Fortune is preparing for us."

Men were slowly ranging themselves on the one side or the other, under the influence of motives as various as their characters. " Pompey," writes Cælius, † " will have the Senate and the jurors, Cæsar all who are in peril or whose outlook is bad." Suetonius ‡ tells us that Cæsar had spared no money and no pains to provide himself with partisans against the day of conflict. " All those who were in his suite, and a large portion of the Senate besides, were bound to him by loans without interest, or at very light charges. Men of other ranks who visited him, either with or without invitation, at his head-quarters, were gratified by handsome donations, which were extended even to the freedmen and slaves of each, according as they had influence with their patron or master. Further he was the sole resort of debtors and persons threatened with prosecution and of spendthrift youths; only to those who

* *Ad Fam.*, viii., 14, 4.
† *Ad Fam.*, viii., 14, 3.
‡ Suet., *Jul.*, 27.

lay under accusations too serious or a weight of em-
barassment and profligacy too great for him to be
able to assist them, he would say outright, 'The
only thing for you is a Civil War.'" Some, such as
Curio and Paullus, who were able to give really valuable assistance, sold their services for enormous sums
of money. Cælius too, it is hinted,* was found to
be in possession of unlikely resources at this moment
of crisis. He was not the man to serve any cause
for nothing, if he could see his way to be paid for
following it; but even apart from money, the creed
which he professes with signal effrontery to Cicero
would naturally carry Cælius into Cæsar's camp.
"One consideration," he says, † "will not, I think,
escape you; namely, that in civil strife, so long as
the contest is waged with the weapons of peace, we
ought to follow the more honourable cause, but when
it comes to camps and armies, then the stronger, and
one should esteem that the better side which is the
safer." As he adds immediately afterwards that
Cæsar's army is incomparably the better of the two,
there can be little doubt to which side he is inclined
to give or sell his services.

The name of Marcus Cælius Rufus calls up the
image of strange and striking personalities, and of
all the pleasures and the passions in which Roman
society revelled on the brink of the Civil War. It
reminds us of his stormy loves with Clodia, the
"Juno of the great eyes," the glorious "Lesbia"
who broke the heart of Catullus, while she inspired

* *Ad Att.*, vii., 3, 6.
† *Ad Fam.* viii., 14, 3.

him with the passion which has made his verse immortal, and of the bitter and tearful reproaches
which Catullus addresses to the friend who has sup-
planted him; then of Cælius' deadly quarrel with
this terrible mistress, of the charge of poisoning
which Lesbia brought against him, and of Cicero's
tremendous onslaught on her, while he defended
Cælius at the bar, and took revenge at the same
time for her share in the wrong, which her brother,
Publius Clodius, had inflicted on Cicero himself.
"It would seem," writes Mr. Tyrrell, "that Cælius
ultimately escaped both from her love and her
hatred after a long struggle; but we question if he
ever forgot her." We might dwell on Cælius' daring
but unchastened eloquence, his keenness of political
insight, his able administration as ædile, his charming letters to Cicero, his recklessness, his unscrupulous cynicism, and finally on his insane attempts at
revolution and his miserable end during the Civil
War; all these make up together one of the most
interesting episodes of the last age of the Roman
Republic. But another biography, or better still a
historical romance,* would be needed to do justice
to Cælius, Clodia, and Catullus. We have here to
do with the stern realities of politics and of war,
which underlay the genius and the wantonness of
that brilliant society.

The situation of Cicero on his return to Italy in

---

* This suggestion is borrowed from Messrs. Tyrrell & Purser who
have included a charming paper on Cælius in the third volume of
their edition of the Letters. There is also a very interesting account
of him in Boissier, *Ciceron et ses Amis.*

50 B.C. was necessarily one of peculiar anxiety. He
had embraced the friendship of Cæsar in order to
please Pompey, and he never seems to have contemplated the possibility of having to choose between
the two. He lays his difficulty with all frankness
before his friend in a letter written from Athens in
October.* " I adjure you, bring to bear all the
affection you have for me, and all the sagacity in
which I know not your equal, bring them all, I say,
to the task of considering my whole position. For I
seem to see such a conflict impending—unless the
same Providence which extricated us better than
we dared to hope from the Parthian war should
again take pity on the State—such a conflict, I say,
as the world has never witnessed before. Well, that
is a peril I share with the rest, and I do not bid you
think of that. It is my own personal problem which
I beg you to solve. You see that by your advice I
have linked myself to each of them. . . . I have
succeeded, and that by constant observances, in
making myself a prime friend of both. For my
calculation was that, while allied with Pompey, I
should never be forced to act against the right, and
that in supporting Cæsar I should never find myself
in collision with Pompey; so firmly were the two
bound together. And now, as you prove to me and
as I see, a death-struggle between the two is at
hand. . . . What am I to do? I do not mean
in the last extremity; for if it comes to war, I see
well enough that it is better to be conquered along

---

* *Ad Att.*, vii., 1, 2.

with Pompey, than to conquer with Cæsar; but
what of the questions which I shall find open on my
arrival? Whether Cæsar is to be allowed to stand
for the consulship in his absence? And whether he
must dismiss his army?."

On all the questions at issue Cicero feels that gross
blunders have been made. It is too late now to think
of defending the commonwealth against Cæsar in his
strength. "That cause," he writes, "has nothing
wanting to it except a cause." Since it has come to
this, he feels that "there is no ship for him, except
that one which has Pompey at the helm," * but that
he will privately use his influence with Pompey for
peace. This resolution is recorded on the 6th of
December. In a letter to Tiro † six weeks later Cicero
sums up his proceedings. "For my own part, since
I drew near to the city, I have been incessantly plan-
ning and speaking and acting for peace; but a
strange madness has possessed not only bad men,
but even those who are esteemed good, so that all
desire to fight, while I cry out in vain that nothing
is more wretched than a civil war."

Thus by a strange irony of fate that union of
Pompey and the Optimates, which had been the
dream of Cicero's politics, realised itself now, when
it was too late, and under circumstances which moved
him to despair.

After stormy discussions during the first days of
the new year, the Senate on the 7th of January met

---

* *Ad Att.*, vii., 3, 5.
† *Ad Fam.*, xvi., 12, 2.

21

the persistent veto of Cæsar's tribunes by the proclamation of martial law. The tribunes fled away, as Metellus Nepos had done 49 B.C. thirteen years before (see p. 170) to their master's camp. Cæsar had now the pretext for which he had been waiting. He appealed to the legion which he had with him at Ravenna, and led his advanced guard at once across the river Rubicon, the frontier of his province. "The die was cast," and the Civil War had begun.

CHAPTER XI.

THE CIVIL WAR.

49-47 B.C.

THE first moves in this terrible game were highly successful for Cæsar. Though he had at the moment only a small force south of the Alps, it consisted of seasoned veterans, and he pushed it forward without intermission. "We still hold Cingulum," writes Cicero on the 18th of January,* "we have lost Ancona; Labienus has deserted Cæsar. Are we speaking of an officer of the Roman People, or of Hannibal? Insensate and unhappy man that he is! he has never had sight of so much as the shadow of true honour." Ariminum, Pisaurum, and Arretium also opened their gates to Cæsar. Pompey seems to have been taken by surprise. The city of Rome was manifestly untenable in any case, but it was deserted in such

B.C. 49.

* Ad Att., vii., 11, 1.

hurry and confusion that even the money in the Treasury was forgotten and left to fall into Cæsar's hands.

Pompey soon recovered himself and took the only course open to a prudent general under the circumstances. The young men of age to serve throughout Italy had already taken the oath of military allegiance to him, and he now ordered a general levy, and directed that the recruits should concentrate at Canusium and Luceria in Apulia, so that they could fall back on the port of Brundisium. He had full command of the sea, and had collected abundance of transports. His orders however were not obeyed. Domitius Ahenobarbus, who had charge of Picenum and Umbria, in spite of the most urgent commands * to march south with every man whom he could raise, chose to believe that he could make a stand against Cæsar at Corfinium. He had promised † to start from thence on the 9th of February, and if he had done so all might have been well. Later on he changed his mind, and announced that he should remain. He seems to have thought that he would force Pompey's hand, and compel him to advance to his support. Pompey, of course, knew better than to expose his raw recruits to Cæsar's veterans. Cæsar cut off Domitius' army at Corfinium, and it surrendered on the 21st of February. Cæsar dismissed the officers, including Domitius and Lentulus Spinther, unharmed, and enlisted the soldiers under his own standard.

* *Ad Att.*, viii., 12, A, B and C.
† *Ad Att.*, viii., 11, A.

In this signal act of clemency Cæsar acted both
nobly and wisely. He had indeed every reason to
be thankful to Domitius, who had done his best to
give him the opportunity of finishing the war at a
stroke, and who actually succeeded in disconcerting
all Pompey's plans. In any modern army Domitius
would have been shot by sentence of court-martial;
but it is doubtful how far Pompey's power extended
in matters of military discipline ; and even if he had
the power, after Cæsar had spared Domitius, Pompey
could hardly help doing the same. In letting loose
on him again so mutinous and incompetent a colleague, Cæsar was at once embarrassing his adversary,
and gaining great credit for moderation himself. He
had good cause to remark five weeks later in a letter
to Cicero *: " I am quite indifferent to the fact that
those whom I released are said to have gone away
to make war with me again. All my wish is, that I
should act like myself, and they like what they are."
Cæsar little knew that Domitius Ahenobarbus was
destined to play the part of Banquo to his Macbeth.
The great-grandson in direct male line of this Domitius married Agrippina the great-granddaughter of
Augustus, and became the father of Nero, the last
Emperor of Cæsar's House.

It is possible that, if Domitius had obeyed orders,
Pompey might have been able with the sea open behind him at Brundisium to make a stand within lines
erected there, just as he did a year later at Dyrrachium. As it was, there was nothing for him but
to evacuate Italy. Cæsar pressed close upon him

* *Ad Att.,* ix., 16, A.

and tried to block the harbour of Brundisium; but
Pompey effected his escape with great skill, and
crossed the Adriatic with the remainder of his force
on the 10th of March.   Cæsar was unable from
want of ships to follow up the pursuit; and he
resolved to transfer the war at once to Spain, which
was held with a strong army by Pompey's lieutenants,
Afranius and Petreius.   Pompey might have availed
himself of his command of the sea to reach Spain
before Cæsar, and to face him again on this new
battle-ground.   Cæsar seems to have thought that
this would have been his adversary's best move;
" as it is," he said,* " I shall go to Spain to fight an
army without a general, and shall return to fight a
general without an army."   Pompey had however
no reason to expect that Afranius and Petreius, who
were esteemed competent officers, would be so
completely out-generaled by Cæsar; and he hoped
that the war in that quarter would at least be prolonged.   He judged that he would be more usefully
employed in using his great influence in the East to
raise and train a fresh army, which might perhaps be
able to restore his power in Italy, while Cæsar was
occupied in Spain, and would at the worst form a
second line of defence.

Cæsar returned from Brundisium to Rome, where
he arrived about the end of March, and then set out
for Spain.   The Spanish campaign, after some weeks
of much danger and anxiety for Cæsar, ended tri-
umphantly in the month of August by the surrender
of all the Pompeian forces.   The failure of his lieu

* Suetonius, *Jul.*, 34.

COIN OF CÆSAR.
(Cohen.)

NERO AND CLAUDIUS.
(Cohen.)

NERO AND AGRIPPINA.
(Cohen.)

tenants in Illyricum and the overthrow of Curio's
army in Africa were drawbacks which Cæsar's personal success far more than compensated. By the
end of the year he was again at Brundisium, ready to
cross over for the decisive struggle on the other side
of the Adriatic.

Cicero's letters to Atticus enable us to trace,
almost day by day, the fluctuations in the hopes,
the wishes, and the opinions of the people of
Italy during these eventful months.
The first news that Cæsar was actually   49 B.C.
in armed rebellion shocked and disgusted all moderate men. They were moved by the spectacle
of the city left without Senate or magistrates,
and of Pompey in flight—" the whole
aspect of opinion is changed; every   Jan. 18.
one now thinks that no terms should be made
with Cæsar." * The Italians however showed
themselves by no means ready to take
arms in the quarrel, and the conscripts   Jan. 23.
came in slowly and unwillingly.† A month later the
feeling against Cæsar has considerably cooled down.
Cicero reports from Capua‡—"there is no indignation of any class, nor even of
individuals publicly expressed. There   Feb. 19.
is some feeling among loyal men, but it is blunted
as usual; and (as I have clear evidence) the rabble
and the lowest classes are keen on the other side,
and many anxious for revolution."

---

* *Ad Att.*, vii., 11, 4.
† *Ad Att.*, vii., 13, 2.
‡ *Ad Att.*, viii., 3, 4.

By the 1st of March the news of Cæsar's great success at Corfinium and of the generosity he

49 B.C.

showed to his prisoners has caused a strong revulsion in his favour.* " Just see what a man this is into whose power the commonwealth has fallen, how keen, how

Mar. 1.

watchful, how well prepared! I declare that if he puts no one to death and robs no one of his goods, he will become the object of affection to those who were most in dread of him. I have much conversation with men from the borough-towns and with the country people. They care for absolutely nothing except their farms, and their bits of houses and money." The threatening language reported from the Republican headquarters, and the determination which the Optimates expressed, to regard all neutrals as enemies, heightened by contrast the impression made by Cæsar's moderation. " The one, alas that it should be so, earns applause in the worst of causes ; the other in the best of causes nothing but reproach." † By the 4th of March we find this

Mar. 4.

current of opinion in full flood. " The country towns," writes Cicero,‡ " hold Cæsar for a god ; and there is no pretence about their feelings, as there was when they made vows for Pompey in his sickness. It comes to this ; whatever mischief this Pisistratus refrains from committing, they are as grateful to him as if he had stopped

---

* *Ad Att.*, viii., 13.

† *Ad Att.*, viii., 9, 3.

‡ *Ad Att.*, viii., 16.

some one else from committing it. They hope that
he will be all that is kindly; whereas they dread
Pompey in his anger."

Cæsar was particularly happy in allaying the fears
of the monied men, who had expected a national
bankruptcy as the result of his victory. He devised
an excellent plan for tiding over the difficulties of
the money market, while doing substantial justice
both to debtors and creditors. He ordained that it
should be open to debtors to discharge their obligations by the tender of land, which was to be
received at a valuation, calculated on what it would
have fetched before the Civil War broke out.* This
was a bitter disappointment to many of Cæsar's
bankrupt supporters, who seem to have forgotten
that Cæsar was now no longer the penniless prætor
of thirteen years ago. Early in the next year Cælius
Rufus, the most audacious of the malcontents,
ventured to bring forward revolutionary proposals on
his own account, and, when they failed, to attempt,
along with the exile Milo, an insurrection in which
both lost their lives. In a wild letter to Cicero, †

---

* Cicero, writing after Cæsar's death, blames his law of debt as
impairing the sanctity of contracts (*De Off.*, ii., 24). This has generally been explained by the statement of Suetonius (*Jul.*, 42), that
all interest hitherto paid was to be deducted from the principal. If,
however, Cæsar's law really contained such a clause, his silence
about it in his own account of the law (*Bell. Civ.*, iii., 1) and his
severe comments on Cælius' schemes of repudiation (*Bell. Civ.*, iii.,
20) are difficult to interpret. I am inclined to think that Suetonius
has been misinformed, and that Cicero's criticisms apply to the
measure as Cæsar himself describes it.

† *Ad Fam.*, viii., 17.

written immediately before his revolt, Cælius gave unconscious testimony to the sagacity with which Cæsar had discarded the bad traditions of his party, while declaring that every one at Rome is now for Pompey, he is obliged to add "except a few money-lenders." From this time onward the equestrian order may be counted as among Cæsar's partisans.

In the midst of a people thus drifting, how was Cicero to act? Honour and duty showed him his place in the Republican camp; but many accidents and many doubts delayed his arrival there. He had been nominated by Pompey to take charge of the Campanian coast; and partly owing to a misunderstanding he had not quitted his post to join his leader, when the disaster of Corfinium occurred.

49 B.C. Cæsar advanced on the very day of the surrender (21st of February) and Cicero's road to Brundisium was barred. In any case he would not have gone,* for he was at the moment in the very depths of trouble and perplexity, and wanted time to recognise his duty and to steady his resolution. Meanwhile he had been constantly deluded by the hope that a peace might still be arranged. After crossing the Rubicon, Cæsar made fresh proposals through his cousin Lucius, which reached Pompey in Samnium on the 22d of January.† By these, Cæsar offered to give up all the points at issue ‡; he would surrender his provinces to the successors nominated by the Senate, and would come

* *Ad Att.*, viii., 12, 3.
† *Ad Att.*, vii., 14, 1.
‡ *Ad Fam.*, xvi., 12, 3.

himself to Rome to sue personally for the consulship ;
Pompey was to retire to his Spanish province. The
only condition attached was that the Republicans
should dismiss their levies. The terms were accepted
by Pompey and the consuls with the sole proviso
that Cæsar should likewise withdraw from the posts
he had occupied in Italy. But Cæsar, like Napoleon,
made it his practice to push on his military operations all the more vigorously when he had begun to
negotiate. He was advancing day by day ; and when
Lucius arrived at his camp, he rejected the condition
that he should withdraw his garrisons. His offer
certainly had not been sincere. It is probable, indeed, that at this time neither party trusted the
other, and that each suspected that the adversary
would take advantage of the preliminaries of peace
only to strengthen his military position. Cicero, however, seems to have had no suspicion of this, and so
late as the 3d of February * he evidently believes
that Cæsar will stand to his offer ; " he is a lost man
else." Cicero's intention during these days was to
go with Pompey to Spain, that he might have no
part in the coming iniquities of Cæsar as consul.
Even when this negotiation had fallen through,
Cæsar continued to amuse Cicero with hopes that a
peace might still be arranged, and that he himself
might act as mediator. Balbus and Oppius, Cæsar's

---

* *Ad Att.*, vii., 18, 1. It is to be noticed that next day he received
by enclosure from Atticus a letter written by Curio to Furnius (pre-
sumably a few days earlier) in which Curio, with a frankness for which
Cæsar would not have thanked him, openly scoffed at the mission of
Lucius. (*Ad Att.*, vii., 19.)

confidential agents, were constantly urging Cicero to
this course,* and protesting that Cæsar would be
only too happy to put an end to the war; they likewise enclose letters of Cæsar, appealing to the clemency he has shown as an evidence of his desire for
reconciliation.　Cicero wrote and published † an
elaborate letter to Cæsar which he hoped might
pave the way for peace; and in the meantime he
preserved, so far as might be, the neutral attitude
proper to a possible mediator between the parties.
" I have refused," he writes, ‡ " to be a leader in a
civil war, so long as any negotiations for peace are
afoot. . . . If there is war, as I think there will
be, I shall not be found wanting in my duty."

These last words give a faithful presentation of
Cicero's deliberate resolve, and his action never
really swerves from the path thus marked out; but
in his constant exchange of letters with Atticus, his
only consolation in this dreary time, we find his mind
working over every possible topic of hesitation and
anxiety.　He criticises Pompey's strategy in a way
which reveals his own plentiful ignorance of the art
of war.　Cicero seems to have thought that military
movements could be conducted in obedience to
sentimental considerations.　He first urged Pompey
not to abandon the city of Rome, " his country for
which and in which it would have been a noble deed
to die." §　Next he blames him bitterly for not going

---

* *Ad Att.*, viii., 15, A and ix., 7, A.

† *Ad Att.*, ix., 11, A.　Compare viii., o.

‡ *Ad Att.*, vii., 26, 2.

§ *Ad Att.*, viii., 2, 3.

to the support of Domitius at Corfinium ; and when
it comes to Pompey's resolve to leave Italy, he is
almost in despair. How can he join Pompey in
bearing arms against his country ? What does posterity think of Hippias and Tarquin and Coriolanus, who did the same ? * " Is not his cause then a
good one ? Nay, it is the best in the world ; but it
will be played for, mark my words, most foully." †
Pompey will starve out the Roman People ; he will
bring hosts of Thracians and Colchians and Armen-
ians to invade Italy ; he will ravage, burn, and rob.
Again it occurs to him that he is staking too much
on a single life, that Pompey is after all a man, that
he is subject each year to grave sickness,‡ that a
thousand chances might cut him off, " but that our
city and nation ought, so far as in us lies, to be preserved to eternity." § The threatening language of
the Optimates and the prospect of a victory, cruel as
that of Sulla, likewise affect him painfully ; and it is
to be noticed that at this time he is inclined to include Pompey in the same condemnation with his
followers on the score of cruelty. Nay, he sometimes writes as if he fancied that Pompey no less
than Cæsar was aiming at a despotism,‖ or that he
might sacrifice the Republic and Cicero (as he had
done at Luca) to Cæsar as the price of a private
reconciliation.¶ When all was over, and Cicero had

* *Ad Att.*, ix., 10, 3.
† *Ad Att.*, ix., 7, 4.
‡ *Ad Att.*, viii., 2, 3.
§ *Ad Att.*, ix., 10, 3.
‖ *Ad Att.*, viii., 11, 2.
¶ *Ad Att..* x., 8, 5.

gathered by personal intercourse fuller knowledge of the doings and intentions of his associates, he was careful to correct these hasty judgments; he acknowledges Pompey to have been "loyal and stainless and of faith unshaken," * and he expressly exempts him from the charges of savagery which he records against the mass of his party.† But for the moment, these doubts and suspicions added painfully to Cicero's embarrassments.

The blacker the fortunes of the Republicans look, the more Cicero is determined to throw in his lot with them. When Cæsar is swooping down on Brundisium, and Pompey's life seems in danger, he breaks out ‡ in the bitter self-reproach of Achilles: "Let me die at once, since it was not mine to help my friend in death; far from his fatherland he fell, and found not me beside him to ward off woe." §

March 11. A few days later he writes ‖ : "I seem to myself to have lost my wits from the first; and one thing torments me, that I did not follow Pompey, when he was falling or rather rushing headlong to ruin, like any private soldier in the ranks. . . . Now my affection for him re-awakens, now I cannot bear the loss of him, now neither books nor letters nor philosophy give me any relief. Day and night, like the caged bird, I look towards

---

* *Ad Att.*, xi., 6, 5.
† *Ad Fam.*, vii., 3, 2.
‡ *Ad Att.*, ix., 5, 3.
§ Homer, *Iliad*, xviii., 98 (Purves' translation).
‖ *Ad Att.*, ix., 10, 2.

the sea and long to fly away." The climax is reached
on the 20th, when a false report arrives
that Cæsar has succeeded in blocking
up the harbour of Brundisium, and that Pompey
is cut off and surrounded. " Now I lament, now
I am tormented, when some think me prudent
and others think me lucky in not having gone along
with him. It is just the other way ; I never wished
to share his victory, but would that I were the
partner of his disaster." *

The memory of those dreadful days served to
steady Cicero's purpose, and he came to see clearly
that there was no place for him in Italy ; the only
question now was whether he should retire to some
remote spot, to Malta for instance, or whether he
should join Pompey in Epirus. But to leave Italy
at all was no longer easy ; he would not be allowed
to cross over to the east coast; and to escape by
sea from a western port he must wait till the
winter was over, † and in the meantime must conceal his intentions.

Cæsar was strong in all the material elements of
success ; " all the rascals in Italy " writes Cicero, ‡
"seem to have flocked to him ; " and these were useful,
no doubt, in their way to a fighting chief. None
the less, Cæsar seems to have felt keenly the weak

---

* *Ad Att.*, ix., 12, 4.

† The confusion of the Calendar must always be borne in mind.
The 10th of March, when Pompey crossed the Adriatic, was really
the 18th of January, that is to say, it was just twenty-eight days after
the winter solstice.

‡ *Ad Att.*, ix., 19, 1.

point in his own position. All men of character and standing were at heart loyal Republicans: taking a broad view of the matter, they could not but be enemies to Cæsar's cause. Cæsar did his best to remedy this weakness. In the first place he showed scrupulous moderation in all his words and even in all his deeds, so far as these did not interfere with the main military issues. His chivalrous temper always inclined him to spare a fallen enemy, and his cool head and brave heart made it clear to him that his clemency could do him no harm. " I will follow your advice," * Cæsar writes to Balbus and Oppius, " and the more willingly as I had already resolved to act as leniently as possible, and to do my best to effect a reconciliation with Pompey. Let us exert ourselves to recover by such means, if it be possible, the good-will of all men, and so secure a lasting victory; our predecessors did not escape the hatred which their cruelty aroused; none of them could permanently hold his ground, excepting only Sulla, and him I will never imitate. Let us conquer on a new plan, and fortify ourselves with mercy and kindliness." We have already seen how successful this policy was with the rank and file of the Italians.

Secondly, Cæsar was unremitting in his efforts to draw or to keep to his side any of the distinguished citizens who had not yet finally committed themselves against him. His chief success was with the two consulars Volcatius Tullus and Servius

---

* *Ad Att.*, ix., 7, c. 1.

Sulpicius Rufus. Servius was the first lawyer in Rome, but in politics he showed himself wanting in insight and decision. He allowed his son to accompany Cæsar to Brundisium, to take part in peace negotiations, as he hoped, really to assist in attacking and blockading Pompey.* He was next obliged himself to appear in Cæsar's Senate at Rome. His despair and disgust at the situation were overwhelming, and he expressed his sorrows freely in an interview just before Cicero's departure. "He shed so many tears, that I wondered that the fountain of them had not been dried up with his continued affliction."† But his timidity prevented his accompanying his friend in his flight from Italy. He had committed himself too far, and he had to count, sorely against his will, as a Cæsarian.

All Cæsar's efforts were directed to inducing Cicero to acquiesce in the situation as Sulpicius had done. The presence of Cicero would have soothed the minds of many, and would have given weight and dignity to the remnant of the Senate which could still be assembled in Rome. Urgent letters, couched in the most flattering language from Cæsar himself and from his friends pressed Cicero to return, and the hope that he might thus aid the cause of peace was always dangled before him. On this point, however, Cicero was no longer to be deceived, and he stood firm in spite of the ordeal (which he would fain have avoided) of a personal interview with the " master of

---

* *Ad Att.*, ix., 19, 2, and x. 1, 4.

† *Ad Att.*, x., 14, 1.

22

so many legions." This interview took place at
Formiæ. "We were much mistaken,

March 26.

when we supposed that Cæsar would
be easy to deal with ; I never saw any one less so.
He would be discredited, he said, by my refusal, and
the others would be more unwilling to speak if I did
not come. I said their case was different. At length,
' Come,' says he, ' and speak for peace.' ' Am I to
say what I please on the subject ? ' ' Do you suppose,'
says he, ' that I claim to dictate what you shall say ? '
' Then I shall move that the Senate disapproves of
any expedition to Spain, or of any transport of troops
to Greece ; and I shall express many regrets about
Pompey.' ' I should object,' says he, ' to a speech
of that sort.' ' So I supposed, and that is my
reason for not wishing to go to Rome ; I must
either utter, what I have told you, and much more
about which I could not hold my tongue, if I were
on the spot, or else I must stay away.' The end was
that, to put a stop to the discussion, he begged me
to think the matter over. This of course I could
not refuse, and so we parted. I imagine that he is
much displeased with me ; but I am pleased with
myself, a feeling that I have not had for this long
time. . . . Now, if ever, I must call for your
advice. This makes a fresh departure. I almost
forgot to mention an ugly remark with which he
cienched his argument—' that if he were not to have
the benefit of my counsel he must follow the advice
of those who would give it, and stick at nothing.' " *

Cicero's mind was now made up, and he only

* *Ad Att.*, ix., 18.

looked for an opportunity of flight. His daughter
indeed urged him to await the issue of the Spanish
campaign, which was now commencing ; but this
idea he entirely discarded, holding that it would
be even more his duty to shake himself loose from
Cæsar, if he were victorious than if he were beaten.*
There were difficulties in the way of escape.
Antony, who was left in command in Italy, informed
Cicero that he could let no one go without Cæsar's
permission. He pretended acquiescence, and took
precautions to elude the vigilance of Antony's spies,
even dropping during the last fortnight his correspondence with Atticus for fear that the letters
might fall into wrong hands. Meanwhile he secretly
prepared a vessel at Caieta, as soon
" as the first swallow appeared," and
from thence he set sail on the 3d of June (really 19th
of April) for Pompey's headquarters.

The year 48 B.C. saw the conflict between the two
great commanders in person. The strategy was admirable on both sides, full of daring and genius on
the part of Cæsar, and of skill and prudence on the
part of Pompey. The campaign in Epirus after
many vicissitudes ended favourably for Pompey, who
beat Cæsar out of the lines in which he had attempted
to enclose him at Dyrrachium. Cæsar was as great
in defeat as in victory ; he succeeded in extricating
his army from the pursuit, and marched right across
the peninsula, thereby transferring the war to fresh
ground on the eastern coasts of Greece. Pompey,
who had command of the great northern road passed

49 B.C.

* *Ad Att.,* x., 8. 2

by a parallel route into Macedonia, and the two were again face to face. Pompey knew that he ought still to play a waiting game; but he lacked firmness to resist the urgency of his associates, who were elated with the victory which had been gained, and thought themselves now in a position to crush Cæsar at once.* Pompey had indeed performed wonders in raising and training in a single year an army which had held its own, so far, with credit. But his success came to an end, as soon as he allowed his own judgment to be overborne by the clamours of the ignorant Nobles. His troops required every advantage which consummate generalship could give them; they were not fit for a soldier's battle on fair ground with the veteran legions of Gaul, and the day of Pharsalia ended in their utter overthrow. Pompey fled

Aug., 48 B.C.

to Egypt where he was immediately murdered by order of the ministers of the boy-king who had succeeded his father " the Piper."

In spite of great military talents and in spite of honest but clumsy efforts to do his duty, Pompey's life had been a failure, because he aspired to guide the politics of his country without any political principles to carry into effect and without any party to which to be loyal. The errors of the statesman entailed the ruin of the soldier, and fate denied him even a soldier's grave. It was given to one of the petty Eastern Courts, so long the creatures of Pompey's will, to extinguish a personality which ever since the death of Sulla had occupied the fore-

* Plutarch, *Pomp.*, 67.

most place on the great stage of the Roman world—

"Sunt lacrimæ rerum, et mentem mortalia tangunt."

Cicero had remained in Epirus along with Cato
and Varro, and the news of Pharsalia reached them
at Dyrrachium.* Cato resolved to fight to the last,
and took refuge with the more obstinate of his adherents in Africa, where the Cæsarian governor Curio
had been overwhelmed and slain the year before by
the help of Juba, King of Numidia. Cicero and
Varro considered that the issue of the conflict must
be held to have been decided by the defeat of
Pompey. Cicero returned once more to Italy, landing at Brundisium about the end of October in the
year 48 B.C.

It was doubtful at first whether he would be allowed to remain. Antony, who held Italy as Master
of the Horse (for Cæsar had been proclaimed Dictator immediately after the battle of Pharsalia), had
received orders that no Pompeians were to return to
Italy without leave. Cicero, however, was able to
show that Dolabella had written to him by Cæsar's
direction, requesting him to return at once.† This
caused an exception to be made for him in the general edict of prohibition. He remained,
therefore, at Brundisium for the next   Nov., 48-
Sept., 47. B.C.
ten months in a miserable condition of
mind and body. The climate affected his health,
and his nerves seem to have completely broken
down under the doubts and difficulties of the situa-

---

* *De Div.*, i., 32, 68, and ii., 55, 114.

† *Ad Att.*, xi., 7, 2.

tion. His complaints are consistent only so far as
they are always directed against what he esteems
his own blindness and folly. Sometimes he blames
himself for having taken arms at all ; more often
he is afraid that he has disgraced himself by not
following the fortunes of his party to the last in
Africa. Cæsar is detained in Egypt and in Asia, so
that he cannot come to speech with him, and he
fears that this will prevent a reconciliation. He
hears that his brother and nephew have turned
against him, and mean to make their own peace
by accusing him to Cæsar.* This does not prevent
his writing to the Dictator on behalf of
March, 47 B.C. Quintus, protesting that the responsibility of the flight from Italy was all his own, and
that his brother had only borne him company. †

At the same time some action of his wife, as to
which we have only obscure hints, caused him much
displeasure. His beloved daughter was in distress
on account of the neglect and infidelities of her husband, and Dolabella's conduct in public matters was
also most painful to his father-in-law. He took advantage of Cæsar's absence to dabble in socialistic
and revolutionary legislation, much as Cælius had
done a year before. This led to riots which Antony
put down by military force ; eight hundred persons
are said to have been killed in these disturbances.
Dolabella, however, stopped short of the extrava-
gances of Cælius, and Cæsar checked and forgave
him. ● In the meantime his actions appear to Cicero

* See above, p. 79.

† *Ad Att.*, xi., 12, 2.

only a foretaste of the general reign of rascality
which is to be expected from the victory of such a
crew. This adds to Cicero's despair. " I see no
chance of peace," he writes,* "and the
party now in power will, I think, bring
itself to ruin, even if there be no adversary to
oppose it."

July, 47 B.C.

Cæsar was occupied with war and pleasure in
Egypt during the first half of the year 47, and trustworthy news from him was wanting. When he did
write, Cicero doubted † whether the letter was really
Cæsar's. Thus the comfort to be derived from the
Dictator's intentions regarding him was delayed.
Cæsar, when he had time to attend to the matter,
behaved as generously as possible. He pardoned
Quintus at a word, " would not even allow himself
to be entreated," ‡ and expressed himself so kindly
about Marcus Cicero that his brother wrote heartily
in congratulation. § Cæsar likewise sent word to
Cicero to keep his laurelled fasces, ‖ thus ignoring
the part he had taken in the Civil War, and indicating that he looked on him merely as the pro-consul
on his way home from Cilicia and claiming the honour of a triumph.

After settling the affairs of Egypt and Asia Cæsar
returned in the month of September, and Cicero
met him somewhere in southern Italy. When he

---

* *Ad Att.*, xi., 25, 3.
† *Ad Att.*, xi., 16, 1.
‡ *Ad Att.*, xi., 22, 1.
§ *Ad Att.*, xi., 23, 2.
‖ *Pro Lig.*, 3, 7.

perceived Cicero advancing to meet him, Cæsar dismounted from his horse and came forward to salute him, and the two walked together conversing alone far along the road.* The reconciliation was complete, and Cicero was free to return to his home and his family.

* Plutarch, *Cicero*, 39.

CHAPTER XII.

CÆSAR'S DICTATORSHIP.

47–44 B.C.

ROM Cæsar's return to Rome at the end of September 47 B.C., we may date the commencement of his direct responsibility for the central government of the Empire. His rule lasted for thirty-two [*] months in all, but of these eighteen were passed in Africa and Spain, and two dangerous wars had to be waged in the course of them.

In this brief period Cæsar showed great activity as a legislator. Besides a number of laws called by the name of Julius, [†] which defined or consolidated existing arrangements with slight modifications of detail, we find many fresh projects, from the increase

---

[*] It must be remembered that three extra months were given to the year 46 B.C. in order to bring the Calendar straight.

[†] *E. g.*, the Leges Juliæ *Municipalis, de vi, de majestate, de liberis legationibus* (modifying Cicero's), *de provinciis* (of length of tenure), *de sacerdotiis*, and *de judiciis* (abolishing Pompey's third decury).

of the patriciate and the borrowing of an amended Egyptian * Calendar to sumptuary laws and plans for roads and drainage works. Cæsar, as Dictator, undid two pieces of mischief which had been the work of his creature Clodius, by dissolving the "collegia" or street-guilds (see p. 230) and by restricting the distribution of corn. The enlargement of the boundary of Italy by the grant of the Roman franchise to the inhabitants of the country between the river Po and the Alps was a necessary consequence of Cæsar's victory. These "Transpadanes" had been his warm supporters, and he had always maintained that they were already by right Roman citizens. † Outside the natural limits of Italy, Cæsar likewise made certain amplifications both of the Roman and of the Latin franchise; the most important was the grant of Latin rights to Sicily. He extended to the province of Asia a wise system, which had long ruled in Spain, by which the subject communities collected their own taxes, and paid out of them the tribute due to Rome; and he revived an excellent project of Caius Gracchus by founding Roman colonies at Carthage and at Corinth.

---

* The principle of the Julian Year (*i. e.*, 365 days with an extra day added every fourth year) is to be found in a bilingual inscription of 238 B.C. (the decree of Canopus) now in the Museum of Cairo. The distinguished mathematicians and astronomers whom Cæsar consulted (Plutarch, *Cæs.*, 59) perhaps did not think it necessary to inform him that the work had been done two centuries before.

† It is difficult to say on what the claim was founded, but that it must have been very strong is proved by the admission of so rigid an aristocrat as the elder Curio. Cicero informs us (*De Off.*, iii., 22, 88) that Curio used to say : " The claim of the Transpadanes has right on its side, but expediency forbids, and that is enough."

BUST OF CÆSAR IN THE BRITISH MUSEUM.

The subject peoples gained incidentally by the establishment of a despotism. Cicero hits the truth when he calls the provinces of Rome " Cæsar's estates." " Sardinia," he says,* " is the worst farm which Cæsar owns, but he does not neglect it for all that." It is clear that it could not be in the interests of a master that anyone except himself should shear his sheep. No despot, unless he were a man of feeble will and character, would tolerate such vicegerents as we have seen the Roman Republic tolerate in Verres and Appius Claudius. It is recorded even of Domitian, that he kept the provincial governors from misdoing. We have no record of Cæsar's dealings with the proconsuls, but we may be sure that the control he exercised would be firm and intelligent. Thus in the mere abolition of the rule of persons who were members of a sovereign corporation and the substitution of governors, who were hardly less absolutely at the mercy of Cæsar than the subjects over whom they ruled, a new guaranty was found for tolerable administration. The provincials soon learned to appreciate their own interests in these matters. They had mostly stood for Pompey against Cæsar, but they showed a very different temper when in the next Civil War Cæsarism was ranged against the Republic. By their experience of Cæsar's rule they had learned that their servitude was likely to be more endurable, if no freedom were left in the world to contrast with it.

The changes which I have been recording were not unimportant in themselves, but they are hardly

* *Ad Fam.,* ix., 7, 2.

mentioned in Cicero's correspondence. Their interest was in truth eclipsed by the presence of the
great problem which called on Cæsar and the
Romans for solution.*   The world stood at the
parting of two ways; Rome was destined, for good
or for evil, to absorb into her citizenship all civilised
men; and it rested with Cæsar to decide what should
be the nature of the new Cosmopolitan State.   The
Roman Empire might be organised on one of two
systems.   The first was the obvious and easy expedient, familiar to the world since the days of the
Pyramids, of a despotism, dependent only on the
swords of a professional soldiery.   This required
nothing but a trained army and a skilful general for
its inception.   Its results were equally sure: the
periodical recurrence of civil war whenever the
soldiers could not agree on a chief; occasional
stretches of decent government when accident
brought a skilful administrator to the head of
affairs; wild freaks of tyranny when the chances of
the succession turned out unluckily; and throughout a steady degradation of character, the loss of
manhood, and the destruction of the capacity for
self-government in the civilised human being.   All
hopes of freemen, all ideals of political aspiration,
all causes worth fighting for, perished along with the
Roman Republic, and the world entered on a period
of its history, in which its life seems to be " weary,
stale, flat, and unprofitable."   The unmixed despotism which Cæsar established was somewhat tempered
by the wisdom of Augustus; yet the essential mis-

* See above, p. 167.

chief remained, and the result was inevitable. Three
out of four of the Roman emperors perished by violence, and each mutiny or assassination or civil war
was the occasion for fresh degradation of the citizens.
The Italian nation, which under happier auspices
would have been the centre from which liberty and
self-government might spread over the civilised
world, only led the way in abasement and servility.
Gibbon has summed up for us the story of its fate
in words which may be repeated with little change
for each of the nations which lay beneath the shadow
of the Roman Empire. " The forms of the constitution, which alleviated or disguised their abject
slavery, were abolished by time or violence ; the
Italians alternately lamented the presence or the
absence of the sovereigns whom they detested or
despised ; and the succession of five centuries inflicted the various evils of military license, capricious
despotism, and elaborate oppression." * It has even
been argued, though the argument is to my mind
far from convincing, that the fragments of liberty
which Augustus retained cost more than they were
worth in friction and inconvenience, and that if the
ideas of freedom and self-government, the only
political ideas worth having, were in truth absolutely
beyond realisation in practice for the world as it was,
then the more outspoken despotism of Julius or of
Diocletian was the lesser of the two evils. Even so,
such a plea serves but to extenuate. The work of
Cæsar may be excused as a miserable necessity : it

* Gibbon, ch. 36.

is not, like the work of Washington or of Cavour ol of Bismarck, an achievement to glory in.

It is not without regret that we contemplate this lame and impotent conclusion to the life-long toil of a great man. Cæsar was unsurpassed as a soldier, as a scholar, as a gentleman, as a leader and manager of men ; in him the saying of Cervantes finds its fullest realisation, that "the lance has not dulled the pen, nor the pen the lance." But after all the tree is known by its fruit, and Cæsarism is condemned by the character which the despotism necessarily stamped upon the generations bred under it. We must look for its perfect work in the subjects of the later Empire, ground down by an intolerable burden of taxation, with souls which had lost all nobler political interests, trusting to hired soldiers to fight for them, no longer capable of managing their own concerns nor of striking a blow in defence of their own hearths. All the horrors of the barbarian invasion and all the darkness of the Middle Ages were not a price too heavy to pay for the infusion of fresher and stronger blood, and the revival of the sense of dignity in mankind.

Such was the path in which Cæsar willed that the world should walk. The other alternative before him was to undertake a complicated and difficult task, requiring the highest constructive statesmanship. The Italian people was still sound at heart ; Italy still loved liberty and hated despotism ; her sons could still endure with patience, and dare with energy, and die with heroism around the eagles. When a people displays such qualities, a statesman need not despair of organising it into a free nation.

COIN OF CÆSAR.
(*Babelon.*)

JULIUS CÆSAR.
FROM COIN IN BRITISH MUSEUM.

COIN OF CÆSAR.

HEAD OF VENUS.   ÆNEAS AND ANCHISES.
(*Cohen.*)

In this case it was no ordinary nation which called for organisation, but one whose fate must determine likewise the fate of the world.   Never in the history of the race has such an opportunity been laid in the hands of a legislator; but a man was wanting to take advantage of it.   That Cæsar, with all his genius, could not rise to the height of this task is a matter for sorrow, not for anger.   For such a construction was in truth no simple or easy thing.   It would have required a modification at least of slavery, and the extinction of the slave-trade, personal military service as the duty, and the power of choosing and controlling his rulers as the right of every Roman, and, finally, the gradual extension of the citizenship with political as well as personal privileges to the subjects of the Empire.   A constitution was called for, which would have given room for the personal policy of a great statesman, while it carefully cherished every germ of independence and self-reliance in the citizens. Despotic methods of government may possibly find justification under certain circumstances, as a necessary transition to something better; the damning fact about Cæsarism is, that it left no niche in which any fresh growth of freedom could find root.

In a very half-hearted and imperfect way Cæsar's great successor seems to have recognised some of the needs of the world in this matter, and to have striven to find a place in his system for other powers and activities beside his own.   Thus he averted for a time the full degradation of life under a despotism. The elder Cæsar had much better chances than his nephew.   He had never been under the necessity of shedding blood except on the battle-field; his wise and noble clemency predisposed all hearts in his favour; even Republicans were not anxious for his defeat in the last struggle in Spain, and preferred, as Cassius said to Cicero, "the old kindly master to an untried and angry one." * The Romans were willing to accept any tolerable compromise at his hands. But of compromise Cæsar would not hear a word. He seems to have been utterly blind to the evils of a despotism, and utterly indifferent to the preservation of the dignity and manliness of the Romans. With relentless and foolish consistency he pushed the doctrine of his own supremacy to its uttermost conclusions. The first act of this so-called democratic leader was to deprive the popular assemblies of the little power that had remained to them under the later Republic. In legislation, the assent of the people had already become merely formal, and so it remained; but in elections some power of choice had hitherto really lain with the voters. This was now taken away by the Dictator, who granted letters of recommendation to his candidates, and so had them returned without opposition. The elections indeed might as well not have been held at all. Cæsar lost no opportunity of degrading the Republican magistracies in the eyes of the people. Sometimes the State was left for

Jan. 45 B.C.

---

* *Ad Fam.*, xv., 19, 4. The reference is to Pompey's son Cnæus, who was killed in Spain. Cassius was much in dread of him. " You know how foolish he is, and how apt to mistake cruelty for manliness. He always thought we were laughing at him, and I fear repartees delivered in boorish fashion at point of sword

months without consuls or prætors, and Cæsar nominated prefects to do their work; sometimes a number of consulships were crowded into a short space, and Rome now contained a consular * in whose term of office "no one had breakfasted."

Cæsar's treatment of the Senate was even more inexcusable than his action towards the People or towards the magistrates. It can only be explained on the supposition that his head was turned by the giddy height of supreme power, and that he was no longer the cool and sober politician who had trod the upward way so skilfully. The Senate was the only possible home of free speech and independent counsel, yet we find it exposed in the person of its most distinguished members to wanton insult. Cicero writes † to his friend Pætus, who has urged him to remain at Rome and take part in public business: "You cite the example of Catulus and his time. Where is the resemblance? In those days I too was loath to be long away from my post in the State. For then we sat on the poop of the vessel with our hands to the tiller; now there is scarcely a place for us in the hold. Do you suppose that any fewer decrees of the Senate will be passed if I stay at Naples? Why, when I am in Rome, and in the thick of the Forum, the decrees of the Senate are written out at our friend's house‡; aye, and if it comes into his head, I am set down as one of those who attested the registration, and I get

---

* See below, p. 378.

† *Ad Fam.*, ix., 15, 4.

‡ One would fain hope that the person meant is not Cæsar himself.

23

intelligence of the arrival in Armenia or Syria of
decrees, said to have been passed on my proposition,
before I have heard a word about the matter. Pray
do not think I am jesting. I assure you I have
received letters from princes in the uttermost parts
of the earth, returning thanks for the salutation as
'King,' which had been given them on my proposal
—people of whom I was so far from knowing that
they had been saluted kings, that I had never even
heard of their existence."

Cicero was willing, as he said to Varro,* " to lend
a hand, if not as an architect, then even as a mason,
to the reconstruction of the commonwealth." There
is no reason to suppose indeed that he any more
than Cæsar had a solution for the almost inextricable
difficulties which presented themselves in the way of
combining liberty with empire. But Cicero at least
held fast to that which Cæsar ignored. He felt that
it was apostasy and cowardice to slide back from
the political faith which Greece had delivered once
for all to the world, that it was of the essence of the
higher civilisation of the West to protest against
arbitrary power, to believe in government by discussion and consent, and in the rule of reason and of
law. " From the man," he writes,† "who has all
power in his hands, I see no reason to fear anything,
except that everything is uncertain when once you
set law on one side : it is impossible to guarantee a
future which depends on the will, not to say on the
caprice, of a single man."

* *Ad Fam.*, ix., 2, 5.

† *Ad Fam.*, ix., 16, 3.

It was long before Cicero gave up the hope that after all there was to be " some sort of Free State," and that Cæsar was destined to be its founder. This delusion was fostered, and not unnaturally, by the spectacle of Cæsar's constant clemency and kindness to the conquered. "The all-powerful ruler," he writes to an exiled Pompeian * in January, 45 B.C., "seems to me to be daily inclining more and more to justice and to a reasonable view of things . . . Every day something is done with more of lenity and liberality than we were expecting." "No one," he says in another letter, † " is so much an enemy to the cause which Pompey supported with more spirit than prudence, as to venture to call us bad men or unworthy citizens ; and in this I always admire the rectitude, fairness, and good sense of Cæsar. He never speaks of Pompey, but in the most honourable terms." Cicero is eager to make excuses for Cæsar. If he delays the restoration of the Republic, it is because "Cæsar himself is the slave of the situation." ‡ " Since," he says, § "I have judged it right to live on, I cannot but feel a kindness for the man by whose favour life has been granted me. If that man desires that there should be a commonwealth such as perhaps he wishes, and such as we are all bound to pray for, he has no power to realise it, so hampered is he by obligations to his followers."

---

* Trebianus, *Ad Fam.*, vi., 10, 5.

† *Ad Fam.*, vi., 6, 10.

‡ *Ad Fam.*, ix., 17, 3.

§ *Ad Fam.*, ix., 17, 2.

Cicero became a main channel of Cæsar's grace towards his old comrades, and in the delight of serving them committed himself more and more to acquiescence in the new government, and to hopes based on the personal character and conduct of its chief—" nothing * can be better than the ruler himself ; for the rest, men and things are such that, if needs be, it is better to hear of them than to see them."

Cicero is the main hope and stay of the exiled Pompeians. He is ever writing them letters of solace and encouragement, and working assiduously for their restoration. "You," writes Aulus Cæcina † to Cicero, "must bear the whole burden ; all my hopes are staked on you. . . . Only persuade yourself that your part is not to do whatever you are asked in this business (though that were favour enough), but that the whole is your own work ; then you will succeed. I fear that my misery makes me foolish, or my friendship shameless in heaping burdens on you : your own conduct must serve as my excuse ; all your life long you have so accustomed us to see you labouring for your friends, that now we who may claim that title do not so much beg as requisition your services." To another exile, Ampius Balbus, Cicero writes ‡ : " I spoke in your cause with more bluntness than my present situation justifies ; but the very ill-luck proper to my shipwrecked fortunes was overborne by your dearness to

---

* *Ad Fam.*, iv., 4, 5 (to Ser. Sulpicius).

† *Ad Fam.*, vi., 7, 5.

‡ *Ad Fam.*, vi., 12, 1.

me, and by the long friendship between us which
you have so sedulously cherished. Everything which
relates to your restoration is promised, pledged,
guaranteed, determined. I speak from my own
sight, and knowledge, and participation."

Cæsar was ready enough to pardon on his own
account; but even in cases where he felt specially
displeased, he was generally willing to give up his
resentment at Cicero's request. It was thus that
Cicero saved Quintus Ligarius, the only one of the
Pompeians, so far as we know, who was publicly and
formally put on his trial. Cicero defended him at
Cæsar's bar in a brief but interesting speech, which
he afterwards published by the advice * of Balbus
and Oppius, and which still survives. The circumstances may best be described in the words of
Plutarch. † " The story goes that when Quintus
Ligarius was put on his trial as an enemy to Cæsar,
and Cicero appeared as his advocate, Cæsar said to
his friends : ' We know beforehand that the prisoner
is a pestilent fellow and a public enemy : what harm
can it do to listen once again to a speech of Cicero ? '
But soon he felt himself strangely stirred by Cicero's
opening words, and as the speech proceeded, instinct with passion and exquisite in grace, one might
see rapid changes of colour pass over Cæsar's face,
bearing witness to the tide of emotions ebbing and
flowing through his mind. At length, when the
speaker touched on the struggle at Pharsalia, Cæsar
became so agitated that his body trembled, and

* *Ad Att.*, xiii., 19, 2.
† Plutarch, *Cic.*, 39.

some papers which he was holding dropped from his hand. In the end he was carried by storm, and acquitted the accused."

Another notable instance of clemency, the pardon of Marcus Marcellus, who, as consul in the year 51, had taken a prominent part in the opposition to Cæsar, overpowered the resolution of Cicero not to open his lips again in the Senate. " This day," he writes * to Servius Sulpicius, "seemed to dawn so fairly on me, that I fancied I could see, as it were, some vision of the Republic springing to life again. . . . When my turn came, I departed from my original intention. For I had resolved, not, I assure you, from sloth, but from a sense of the aching void left by the loss of my old independence, to hold my peace for ever. My resolution broke down in the presence of Cæsar's magnanimity and of the loyalty with which the Senate had pressed our friend's cause. And so I made a long speech of thanks to Cæsar ; I only fear that by so doing I have debarred myself for the future from that decent quiescence which was my only consolation in these bad times."

This speech, too, has been preserved. From the enthusiasm with which Cicero speaks of the occasion in the confidential letter to his friend, it will readily be conceived that the public expression of thanks is conveyed in language whose fervour knows no bounds. The hyperbolical protestations of gratitude and devotion are in painful contrast to the satisfaction which Cicero afterwards took in Cæsar's assassination ; but at the moment the speaker was doubtless

---

* *Ad Fam.*, iv., 4, 3.

sincere in his declarations, as in his hopes. The real interest of the speech *Pro Marcello* lies in the expression of these hopes, which Cicero still cherished in the summer of the year 46, though Cæsar had killed them before he himself fell on the fatal Ides of March, twenty months later. Cicero told the Dictator in language guarded indeed, but sufficiently explicit, that Rome expected something more from him.

"At this moment, though your achievements have embraced the whole State and the preservation of all its citizens, yet so far are you from setting the coping-stone on your greatest work, that you have not yet laid the foundation-stone of that which you design. . . . If, Cæsar, after all your splendid deeds, this were to be the final result, that now your adversaries are overpowered you should leave the commonwealth in the condition in which it at present lies, consider, I pray you, whether your career will not seem famous, indeed, but scarcely glorious; for glory, I take it, consists in the tidings, spread through the world, of great services done to friends or to country or to mankind. This portion, then, of your task, is still before you; this act is still to be played; this work is still unwrought; you have yet to reconstruct the Republic; you have yet to enter on and share with us, amidst all peace and quiet, the fruition of your labours. Then, and not till then, when you have paid to your country her due, and filled up the measure allotted by nature to man, it will be time to say that you 'have lived long enough.' . . . And yet why count this as your

life, which is hemmed in by the bounds of body and
of breath?   Your life is there, there, I say, where it
will be fresh in the memory of all ages, where posterity will cherish it, where eternity itself will claim
it for its own.   It is the approval of that time to
come which you must court, to its good-will you
must commend yourself.   It has much already to
wonder at in you, now it asks for something to
praise.   Future generations will listen awe-struck,
doubtless, as they hear or read the tale of all your
conflicts and all your triumphs.   But unless you
have so designed and framed the constitution as to
set this city on a sure foundation, your name, though
it may go forth into all lands, will find no abiding
resting-place.   Among those who are yet to be born
there will be controversy, as there has been amongst
ourselves; some will extol your deeds, others per-
chance will find something wanting, and that the one
thing needful, unless you quench the coal of civil
war, by giving life to our State, so that men may
ascribe the first to the inexorableness of destiny, the
second to the providence of your design.   Labour,
then, as beneath the eye of that tribunal which will
give its sentence concerning you many ages hence, a
sentence perhaps more disinterested than any which
we can pass to-day; for posterity will pronounce, un-
disturbed by favour or hope of advantage, undis-
turbed, likewise, by passion or by jealousy." *

When Cicero uttered these words it is clear that
the question " is there to be any sort of Free State?"
had not yet received a definite answer in the nega-

* *Pro Marcello,* ch. viii., 25 *seq.*

tive. Cæsar had not yet, to Cicero's mind, finally stamped himself a "tyrant."

Though with many fluctuations and much doubt, the tone of Cicero's mind in the latter part of the year 46 and the first months of 45 B.C. is on the whole cheerful. He has "mourned for the commonwealth longer and more bitterly than ever a mother mourned for her only son," * and now his thoughts dwell by choice on the redeeming features of the situation, or turn to other interests and pursuits. He was on terms of intimacy with many of Cæsar's personal friends, especially with Balbus, Oppius, Matius, Hirtius, Pansa, and Dolabella. These were most useful to him in the negotiations for the pardon of his Pompeian comrades. He gives special credit to Pansa for his help. "He is an example," Cicero writes to Cassius (who "held Epicurus strong "), " of the doctrine † which you have begun to doubt, that righteousness is desirable on its own account. He has relieved many from their distress, and he has shown himself humane in these bad times, and so the good-will of honest men goes with him to a notable degree." Cicero's social intercourse with the younger Cæsarians was cheerful and pleasant; they gathered round the old orator to learn from him the secrets of his craft, and he amused himself and pleased them by giving lessons in declamation, "like Dionysius the tyrant," he says, "keeping school at Corinth," while they in turn instructed him in the new art and science of good living—

* *Ad Fam.*, ix., 20, 3.
† *Ad Fam.*, xv., 17, 3.

" for they are my pupils in speaking, but my tutors in dining." * Sometimes indeed he is painfully struck by the contrast between these empty rhetorical displays and the glorious strife of his old days in the Senate and the law courts. "If I ever utter anything worthy of my ancient name, then I groan like Philoctetes in the play, to think that 'these shafts are spent inglorious on a feathered not an armed prey.'" † Nevertheless he felt the better for these exertions, "in the first place as regards my health, which had suffered from the want of exercise to my lungs, next because any faculty of speech I may have had would have dried up, unless I had refreshed it by these declamations ; there is another reason, which perhaps you will think worthy of the first place : I have been the death of more peacocks than you have of young pigeons." ‡

With the return of hope, Cicero's sanguine and mercurial temperament recovered its elasticity, and though the despotism bowed it did not crush him. Plutarch says § of Cicero, that "he was by nature framed for mirth and jests, and his countenance expressed smiles and sunshine." At this period his wit played freely on the new situations of politics and society ; and the despotism of Cæsar, like that of Lewis XIV., was "tempered by epigrams." Cæsar could listen with frank and fearless enjoyment to strokes of satire directed against himself and his system. He even prided himself on his

---

* *Ad Fam.*, ix., 16, 7.

† *Ad Fam.*, vii., 33, 1.

‡ *Ad Fam.*, ix., 18, 3.

§ Plutarch, *Comp. Cic. et Dem.*, i., 6.

critical acuteness in detecting the true flavour of Cicero's jests, and in refusing to be taken in by the work of any inferior craftsman.

"Cæsar has a very shrewd literary judgment, and just as your brother Servius, one of the best critics I ever knew, would say off-hand, 'this verse is Plautus', this is not,' because he had an ear trained by habits of study and of noting the style of the various poets, so I am told, that Cæsar, when compiling a collection of jests, would at once reject any spurious ones which were brought to him under my name. He can do this the more easily at present, because his most intimate friends are almost every day in my company. Many things drop out in the course of conversation which my hearers are good enough to consider not devoid of wit and neatness. These are regularly reported to him along with the news of the day—such are his orders—and so he pays no attention to forgeries from outside." *

This period of suspense from active politics was fruitful in literary labour, which was indeed Cicero's most plentiful source of contentment. "I must tell you," he writes to Varro, † "that so soon as I returned home again I was restored to favour by my old friends, my books. . . . They have forgiven my neglect, and summon me back to the old intimacy." The works of the next year and a half are chiefly on the art of rhetoric. In the *Brutus* and the *Orator ad Brutum* Cicero pursues the discussions

Sept., 47—
Dec., 46 B.C.

* *Ad Fam.*, ix., 16, 4.
† *Ad Fam.*, ix., 1, 2.

begun in the dialogue *De Oratore*. The *Brutus* is especially valuable and interesting, on account of the personal experiences which Cicero there records of his training and practice as a speaker. Several extracts from it are to be found in earlier chapters.

In the same year (46 B.C.) Cicero was engaged with a panegyric of Cato. The theme seems to have been suggested to him by his republican friends soon after the suicide of his hero at Utica in April. It was, as he says,* a problem fit for Archimedes, to write on such a topic without giving deadly offence to the party in power. "Cato cannot be fairly treated, unless I make it a theme for praise that he struggled against the state of things which now is and which he saw coming, and that rather than look on its realisation he took refuge in the grave." He succeeded, however, entirely to his satisfaction. Cæsar was too generous to take offence at praises of his fallen enemy, and Brutus was encouraged to follow Cicero's example and publish a work in his uncle's honour. We have a curious record of Cæsar's criticism on the two in a letter to Balbus. He had read Cicero's *Cato*, he said, over and over again, and had enriched his mind in the process, but Brutus' book flattered him with the idea that he could write better himself. †   In the midst of the occupations of his Spanish campaign the Dictator found time to pen an *Anti-Cato* in answer to Cicero's panegyric. While inveighing against Cato, Cæsar spoke in high terms of Cicero, whom he compared for eloquence

---

* *Ad Att.*, xii., 4, 2.
† *Ad Att.*, xiii., 46, 2.

and for statesmanship to Pericles and Theramenes. *
These compliments called forth a suitable letter in
reply from Cicero. "I wrote," he says to Atticus,
"precisely as I should have done to an equal; for I
really think highly of his work, as I mentioned to
you in conversation, so that without flattery I was
able to write what he, I think, will be pleased to
read." †

At some time during the year 46 the estrangement
between Cicero and his wife Terentia ended in a
divorce. We hear very little about this in his letters.
He would hardly write on such a subject to any one
but Atticus, and probably Atticus was with him when
matters came to a crisis. Soon afterwards Cicero
took a second wife, a young and wealthy woman
named Publilia, who had been his ward. In the interest of this new connection, in literature and in the
pleasures of society, graver cares were for the
moment forgotten. "I would write more at length,"
he says in a letter ‡ to Cassius, "if I had any non-
sense to write about, for we can hardly discuss serious topics without danger. Well at any rate, you
say, we can laugh. That is not so easy after all; but

---

* Plutarch, *Cic.*, 39. Cæsar probably had in mind the verdict of
Aristotle on Theramenes, which in its complete shape has just come
to light in the newly discovered *Constitution of Athens*, ch. xxviii
"Those who weigh their judgments are agreed that he did not, as
was said against him, wreck all governments, but that rather he
furthered all so long as they kept within the limits of the law, being
capable of serving under all, as a good citizen should, but that when
they crossed these limits he resisted and repudiated them."

† *Ad Att.*, xiii., 51.
‡ *Ad Fam.*, xv., 18, 1.

there is no other way of forgetting our anxieties. But where, you say, is philosophy gone? Yours to the kitchen, and mine to the rhetoric school. I am ashamed to be a slave, and so I make believe to be busy, that I may shut my ears to the reproaches of Plato." To another friend * he describes a dinner with Volumnius Eutrapelus, where Cicero and Atticus and other grey-beards found that they had been invited to meet a lively person, hardly fit company for a consular of Rome. "You wonder that we can make our slavery so merry. Well, what am I to do? I ask you, the student of philosophy. Shall I wring my heart and torment myself? Who will be the better for that? and how long am I to go on with it? . . . I never was much attracted by women of that class even when I was young, to say nothing of my old age: but I do enjoy the dinner table; there I speak whatever comes uppermost, and turn all my lamentations into hearty laughter."

This easy life was rudely cut short by a great and unexpected calamity. Cicero's daughter Tullia, died suddenly at Rome about the end of March in the year 45 B.C. Tullia was her father's darling, the only one of his family of whose conduct he never complains, his consolation in all his troubles, and his tender and sympathising companion in all his pursuits. Cicero was overwhelmed with grief, and sought refuge in tears and seclusion. "In this desolate spot," he writes† to Atticus from Astura soon after his bereavement, "I avoid speaking a word to any one

---

* Pætus, *Ad Fam.*, ix., 26. 2.

† *Ad Att.*, xii., 15.

Early in the morning I hide myself away in a thick
wood and do not quit it till evening. Next to yourself my best friend is solitude." He attempted to
beguile his grief by a project of erecting a shrine for
Tullia, and so deifying her memory. His letters are
full of schemes for the purchase of gardens near
Rome suitable for the purpose. It does not appear
that Cicero's wish was ever realised, and the disturbances after Cæsar's death interrupted all his plans.

Cicero's young wife Publilia had been jealous of
her stepdaughter, and she was unable to conceal her
satisfaction when Tullia died. This heartlessness
deeply offended Cicero. He at once divorced Publilia, and though she and her friends made several
overtures for a reconciliation, he would never see her
again.

In this great trouble Cicero found much consolation in literature. "Those old friends," his books
now once again proved true to him. "There is not
a treatise on consolation under bereavement, that I
did not read through when I was in your house ; but
my grief was too strong for the medicine. Nay, l
did what I believe no one ever did before ; I wrote
a treatise on consolation myself. I will send you
this book if the copyists have written it out. I declare to you, this has given more relief than anything. Now I write from morning to night ; not
that what I write is good for much, but it checks my
grief to a certain extent." * These words were written soon after his loss. Some two months later
Cicero can appeal unhesitatingly to his literary

* *Ad Att.* xii., 14, 3.

activity, which is producing the *Tusculan Disputations*, as a proof that he is not yielding an unmanly subjection to his grief. " Those cheerful souls," he writes, " who find fault with me, cannot read as much as I have written in the time. Whether the work is good or bad, is nothing to the point; it could not have been attempted by anyone who had abandoned himself to despair." *

Almost all Cicero's philosophical works belong to this (45 B.C.) and the following year. His writing was hardly interrupted by Cæsar's death and ceased only with his own recall to the active labours of a statesman at the end of the year 44. Not to mention several works which are lost, we have from this period the *Academic Questions*, the treatise *On the Definitions of Good and Evil*, the *Tusculan Disputations*, the dialogues *On the Nature of the Gods, On Divination, On Old Age*, and *On Friendship*, and finally the treatise *On Duty* (De Officiis) addressed to his son Marcus. Cicero found the materials for most of these works in the writings of the Greek philosophers : " I have to supply little but the words," he writes, † " and for these I am never at a loss." Though Cicero has no pretensions to be considered a thinker of original and inventive genius in the region of philosophy, it was no small achievement thus to mould the Latin tongue to be a vehicle for Greek philosophic thought. Cicero wiped away the reproach of "the poverty of our native speech," of which Lucretius complains, and in so doing he se

* *Ad Att.*, xii., 40, 2.
† *Ad Att.*, xii., 52, 3.

cured the tradition of ideas and modes of thought which must otherwise have missed their influence on the world. There have been ages during which Plato and Aristotle have suffered eclipse; but perhaps hardly one in which Cicero's philosophic writings have not been cherished by at least a few men of letters. They have thus kept alive the memory of ancient philosophy, and have humanised the thoughts and words of one generation after another. If we were required to decide what ancient writings have most directly influenced the modern world, the award must probably go in favour of Plutarch's *Lives* and of the philosophic works of Cicero.*

Tullia's death marks a turning-point in Cicero's appreciation of Cæsar and his work. He is resolved that patience shall not be wanting, but he "has lost for ever that cheerfulness with which we used to season the bitterness of the time." It is characteristic of the man, that his private sorrow opens his eyes to the fact that the hopes which he has been indulging for the commonwealth are all delusions. When once the truth is grasped, Cæsar's proceedings during the last months of his life serve to confirm Cicero's melancholy conviction, and to bring him to the state of mind in which he is ready to approve the deed of the Ides of March.

"All is lost, my dear Atticus," he writes † in the month of his daughter's death, "all is lost; that is

---

* On the absorption of Greek moral doctrine into the ethics of the Christian Church, effected mainly through the influence of Cicero on St. Ambrose, see *Hibbert Lectures*, 1888, by Edwin Hatch, ch. vi.

† *Ad Att.*, xii., 23, 1.

24

no new thing; but now that my one hold on life is gone, I am fain to acknowledge it." His reply * to the consolations of his friend Lucceius, a month later, breathes the same spirit. "In one respect I think that I am even more courageous than yourself, who exhort me to courage; for you seem to be cherishing some hope that better days may be in store. Your illustrations from the chances of combat and the like, and the arguments you adduce, seem intended to forbid me from despairing utterly for the commonwealth. I do not wonder then that you are braver than I, since you have some hope; but I do wonder that you should still hope on. What remains that is not so stricken, that we must needs confess it to be doomed and blasted? Look round on all the limbs of the State which you know so well; where will you find one that is not crushed and crippled . . . So I will bear my private grief, as you bid me, and the public grief perhaps even more patiently than you, my preceptor. For you have some hope to comfort you, I am resolved to be strong amidst absolute despair."

The misery and hopelessness, which was entailed on the Romans by Cæsar's government, may be well illustrated by Cicero's correspondence with his old friend Servius Sulpicius Rufus. Servius had taken no part against Cæsar in the Civil War (see above, p. 337), and at its close he was nominated by the Dictator to the governorship of Greece. This appointment was a kindly and delicate action on Cæsar's part. He must have known that Servius

* *Ad Fam.*, v., 13, 3.

was at heart a Pompeian, and Greece was full of re-publican exiles to whom the presence of a sympa-thetic proconsul was a great comfort and protection. Nevertheless, Servius, far from congratulating him-self that he has played his cards well, is "deeply troubled, and in the midst of the public misery is tormented by a grief peculiar to himself." * The reproaches of conscience, felt by one who had been hardly more than a neutral, may serve to explain the bitter wrath of those members of the democratic party who had actively aided Cæsar in arms, and who now found that they had been unconsciously con-spiring to destroy the last remnant of popular gov-ernment, and to set up an unmitigated despotism. This disappointment, sharpened by self-reproach, armed against Cæsar the daggers of some of his best officers, Decimus Brutus, Trebonius, and Galba.

Servius Sulpicius is best known to modern readers as "the Roman friend of Rome's least mortal mind," part of whose beautiful letter of consolation on the death of Tullia is paraphrased by Byron:

> "Wandering in youth, I traced the path of him,
>   The Roman friend of Rome's least mortal mind,
> The friend of Tully : as my bark did skim
>   The bright blue waters with a fanning wind,
> Came Megara before me, and behind
>   Ægina lay, Piræus on the right
> And Corinth on the left ; I lay reclined
>   Along the prow, and saw all these unite
> In ruin, even as he had seen the desolate sight.
>
>   .   .   .   .   .   .
>
> The Roman saw these tombs in his own age
>   These sepulchres of cities, which excite

---

* *Ad Fam.*, iv., 3. 1.

Sad wonder, and his yet surviving page
The moral lesson bears, drawn from such pilgrimage."

The reflection on human nothingness by one who contemplates the ruins of by-gone cities and empires is a topic for every age. But Servius has special considerations to urge, which are happily not of so universal application: "Do you grieve for her lot, who is taken away from the evil to come? who has seen the great days of the Republic, and has expired with its expiration? Does it not often occur to you, as it does to me, that we have fallen on times in which those are to be congratulated who can pass painlessly from life to death? Why be so deeply stirred by a private grief? Consider how fortune has buffeted us already. We have been bereft of those things which men should hold not less dear than their children—our country, our reputation, our dignity,—everything which made life honourable. What can one blow more add to our pain? Schooled in such a fate as ours, ought not the mind to become callous, and hold whatever may befall as insignificant." *

In sentences such as these we seem to catch the note of dull, passive despair, which Tacitus has taught us to recognise as the tone appropriate to the Romans under the Empire. The inexorable, unapproachable despotism already throws its chill shadow over the world, and the "petty men," as Cassius says, "peep about, to find themselves dishonourable graves."

* Extract from *Ad Fam.*, iv., 5.

Every incident of monarchy was galling and degrading to those who had been nurtured in the proud atmosphere of aristocratic republicanism. There are indications that Cæsar himself was not blind to the feelings which his domination inspired, though he lacked the energy of purpose to correct the faults of which such feelings were the natural outcome. Cicero was dancing attendance one day in the antechamber of the Dictator, waiting for his turn of audience. "Can I doubt," exclaimed Cæsar, "that I am cordially hated, when Marcus Cicero has to sit there waiting, and cannot see me at his own convenience? Well if any one is good-natured it is Cicero, but no doubt he must hate me bitterly." * Cicero had certainly no personal reason for disliking Cæsar, and those who have followed his utterances so far, have before them abundant evidence that personally he revered and admired him. What he hated was not the man but the monarch; yet his hatred of the monarch was sufficient to cause him not only to accept Cæsar's assassination as a necessary measure, but to triumph over it as a righteous retribution. Even when he doubts whether its practical results will not prove worthless, he sets down as clear gain "the exultation in the deed, and the exaction of the penalty desired by our hatred and indignation." † Even "this same easy-tempered man," had felt the iron enter into his soul. To men of sterner mould the thrust of the dagger seemed the only possible answer to the ignominy under which they suffered.

---

* *Ad Att.*, xiv., 1, 2.

† *Ad Att.*, xiv., 12, 1.

"It makes a world of difference, what his will is," Cæsar was wont to say of Marcus Brutus; "whatever he wills, he wills it strongly." * Such wills Cæsar had set in deadly opposition to himself and his policy.

In the latter part of the year 45 we find Cicero engaged, though with little hope of any profitable result, on a letter of political advice addressed to Cæsar. His model was to be a treatise dedicated to Alexander by Aristotle. "There is nothing in it," he writes,† "which may not become a good citizen, but a citizen such as the facts of the time admit of ; and all political philosophers bid us adapt our course to the circumstances." Balbus and Oppius, who always knew Cæsar's mind, objected to some portions of the letter. "Some improvements," Cicero writes, ‡ "were suggested on the present order of things; and because they are improvements they are found fault with." He declined to alter what he had written, and preferred to withdraw the letter altogether. "Let us throw all these futilities to the winds," he exclaims, § "and hold to the half-freedom of submitting in silence and retirement."

Thus ended the last effort to deter the Dictator from the line of action which was leading him to his death. Cæsar paid a visit to Cicero at his villa near

* *Ad Att.*, xiv., 1, 2.
† *Ad Att.*, xii., 51, 2.
‡ *Ad Att.*, xiii., 28, 2.
§ *Ad Att.*, xiii., 31, 3.

Puteoli in the month of December, 45 ; but the conversation was all on literary topics, " of serious matters not a word " * ; on these " serious matters " Cæsar had no intention of listening to counsel, and he was daily revealing to the eyes of the Romans that he had spoken his last word in politics, and that the yoke which they abhorred was to be fixed on their necks for ever. " There could be no complaint," writes Mommsen, " at least on the score that Cæsar left the public in the dark as to his view of his position ; as distinctly and formally as possible he came forward not merely as monarch but as very King of Rome." After the Spanish War was over, he accepted for the first time, under the title of Dictator for life, absolute and unlimited dominion ; and he never even pretended that he would voluntarily set a term to his power, as Sulla had done. Cæsar was not only greedy of the substance of power, but was caught by the glitter of its trappings. Though he knew the hatred which the Romans had cherished for centuries to the name of King, he suffered his partisans to play with the offer of the diadem, the symbol of Oriental monarchy. This offer which took place in January, 44, (see below p. 397) really, says Cicero,† cost Cæsar his life. Meanwhile he set up his statue along with those of the Seven Kings of Rome, and adopted the golden throne and the robes which tradition assigned to them.‡ He thus wilfully trampled on the suscepti-

---

* *Ad Att.*, xiii., 52, 2.

† *Phil.*, xiii., 19, 41.

‡ *De Div.*, i., 52, 119.

bilities of men, who dwelt proudly on the recollection of the long centuries of glory, in which freedom
and self-government had made them masters of the
world. He attempted to force on them the show of
despotism for which the Roman world was not ripe
for yet three hundred years. The setting up of
Cæsar's statue beside that of Quirinus, the deified
Romulus, brings to Cicero's lips the sharp retort:
"I am better pleased to see him the neighbour of
Quirinus, than as sharing the temple of Safety."*
The legend ran that Romulus had governed tyran-
nically, and had been torn in pieces by the Senators.
In indicating such an omen for the new monarch of
Rome, Cicero shows that the idea was already (May
45 B.C.) floating before his mind that the effort to
reconstruct the Republic might have to be made over
the dead body of Cæsar.

While on the one hand Cæsar accepted the odious
memory of the office which the free State had renounced for ever, on the other hand we see in him a
hankering after the barbaric expressions by which
Eastern potentates were wont to attempt to realise
to themselves the plenitude of their power. He
aspired to a "Divine Right," not in that comparatively innocent form in which the ruler is regarded
as the special servant and delegate of Heaven, but in
the slavish sense in which the prostrate Asiatic deifies
the person of his master. Cæsar must have his
statue borne in procession among the images of the
gods, he must have temples and a flamen to offer incense to his divinity and a statue inscribed, "the

* *Ad Att.*, xii., 45, 3.

invincible god."* These pretensions would have
seemed impious to the believers in a dogmatic
theology; but this was hardly the case with the
Romans; their objection was not so much religious
as political. Such conduct in a man was " incivism ";
it was to claim submission as to a being of higher
nature; it was to arrogate a pre-eminence, injurious
and insulting to his fellows.

About the same time when Cæsar was parading
his image among the gods, Aurelius Cotta was employed to discover a Sibylline oracle which might
justify the Dictator in assuming the title of King.
The hurried sentences of a note scribbled to Atticus†
give us a glimpse of Cicero's feelings. " How I delighted in your letter! but this procession is a bitter
business. However, it is well to be kept informed
about everything, even about Cotta. Well done the
people! that they would not lend a hand even to
clap the Victory, because of the bad company she
was in. Brutus is here; he wants me to write to
Cæsar. I had promised to do so, but now I tell him
to look at this procession."

The Ides of March were now drawing on. Cæsar
had not allowed the old year to expire without a

---

* Appian, *Bell. Civ.*, ii., 106 ; Dio Cassius, xliii., 45, 3 ; Suetonius,
Jul., 76. Mommsen's comments are characteristic of the modern
Cæsarian school. " Since the principle of the monarchy leads by
logical sequence either from its religious side up to the king-god, or
from its legal side up to the king-master, we must recognise in this
procedure that absolute and unshrinking thoroughness of thought and
action, which, here as elsewhere, vindicates for Cæsar a unique station
in history."—*Römische Staats-Recht*, vol. ii., p. 755.

† *Ad Att.*, xiii., 44, 1.

deadly insult to the memory of the chief magistracy
of republican Rome. Caninius Rebilus was elected
consul for a few hours of the last day of the year 45.
It was the public proclamation of the fact that the
consulship was now only a mockery and a farce.
The account of the spectacle which Cicero gives to
his friend Curius in one of the last letters* written
before Cæsar's death, may serve as a fitting close to
his experiences of the government of the Dictator :

"I give up pressing you or even inviting you
to return home. All I wish is that I, too, could take
to myself wings, and come at some land ' where I
shall never hear of the name nor the deeds of the
sons of Pelops.'†   I cannot tell you how mean I feel
for having any part in these things. Verily you seem
to me to have had a foresight long ago of what was
coming on us, when you took your flight from these
parts. Bitter as things are to hear of, they are a
thousand times worse to see. At any rate you
have escaped being present in the Campus Martius
at eight o'clock in the morning when the elections
for quæstors were being held. The curule chair of
Fabius, whom they were pleased to call consul, was
duly set. There comes a messenger to say the man
is dead, and away goes his chair. Thereupon, Cæsar,
who had taken the auspices for an assembly by
tribes, held an assembly by centuries instead. At
twelve o'clock he returned a consul duly elected to
hold office till the 1st of January, that is to say, for
the remainder of the day of election. So you are to

* *Ad Fam.*, vii., 30.
† From an unknown Latin tragedian.

know that in the consulship of Caninius no one
breakfasted. It must be granted that his consulship
was remarkably free from crime, owing to his marvellous vigilance, for during his term of office he
never closed an eye. This seems a joke to you. Yes,
for you are far away; if you were here to see it, you
could not refrain from tears. Am I to write anything
more of the sort? for plenty of the sort is happening.
I could not bear it at all, were it not that I take
refuge in the haven of philosophy, and that I have
our dear Atticus as the companion of my studies."

CHAPTER XIII.

CICERO AND ANTONY.

44–43 B.C.

ITH the assassination of Cæsar on the Ides of March in the year 44 B.C. begins the last act in the drama of Cicero's life. One year and three quarters still remained to him before he too met his death, and these months, though full of cruel anxieties, and bitter disappointments, are the most glorious in his whole career. For the first time since the coalition of Cæsar and Pompey, seventeen years before, he sees the path of duty clear, he feels the power to act and to speak freely in the cause of the commonwealth, and for the sake of that cause he is willing cheerfully to lay down his life. This consciousness puts every thought of self aside and gives vigour and dignity to all his words and actions.

44 B.C.

After the assassination the Liberators retired to

the Capitol, where they were joined later in the day
by Cicero and by Dolabella, who took
up the consulship which had been de- March 15.
creed to him in succession to Cæsar. Antony, the
other consul, seized on Cæsar's treasury at the
temple of Ops, and Cæsar's State papers were also
committed to him by Calpurnia, the widow of the
Dictator. Lepidus, the Master of the Horse, who
had under his command a legion encamped on the
island of the Tiber, transferred his troops to the left
bank of the river, and occupied the Campus Martius. Next day negotiations took
place between the several parties March 16.
which resulted in a meeting of the Senate in the
temple of Earth on the 17th, two days after the
assassination.

At this meeting Cicero proposed that, as at Athens
after the tyranny of the Thirty, a general Act of
Oblivion should be passed. The assassins of Cæsar were relieved from all March 17.
pains and penalties for their deed, but on the other
hand all the Acts of Cæsar were confirmed. This
confirmation led to much awkwardness and many
confusions, but * the thing was absolutely necessary. Lepidus' veteran legion was there in arms,
and the soldiers could only be kept quiet by a guaranty that the scheme under which Cæsar had provided lands for them should not be disturbed. A
public funeral was also granted for Cæsar's body.

This compromise, put forward as a basis of reconciliation, was really only the beginning of a fresh

---

* *Ad. Att.*, xiv., 14, 2.

complication of intrigues and disturbances. It is
impossible to trace any consistent policy in the
actions of the leaders of the Cæsarian party. We
find Antony one day agreeing to a general amnesty,
and the next day making inflammatory speeches at
Cæsar's funeral ; then with an equally sudden change
proposing that the office of Dictator should be forever abolished, as if the very name had been defiled
by having been made the title of the despotism.
Immediately after this he is found making a circuit
among the veterans, urging them to swear to the
maintenance of Cæsar's Acts; but this does not
prevent his making overtures to Sextus Pompeius
later on.   These negotiations with Sextus were
conducted through Lepidus, who after obtaining the
office of Pontifex Maximus, as a reward of his
services to Antony, had assumed the command of
Northern Spain and the southern portion of Transalpine Gaul.   His legions thus occupied the passes
both of the Pyrenees and of the Maritime Alps, and
by this commanding position Lepidus exercised an
important influence on the issue of the coming
struggle.   Pollio, the governor of Southern Spain,
and Plancus who held Northern Gaul with five
legions, waited on events along with Lepidus. They
were eager in their protestations of loyalty to the
Senate, but turned without scruple in favour of
Antony the moment his cause appeared the stronger.
Dolabella showed himself at first vigorous on the
Republican side.   When a riotous mob, largely composed of slaves, attempted to raise a column and to
offer sacrifices on the spot where Cæsar's body had

COIN OF CÆSAR.
(*Cohen.*)

COIN OF BRUTUS.
CAP OF LIBERTY, AND DAGGERS.
(*Cohen.*)

ANTONY AND CÆSAR.
(*Cohen.*)

COIN OF SEXTUS POMPEIUS.
(*Babelon.*)

been burned, Dolabella intervened with armed force and put many of them to death. Nevertheless we find him soon after accepting Antony's money,[*] and early next year he led an army against the Liberators in Asia, put to death Trebonius who had fallen into his hands, and was himself defeated and killed by Cassius. All these old officers of Cæsar appear to have been merely time-servers and self-seekers, and to have had no policy except that which suited their own interests for the moment.

There were, however, more honest Cæsarians, who sincerely mourned their lost chief, and were unwilling that his death should go unavenged. Among these were Cicero's friends, Balbus, Oppius, Postumius, and Matius, and in the same category must be counted the consuls-elect Hirtius and Pansa, who, however, were brought later on in the interests of the commonwealth to renounce the prospect of vengeance. Men of this type generally followed the lead of Octavian, as soon as he was able to assert himself. Meanwhile their language was threatening and gave much anxiety to Cicero. Cicero visited Matius early in April,[†] and found him maintaining, "that the entanglement is hopeless: if Cæsar with all his genius could not find a solution, who is to do so now?" "He protested," continues Cicero, "that all is ruined, in which he is very likely right: but he rejoiced at it, and declared that there will be an invasion of Gauls within twenty days. . . . To conclude, he said, 'the matter could not end here.'

[*] *Ad Att.*, xiv., 18, 1.
[†] *Ad Att.*, xiv.. I.

Our friend Oppius is more modest; he laments for Cæsar as much as the other, but says not a word that can offend the loyalists." " Can I," writes Matius * himself a little later, " can I, who wished the lives of all to be spared, fail to be indignant, when that man is slain from whom I gained the fulfilment of my wish? . . . What right have they to be angry with me, if my desire is that they shall repent what they have done? I wish that Cæsar's death should be a bitter thing to everyone." Cicero had good reason to observe,† "You see our bald friend has no mind for peace; in other words, no mind for Brutus." Of Balbus he writes ‡ much in the same tone. " Heavens! how clear it was that he disliked the idea of peace; and you know the man, how circumspect he is." Hirtius, too, as late as the 11th of May, appears of the same mind §: " These fellows make no secret of their intentions; my pupil for instance, who is to dine with me to-day, dearly loves him whom Brutus pierced. If you ask what they are after, I see clearly enough that they do not wish for peace: the burden of their discourse is, that a great man has been murdered, that by his fall the whole commonwealth has been thrown into confusion; that all his Acts will be set aside so soon as the pressure of fear is removed from us: that his clemency ruined him; if it had not been for that, nothing of the kind could have happened to him."

* *Ad Fam.*, xi., 28, 3.
† *Ad Att.*, xiv., 2, 3.
‡ *Ad Att.*, xiv., 21, 2.
§ *Ad Att.*, xiv., 22, 1.

Such were the feelings of Cæsar's friends with regard to his assassination. It proved in the end that these feelings were shared by the veteran soldiers, with whom lay the last word in the contest; but the public opinion of the great body of the Romans was on the other side. As regards the dwellers in the city itself we have very conflicting accounts. Shakespeare's picture of the " first, second, and third citizens," who after applauding Brutus' speech are forthwith roused by Mark Antony to mutiny for the dead Dictator, is only a dramatic exaggeration of what really occurred. The veterans mingled with the multitude at Cæsar's funeral, and the Liberators found it necessary to barricade themselves in their own houses. * On the other hand, the attempt to raise a column and altar to Cæsar's memory seems to have attracted no general sympathy, and Dolabella's stern and even cruel suppression of the movement was applauded by all classes. † At public games, either side could command a sympathetic audience. Those given by the agents of Octavian in honour of his adoptive father were a great success, ‡ but so were those which Brutus provided as prætor. § A few months later, Cicero's harangues were even more effective with the people than with the Senate.

The public opinion of the Romans of Italy was from the first clearly pronounced, and never wavered

---

* *Ad Att.*, xiv., 5, 2.
† *Ad Att.*, xiv., 16, 2, and *Phil.*, i., 12, 30.
‡ Suetonius, *Jul.*, 84.
§ *Phil.*, x., 4, 8, and *Ad Att.*, xvi., 2, 3 ; *cf.* also xiv., 2, 1.

25

until it was overborne by armed force. "In the country-towns," writes Cicero just a month after the assassination, "people rejoice to their heart's content. I cannot describe how delighted they are, how they throng around me, and beg me to tell them the story, how the deed was done." * "Nothing," he writes, † some months later, "can be firmer or better than the temper shown by the people and by the whole of Italy." We find the corporations of the country-towns offering men and money and passing decrees of ignominy and deprivation against anyone who should refuse to enlist. ‡ Even the newly enfranchised Transpadanes received Decimus Brutus heartily, and enrolled themselves under his standard. The first taste of despotism had been bitter to the Roman people, and we hear no more of that apathy which had been so conspicuous in the struggle between Cæsar and Pompey (see p. 327). "This much I must write," says Cicero to Decimus Brutus in the following January, § "that the Senate and people of Rome take the deepest interest not only in your safety but in your glory. I am much struck to see how precious your name is held, and how notable is the affection which all the citizens have for you. All hope and trust that as once you rid the State of the despot, so now you will rid her of the despotism. At Rome and throughout all Italy we are raising a conscription, if it be right to

---

* *Ad Att.*, xiv., 6, 2 (reading " ea de re ").
† *Ad Fam.*, xii., 4, 1.
‡ *Phil.*, vii., 8, 23.
§ *Ad Fam.*, xi., 8

call that a conscription, where everyone comes forward of his own accord ; men's minds are all ablaze with a craving for liberty and with hatred of the slavery we have borne so long." The legions of recruits thus raised find constant mention during the course of the war around Mutina. The consul Pansa had four of them under his command,* and Decimus Brutus at least as many more. Cicero himself placed only too much confidence in them.†
"For my own part, Senators, if I may speak my mind, I think that instead of looking only to the veterans, we should rather ask, what will the young soldiers, the flower of Italy, the newly levied legions who have come forward so readily to defend the State, what will the whole of Italy think of the firmness of your action ? For nothing remains forever at its best ; one generation succeeds another. For many years the legions of Cæsar were in their prime ; now the same is true of the legions of Pansa, of Hirtius, of Octavian, and of Plancus. They are superior to the others in numbers, they are superior by reason of their time of life, and above all superior in the goodness of their cause." Cicero's reliance on the new levies proved to be ill-placed, but their forwardness is a sure token of the depth of republican feeling which had survived Cæsar's victory. The hypocritical utterances of Pollio, show clearly enough what were the thoughts of honest and loyal citizens whose language he strives

---

* *Ad Fam.*, x., 30. 1.
† *Phil.*, xi., 15, 39.

to imitate. He complains * that though he had no choice but to obey Cæsar's commands, this has not shielded him from the blame of his fellow-citizens. "The unpopularity which attached to my conduct, most undeserved though it was, gave me a lesson how delightful liberty is, and how wretched a life passed under the dominion of another. Therefore if the question is of the revival of the absolute power of one man, whosoever that man may be, I profess myself his enemy."

The conspirators during the first weeks after the assassination seem to have been without any intelligent plan of action. Decimus Brutus writes † at the beginning of April as if there were no resource for them but exile, and Marcus Brutus and Cassius were thankful to accept a commission to look after the corn-supply as a pretext for retirement. Trebonius seems to have gone at his leisure to the East. ‡ Cicero himself is perplexed and baffled. Arguing from the precedents of Greek politics, the free State ought to have resumed its life on the removal of the despot, but on the contrary he has to "grieve over a fate which has never befallen any nation before, to have rid ourselves of our master, and yet not to have restored the Republic." §

Antony, whom the chance of the Dictator's dispositions had left as consul, squandered the treasures

---

* *Ad Fam.*, x., 31, 3.

† *Ad Fam.*, xi., 1.

‡ There is a letter (*Ad Fam.*, xii., 16) of his dated May 24th from Athens.

§ *Ad Att.*, xiv., 4, 1.

of Cæsar and used the validity accorded to his Acts
as a sanction for any forgery which he chose to
insert in the dead man's notebooks. Shakespeare
has hit the mark when he makes Antony say:

> " Fortune is merry,
> And in this mood will give us anything."

Laws, immunities, decrees, kingdoms were all to be
bought from the new master of the State. " He sometimes makes one wish," writes Cicero,[*] " that we had
Cæsar back again." It seemed at one moment as if
the inheritance of Cæsar's despotism had really fallen
to this shallow-brained soldier. In presence of this
danger the Liberators soon recovered their presence
of mind and set to work with energy to raise forces
for the inevitable conflict. By the middle of April
Decimus Brutus had entered his province of Cisalpine Gaul, where he was received by three legions as
their lawful commander. He made these the nucleus
of a rapidly collected army,[†] and was soon in condition to stand his ground. Marcus Brutus and
Cassius were slower to act, but they too exerted
themselves to provide a base of military operations
in the provinces. By the end of the year almost all
the troops quartered in the East had joined their
standard, and by active enlistment among the
Romans living in the provinces they organised the
army which was destined to strike the last blow for
the commonwealth at the battle of Philippi. Two
young Romans who were pursuing their studies at

[*] *Ad Att.*, xiv., 13, 6.
[†] *Phil.*, v., 13, 36.

the moment in Athens became officers in Brutus' army, the poet Horace and Marcus son of Cicero. It was a proud moment for his father when he had to announce to the Senate amongst other good news from the East, " the legion which was commanded by Lucius Piso, one of Antony's lieutenants, has gone over to my son Cicero, and placed itself at his disposal." *

Though despondent as to the future and bitterly disappointed at the result of a deed which " has taken away the despot but not the despotism," Cicero is absolutely fixed in his moral acceptance of the assassination. Looking back on Cæsar's career as a whole, he now made no question that he was a " tyrant " in the Greek sense of the word, that he had destroyed a free State, and that he meant his own domination to be permanent. This granted, the rest was clear. The Greek philosophers and historians, the recognised expounders of morality, spoke with no uncertain sound of the despot and his fate. The slayer of the " tyrant " was a hero and a public benefactor; honour and gratitude were his due at the hands of every free man. Not only in his public utterances, where we might suspect him of a desire to make the best of the actions of his political allies, but in his most confidential expressions to Atticus, Cicero never wavers in his approval of the deed and in his admiration for the Liberators. " Their name will be glorious as heroes or rather as gods. Though the deed may be barren of good results for the rest of us, yet for themselves

---

* *Phil.*, x., 6, 13.

there is a mighty consolation in the consciousness of a great and splendid action." * In the darkest moments of Antony's domination Cicero looks forward with calmness to the end of life. Personal fears have no longer any place in his mind. "If I remain in Italy," he writes, † "I see that I shall run some risks, but I cannot help thinking that it may lie in my power to do some good for the State." When Atticus suggests that in the end he will have to submit to whichever side may prove the stronger, he sets his friend's counsel quietly aside—"not I indeed; I know a better way than that," ‡ —and again, "Brutus seems to think of retiring into exile. For my part I look to another haven which lies handier to my time of life; all I wish is that I could reach it, leaving Brutus in prosperity and the Republic established." § Happily for Cicero he was to have the opportunity of selling his life dearly. He might well say with Macbeth,

> " Why should I play the Roman fool
> And die on my own sword? while I see foes,
> The gashes look better upon them."

In the month of August Cicero was contemplating a visit to his son at Athens. There seemed no place for him in Rome while Antony was consul; and all that he could hope was that a return by the end of

---

* *Ad Att.*, xiv., 11, 1.
† *Ad Att.*, xiv., 13, 4.
‡ *Ad Att.*, xv., 3, 1.
§ *Ad Att.*, xiv., 19, 1.

the year might bring him to the post of duty at a moment when his exertions would be of use. He crossed to Sicily and had actually set sail from Syracuse, when an adverse wind, to which he declares his profound gratitude, compelled him to touch again on the Italian coast. This happy accident enabled him to receive a letter from Atticus which convinced him that the crisis would come sooner than he expected and that to retire now would be to forsake his post. Brutus, whom he met a few days later, confirmed him in his resolve, and he set his face steadily towards Rome.

On the 2d of September Cicero appeared in the Senate and delivered the speech preserved to us under the title of the *First Philippic.* The tone of this oration is firm but conciliatory. He inveighs against the policy of Antony, but still urges peace, and holds out offers of compromise. The speech was, however, sufficient to rouse the deadly hostility of the consul; he threatened riot or assassination, and Cicero found it necessary to retire for a while from the city.

During the next weeks events followed thick and fast. Antony had forced through a decree for an exchange of provinces, by which he was himself to have command in Cisalpine Gaul, and Decimus Brutus was to be removed to Macedonia. Meanwhile he had ordered that four veteran legions which Cæsar had stationed in Macedonia should cross over into Italy. On the 6th of October he declared his policy in a speech in which he asserted that while he lived there should be no place for Cæsar's assassins in the

State.* Three days later he proceeded to meet the
four legions at Brundisium with the intention of
bringing them down on Rome. But he had to
reckon with an unexpected adversary.

Caius Octavius, destined afterwards to rule the
world under the name of Augustus, was the grand-
son of Cæsar's sister Julia, and was adopted by the
Dictator's Will as his son and heir. At the moment
of his uncle's assassination he was residing at Apol-
lonia in Epirus. He forthwith assumed the name of
Cæsar Octavianus and came to Italy to claim his inheritance. He arrived at Naples on the 17th of
April † and was met by Balbus, Hirtius, and Pansa.
Next day he had an interview with Cicero at Cumæ.
He professed the greatest devotion, and treated
Cicero with all possible respect and friendliness.‡
" I maintain, however," writes Cicero, § "that he
cannot possibly be a loyal citizen; he has around
him so many who threaten death to our friends."
On arriving at Rome, Octavian found that his inheritance was usurped by Antony, who had no
inclination to share his wealth and power with a lad
of eighteen, and who treated his claims with contempt. The first object of the young Cæsar was to
bring Antony to reason, and to this end he proceeded to ally himself with the Republicans. Already
in the month of June he had almost persuaded
Cicero of his sincerity—"Octavian has, I perceive,

---

* *Ad Fam.*, xii., 23, 3.
† *Ad Att.*, xiv., 10, 3.
‡ *Ad Att.*, xiv., 11, 2.
§ *Ad Att.*, xiv., 12, 2.

abundance of talent and abundance of courage. He seems to me to be disposed as I should wish towards our champions. But it is a matter for grave consideration how far we can trust him, at his age, with his name, with such an inheritance and such instructors." *

In the month of October Octavian who had now just completed his nineteenth year, took a bold step forward. His agents stirred up the legions at Brundisium to resist Antony, and he himself meanwhile summoned to his standard the veterans from his adoptive father's army, who were settled on their lands in Campania. Two of the legions from Macedonia (the 2d and 35th) sided with Antony: he had force enough to put to military execution a number of disaffected centurions of the Martian legion, and the rest sullenly submitted for the moment. But as soon as Antony had returned to Rome, the Martian legion, which was now on its way westward, declared for Octavian, and its example was followed by the 4th legion. Octavian took up his position with his small but formidable army at Alba, protecting the city of Rome from any armed attack on the part of Antony.

Thus threatened, Antony changed his plan. On the 20th of November he left the city, collected all the troops which still remained faithful to him, and pressed northward hoping to surprise and crush Decimus Brutus. Decimus' army of recruits, though probably superior to that of Antony in numbers, was not to be trusted to meet the veteran

* *Ad Att.*, xv., 12, 2.

THE YOUNG AUGUSTUS.
FROM THE BUST IN THE VATICAN.
(*Baumeister.*)

warriors in the open field. He therefore awaited
the attack behind the walls of the powerful fortress of Mutina, where he was besieged by Antony
from December till the following April. Octavian
sent messages to Decimus Brutus, urging him to
hold out and promising assistance. Then he
marched slowly northward through Umbria * to
Cisalpine Gaul, and encamped early in the next year
(43 B.C.) at Forum Cornelii, where he maintained his
post of observation until he was reinforced by fresh
troops under Hirtius and Pansa, the new consuls.

In all these proceedings the young Cæsar had been
acting in concert with Cicero. " Every day," writes
Cicero † on the 5th of November, " come letters
from Octavian urging me to take up the cause, to
save the commonwealth a second time, above all
things to go to Rome immediately. . . . The
country-towns are wonderfully enthusiastic for the
lad. In his progress towards Samnium he came to
Cales and stayed at Teanum. The crowds that go
forth to meet and encourage him are marvellous.
Could you have believed this possible? On this account I shall be in Rome earlier than I intended."
There were still grave reasons for distrust, and these
Atticus seems to have urged on his friend with
much force. Cicero contented himself, however,
with informing Oppius, who pressed him to throw
himself heart and soul into the cause of Octavian

---

* He was at Spoletium in Umbria on January 7th ; compare *Inscription*, Orelli, 2489, with Pliny, *Hist. Nat.*, xi., 37, 190, and see
Mommsen's note, *Corp. Inscr. Lat.*, vol. i., p. 383.

† *Ad Att.*, xvi., 11, 6.

and the veterans, that he could not do so unless he
were "satisfied that he would not only renounce all
enmity against the tyrannicides but frankly accept
their friendship." *   This Oppius assures him that
Cæsar will do.

A permanent reconciliation was in truth impossible;
yet Octavian's action had for the present saved Rome
from Antony, and now the one thing needful was
that he should be willing to rescue Decimus Brutus.
Whatever doubts may have presented themselves, it
was clearly Cicero's duty to accept the situation,
and make what use he could of the army, which
Octavian placed for the moment at his disposal. †
As soon then as the danger of falling into Antony's
hands was removed, Cicero again proceeded to
Rome, where he arrived on the 9th of December.

He immediately struck the key-note of the opposition to Antony by the publication of the *Second
Philippic Oration*, which he had been carefully preparing during the last two months.   This great im-
peachment is thrown into the form of a speech,
supposed to be delivered in the Senate in answer to
one which Antony had actually uttered after Cicero's
retirement in the previous September.   In reality
the *Second Philippic* is not a spoken oration at all,
but the most famous and effective of all political
pamphlets.   Cicero pursues Antony with fiery invective through the whole course of his life, from
his dissolute boyhood onward.   Antony's persistent

* *Ad Att.*, xvi., 15, 3.

† These arguments are clearly put by Cicero in a letter to Trebonius, *Ad Fam.*, x., 28, 3.

veto as tribune was, he says, the occasion of the
Civil War ; Antony was the only man who could
be found base enough to bid for the confiscated
property of Pompey the Great, and insolent enough
to occupy his house. " Alas ! alas ! for the fate of
those walls and that roof-tree. What had that
house ever witnessed but actions pure and excellent
and of good report? Its old master, as you,
Senators, know full well, was alike great in the field
and admirable at home, worthy of praise for his
exploits abroad, and no less worthy for his habits in
private life. It is in that man's house that the
chambers are turned into stews, and the halls into
taverns." * But the inexpiable sin of Antony was
that he had attempted to set up a King in Rome by
the offer of the diadem to Cæsar at the Lupercalia. †
" You set the diadem on his head, and the people
groaned ; he put it aside, and they shouted applause.
You then, villain, were the only man to give your
voice for Kingship, to declare that you wished to
take for your master the man who by law was your
fellow-consul, and to make experiment of how much
the Roman People could tolerate or suffer. Aye,
and you would entreat his pity ; you flung yourself
at his feet in supplication. What was your petition?
That you might be permitted to be a slave? Nay,
you should have begged the boon for yourself
alone, you who have submitted to all indignities
from your boyhood, so that slavery comes easy to
you ; from us and from the Roman People you had

---

* *Phil.*, ii., 28, 69.
† *Phil.*, ii., 34, 85.

no such commission. . . . I fear lest I may
seem to be casting a slight on the glorious action of
our great champions, but anger moves me, and I
must speak. I say that it is foul shame that the
man who set on the crown should be permitted to
live, when all agree that the man who set it aside
was righteously put to death." In reverting at the
end of his speech to the same note of warning,
Cicero takes occasion to eulogise by way of contrast
the great qualities of the Dictator. The passage *
may well find a place here as Cicero's last word
respecting Cæsar.

"Is that a life worth living, to be in fear day and
night of your associates? Do you suppose that you
have bound your satellites by any claims stronger
than those which he had on some of the men who
slew him, or do you presume to mate yourself with
him? In Cæsar there was genius, reasoning,
memory, culture, perseverance, reflection, and energy.
His achievements in war had been disastrous indeed
to the commonwealth, but they had been great.
After pondering for many years how to win the
throne, at the cost of much toil and much peril he
had accomplished his design; he had allured the
ignorant multitude by his shows, his buildings, his
largesses; he had bound his followers to him by
great rewards, and his adversaries by fair-seeming
clemency. In a word, he had brought a State, free
till then, to acquiesce, partly through fear, partly
through torpor, in the practice of subjection. I
may liken you to him in your lust for dominion, but

---

* *Phil.*, ii., 45, 116.

in all other respects how unlike you are! Many are the ills which Cæsar has stamped on the commonwealth, but this good has accrued, that the Roman People has learned what reliance it may place on each of us, into whose hands it may trust its fortunes, against whom it must be on its guard. Do you never think on this? Do you not comprehend that for brave men it is sufficient to have learned the lesson once for all, how noble an action, how acceptable a boon, how famous a record is the slaying of a tyrant? We could not bear him, and do you suppose that we are going to endure you. Believe me, men will hasten to such deeds in future, and there will be no tarrying. Turn and think, I entreat you, Mark Antony, at this eleventh hour think for the commonwealth. Forget those with whom you associate, and remember those from whom you are sprung. Be friends again—with me, as you please—only be friends with the State. But you must look to yourself. My part is simple. I defended the Republic when I was young, I will not desert her now that I am old; I despised the daggers of Catiline, I will not quail before yours. Nay, I offer my body willingly, if at the price of my life the freedom of Rome may be purchased. Long has the indignation of the Roman People been in labour; Heaven grant that at length it may bring forth. For myself, twenty years ago I said in this very temple that death could never come untimely to the consular; now I may say that it cannot come untimely to the old man. Death is a thing that I can wish for, now that I have served my time and done my work. Two things alone I crave, first, that dying I may leave the Romans a free people— that is the greatest boon which Heaven can grant me,—and next that as each has earned his recompense from the commonwealth so he may receive."

Cicero's first business in Rome was to come to an understanding with Hirtius and Pansa, who were to enter on their consulship on the 1st of January. He found them excellently disposed, willing cordially to accept the Act of Oblivion, which had been passed nine months before, and to labour for the re-establishment of the commonwealth. For the moment the most pressing need was the conduct of the war around Mutina, and the relief of Decimus Brutus. Much might be done in Rome itself to further these ends. Advantage must be taken of the general feeling against Antony to press on the work of arming Italy; the Senate must be induced to declare its policy unmistakably, to give an utterance to the will of the nation, to uphold the action of Octavian, to use all the power of its name and authority to induce the commanders of the other armies to follow his example, and to make it clear to all the world that war was being waged between Antony and the united Roman People. The office of guide and leader in this movement was one which Cicero was eminently qualified to fill, and he consented without hesitation to undertake the task.

No important business could be formally completed in the Senate till the new consuls should come into office; but Cicero was impatient for action. The tribunes summoned the Senate on the

19th of December, and at this meeting Cicero laid before the House a statement * of the policy which he was prepared to recommend. He protested that there had been already too much delay, and urged the Senate to pledge itself as soon as possible to a decisive line of conduct. His speech ended with a motion, expressing full approval of the action of Decimus Brutus, of Octavian, and of the soldiers who had supported them, and a resolution to this effect was passed by the House.

Following out this policy to its logical conclusion, Cicero on the 1st of January proposed that Octavian should be invested with the "imperium" of a pro-prætor, neces-

43 B.C.

sary to legalise the command he had assumed over his troops. On this occasion he solemnly assured the Senate that the young Cæsar had sacrificed all his private resentments to the good of the commonwealth, and that his loyalty and good faith might be implicitly trusted. "I venture to pledge my word for him to you and to the Roman People. Judge if I have good cause, when I dare to do this without fear lest you should think me rash in hazarding an assertion on a matter of such moment. I promise, I undertake, I go surety, Senators, that Caius Cæsar will always be such a citizen as he shows himself to-day, that is to say such a one as we should most earnestly desire and hope." † This pledge remained unredeemed, but Cicero sealed his words with his

---

* The *Third Philippic Oration.*
† *Phil.*, v., 18, 51.
26

own blood, and may well plead Prince Henry's great exception :

"If not, the end of life cancels all bonds."

The part which Cicero called upon the Senate to play at this crisis of events may best be stated in his own words * : "Antony must be assailed not by arms alone, but likewise by the decrees of this House. Great is the power and awful the majesty of a Senate unanimous in heart and voice. You see how the Forum is thronged, how the Roman People is all astir with the hope of recovering its liberties; now, after so long a space, it sees us once again assembled in our hundreds, and it hopes that it sees us free at last to speak and to act. This is the day for which I have been keeping myself all the time that I screened myself from the accursed weapons of Antony, whilst he thundered against me in my absence, little knowing for what occasion I was reserving myself and husbanding my strength. If I had consented to come and answer him then, when he would fain have inaugurated his massacres with my blood, I should not now have been in case to serve the commonwealth . . . In Heaven's name then I charge you, Senators, grasp this opportunity which is put within your reach, and call to mind at length that you are the peers of the venerable council that keeps watch over the world. Proclaim it to the Roman People that your counsel shall be forthcoming at this hour in which it declares that its manhood shall not be wanting . . . And if,

* *Phil.*, iii., 13, 32.

which Heaven forbid, but if the death-agony of the commonwealth be indeed upon us, then even as gallant gladiators sink beneath their wounds not ingloriously, so let us, who are at our post in the forefront of the world, and of all its peoples, take thought for this that we should die with honour, but never degrade ourselves to be slaves . . . With our noble consuls for champions and leaders, with Heaven our aid, with ourselves watchful and provident for the time to come, with the Roman People at our back, verily it shall not be long before we are free, and our freedom will be the sweeter for the memory of the servitude that is past."

Thus the great conflict began, and Cicero frankly accepted the post of honour and of danger. The outlook at the moment is described in a letter* to Cornificius, the Governor of Africa, who almost alone amongst Cæsar's officers remained staunch to the Republic in its hour of peril. "What is to happen," writes Cicero in the month of December, "I know not. The single hope remains that the Roman People may at last show itself worthy of its ancestors. For my own part I will not be wanting to the State, and whatever happens, so that it be not by my fault, I will bear it with fortitude." A few days later he adds†: "As soon as ever opportunity presented, I used my old freedom in defence of the Republic. I offered my services as leader to the Senate and People of Rome, and when once I had taken up the cause of liberty, I did not let slip a moment which

---

* *Ad Fam.*, xii., 22, 2.

† *Ad Fam.*, xii., 24, 2.

could be used in defence of the common safety and the common freedom."

On the afternoon of December 19th, and again on the 4th of January, Cicero addressed himself to the Roman People in the Forum.* The debate in the Senate on the first days of the new year (43 B.C.) had ended with a disappointment. Instead of at once proclaiming war against Antony, a majority of the Senate resolved first to send envoys, summoning him to desist from his attack on Mutina. Cicero had protested in vain ; but in announcing the result to the People he was obliged to make the best of the situation, and to console them by the prospect that after this at any rate no one will have any excuse for hesitation. "Wherefore, Romans, do you await the return of the envoys, and digest the vexation of these few days' delay. If, when they return, they bring peace along with them, then say that I have been too rash ; if they bring war, then judge that I have seen further than the rest. Am I not bound to be watchful over my countrymen ? Must I not ponder day and night for your liberty and for the safety of the State ? Do I not owe my all to you, Romans, whom you have set—me, a man sprung from your ranks—over the heads of the noblest of the nation ? Am I ungrateful ? Nay, you know that after I had attained my rank I laboured in the law-courts just as I had done when I was striving for it. Am I a novice in the affairs of State ? Nay, it is now twenty years that I have served, ever battling against disloyal citizens. There-

* *Philippics*, iv. and vi.

fore, Romans, with such wisdom as I have, and with efforts perhaps beyond such strength as remains to me, I will keep watch and ward for you. And well I may. Is there any citizen, especially a citizen holding the rank to which you have been pleased to call me, who could so forget your favours, be so unmindful of his country, so indifferent to his honour, that his heart should not stir and kindle at the sight of your resolution? I have addressed, when I was your consul, many great assemblages; I have taken part in many such; but never did I behold such a one as yours to-day. You have one thought and one desire, to ward off the attack of Antony from the commonwealth, to quench his fury, to crush his insolence. The same wish is shared by every rank in the State; on this is set the will of the country-towns, of the colonies, of all Italy. And so the Senate, strong in its own spirit, is made the stronger by your support. The time has come, Romans, later, far later than beseemed the honour of the Roman People; but now it is so ripe that the hour brooks no delay. A fatal spell, if I may so speak, lay on us, which we bore as best we could. Now, if we are to bear, it will be because we choose to bear. Nay, but it is not written that the Roman People shall be in slavery, that people whom the will of Heaven has set to rule over all nations. The supreme hour has come; liberty is at stake. You must conquer, Romans, as you surely shall by virtue of this your devotion and your unanimity, or else you must accept the worst, anything rather than be slaves. Other nations may be able to bear the yoke; the

Roman People has liberty for its peculiar heritage." *

Cicero now stands in the forefront of the battle; his old ideal of "the union of the orders" and the "consent of Italy" is at last realised. From the middle of December onwards his great speeches rapidly succeed one another; he feels that he is giving form and words to the thoughts and aspirations of all that is loyal and true in Rome, and so his eloquence burns free and splendid without reserve or misgiving. Under the Roman constitution, the duty of leading the debates and guiding the counsels of the Senate was not bound up, as it is under our own parliamentary system, with the tenure of executive office. The magistrate might, without any dereliction of duty, confine himself to naming the subject which the Senate was to discuss; it was open to the private Senator to make any motion on the subject in hand, and this motion, if approved by a majority of voices, became a binding instruction to the executive. Thus Cicero, though without any formal office, took the responsibility of the initiative and shaped the policy of the Republic. He was, in fact, prime minister of Rome.

He succeeded, though not without difficulty and delay, in carrying the Senate with him. A state of war was proclaimed, and the citizens assumed their war-cloaks as in a time of imminent danger; Antony's Acts were cancelled; votes of confidence and thanks were passed in favour of his adversaries, and each promise of support from the provincial governors

* *Phil.*, vi., 6, 17 *seq.*

was met by an appropriate acknowledgment, and an
intimation that if they wished well to the State they
must stand firm against Antony. When the news
arrived that Dolabella had murdered Trebonius, he
was declared a public enemy, and Brutus and Cassius
were invested with full powers in the East. All this
was not accomplished without some opposition.
"We have a brave Senate," Cicero writes,* "but all
the courage seems to be on the lower benches." The
consulars were "partly timid and partly ill-disposed."†
Cicero's policy was too straightforward and decided
for them. "They pose‡ as far-seeing citizens and
earnest Senators. They say that I have sounded
the trumpet for war. They are advocates of peace.
They argue, 'It will not do to rouse Antony's displeasure; he is a dangerous man and a bold one;
there are many disloyal persons, and we must be
cautious of them.' Well, they say the truth here;
and, if they wish to count up those persons, they
may begin with themselves who utter words like
these." Cicero would fain stimulate them to action
worthy of their high station. "Heavens!§ what a
task it is to support with dignity the character of a
chief of the Roman commonwealth; those who bear
it should shrink from offending not only the minds
but the eyes of their fellow-citizens. When they
receive the envoy of our enemies at their houses, admit him to their chambers, even draw him apart in

* *Ad Fam.*, xii., 4, 1.

† *Ad Fam.*, x., 28, 3.

‡ *Phil.*, vii., 1, 3.

§ *Phil.*, viii., 10, 29.

conversation, I say that they think too little of their dignity and too much of their danger. But what is this danger after all? If the greatest hazard must be run, it is but liberty that awaits us if we win and death if we lose; the one is to be welcomed, the other is that which we can no one of us avoid."

The position of "princeps," or prime minister, to which Cicero justly lays claim, implied in this hour of peril not only the duties of a parliamentary leader, but other labours which belong rather to the functions of a diplomatist. While the armies of the Republic under Decimus Brutus, Hirtius, Pansa, and Octavian stood face to face with Antony beneath the walls of Mutina, the ring was kept by the legions of Spain and Gaul under the command of Pollio, Lepidus, and Plancus. It was obvious that these armies might come to have a deciding vote in the conflict, and their attitude and that of their generals was dubious and alarming. The despatches which passed between these commanders and Cicero as the virtual head of the government in Rome form the best comment on the progress of events. Cicero's letters to these almost independent powers are admirable in their force and dignity. Not even in the *Philippics* is the tone more sturdy and uncompromising. "You recommend peace," he writes to Plancus, "while your colleague is besieged by a gang of rebels. If they want peace, they should lay down their arms and beg for it; if they demand it by force of arms, then we must win our way to peace through victory, not through negotiation. . . . Show yourself worthy; sever yourself from an ill-

assorted union with bad citizens; next offer yourself as a guide, chief, and leader to the Senate and
to all honest men; lastly believe that peace consists
not in laying down arms, but in flinging off the fear
of arms and of slavery. If you will act and think as
I say, then you shall be not only consul and consular, but a great consul and a great consular; if
otherwise, in the splendid titles of your station
there will be no dignity, but only a pre-eminence in
ignominy." *

To Lepidus he writes † still more sternly: "I am
glad to hear that you profess yourself desirous of
promoting peace between citizens. If you connect
that peace with liberty, you will do good service to
the State and to your own reputation. But if your
peace is to restore a traitor to the possession of an
unbridled tyranny, then let me tell you that all true
men have made up their minds to accept death
rather than servitude. You will therefore act more
wisely, to my judgment, if you decline to meddle
with projects of accommodation which do not commend themselves to the Senate or to the People or
to any loyal man."

Cicero's efforts seemed at one moment likely to be
successful. Lepidus and Pollio promised their assistance; and though it was clear enough that they were
sure to range themselves on the strongest side, yet
even a feigned and temporary adherence was of some
use in encouraging the efforts of the Romans and in
giving them time for preparation. Plancus seems

---

* *Ad Fam.*, x., 6.
† *Ad Fam.*, x., 27.

The essential mischief, the predominance of the professional soldiers in the commonwealth, was not touched. It was of no avail that Italy declared herself with enthusiasm for the cause of the Republic and sent her sons by tens of thousands to fight for freedom. It was now too late to prepare for danger. A nation which will be free, must not trust its defence solely in the hands of a professional soldiery; in spite of the irksomeness and the comparative inefficiency of a short-service system, it must at all risks train the mass of the citizens to the use of arms. This necessity was even more urgent in the ancient than in the modern world, for the use of the rifle can be taught far more rapidly than the use of the shield, the sword, and the javelin; a few highly practised soldiers could in those days put to the rout whole regiments of half-trained men.* In all the civil wars of Rome there is only one instance in which short-service men won a battle from veterans. The exception is the engagement in the lines of Dyrrachium in 48 B.C. (see p. 339), and in that case the credit rests rather with the commander than with the troops. The victory was due to the consummate skill with which Pompey took advantage of Cæsar's rashness in attempting to cover an extent of ground too great for his forces.

---

* " Dans nos combats d'aujourd'hui un particulier n'a guère de confiance qu'en la multitude ; mais chaque Romain, plus robuste et plus aguerri que son ennemi, comptait toujours sur lui-même ; il avait naturellement du courage, c'est à dire de cette vertu qui est le sentiment de ses propres forces."—Montesquieu, *Grandeur des Romains,* ch. ii.

The Italian temperament seems to have been peculiarly susceptible to the effects of long training and peculiarly in need of it.   Cæsar has given us a lively picture of the panic which affected his own army, while still young, at the prospect of meeting the Germans.   Even the officers " could not keep their countenance, nor sometimes refrain even from tears ; they buried themselves in their tents bemoaning the common danger along with their friends. Throughout the camp men were making their wills. . . . Some even reported to Cæsar that, if he ordered an advance, the soldiers would refuse obedience and not dare to go forward with the colours." The tables were now turned ; Cæsar had fashioned these unpromising recruits into invincible warriors, and they in turn would face without hesitation double their number of raw soldiers.   In the account of the first battle at Forum Gallorum, written to Cicero by an officer who took part in it,* we find Antony hastening to take the initiative in attack with two of his legions " because he thinks that he has only four legions of recruits opposed to him." The unexpected intervention of the veteran " Martian " legion turns the scale against him.

The fear of these veteran troops is constantly before the eyes of men, and the need for humouring them is the favourite argument of the trimmers against Cicero's call for vigorous action on the part of the Senate.   Sextus Pompeius is anxious to intervene in the war before Mutina, but abstains " for fear

---

* Servius Sulpicius Galba, one of the assassins of Cæsar, and an ancestor of the future emperor. *Ad Fam.*, x., 30.

to a civil war, and in the meantime were well pleased to have all sides bidding for their support. Antony, as may be supposed, was not behindhand with promises. "I have three strong legions," writes Pollio *: "one of them, the 28th, was solicited by Antony at the beginning of the war with the promise of a donation of 500 denarii † to each soldier on the day they arrived in camp, and in case of victory the same rewards as to his own troops, and these no one supposes will be other than unlimited. The troops were most eager to go, and I kept them in check with much difficulty. . . . The other legions were also constantly tempted by letters and boundless promises." It was in vain for Cicero to propose votes of honour in the Senate for the veterans, and to pledge the State to reward them; their instinct told them that more was to be hoped from a usurper than from the Republic. ‡

The temper of the veterans determined the action of Octavian. Claiming as he did to be Cæsar's heir, he was obliged to satisfy the opinion of the army by avenging his father's death, and could not sincerely desire the restoration of the Republic, in which the men who had killed the Dictator would hold a chief place. From a Cæsarian point of view there was reason in the reproaches which Antony addressed to his young rival. § "Boy! you who owe your all to

---

* *Ad Fam.*, x., 32, 4.

† About £20.

‡ *Phil.*, xii., 12, 29, "credunt improbis, credunt turbulentis, credunt suis."

§ *Phil.*, xiii., 11 *seq.*

his name, is this your object that the condemnation
of Dolabella shall be ratified? that this other assassin here shall be relieved from my blockade? that
Cassius and Brutus shall be all-powerful? . . . It
is hardly likely that those who have declared Dolabella an enemy for his most righteous act, will spare
me who am heart and soul along with him! . . .
Consider within yourself which is the more proper
course, and which the more useful for our side, to
avenge the death of Cæsar or the death of Trebonius,
and whether it is more right for us to battle with
each other that the crushed cause of the Pompeians
may revive again, or to come to terms and cease to
make sport for our enemies." Antony says that
Cicero looks on like a *lanista*, or trainer, who has set
a brace of gladiators to fight, sure to profit whichever falls, and this in fact bluntly represents the real
state of the case. The single chance for Cicero and
the Senate was that Antony and Octavian should
weaken each other and hold each other in check,
until the Republic could possess itself of an effective
army of its own.

It was obvious then that the young Cæsar's
quarrel with Antony admitted of accommodation.
So soon as he had compelled Antony to acknowledge his power and to treat with him as an equal,
he had no desire to crush him, and their union
against the Republic only awaited time and opportunity. The position of Octavian was greatly
strengthened by the death of both the consuls in the
moment of victory before Mutina; he retained all
the veteran troops under his command, and Decimus

27

Brutus was left, as he says, "with only starveling recruits." Octavian was in no hurry to throw off the mask, and affected to be on cordial terms with Decimus.* But he would not press the pursuit. "If," writes Decimus Brutus,† "Cæsar would have listened to me and crossed the Apennines, I could have hemmed in Antony so completely that he would have perished for lack of supplies; but I cannot command Cæsar, and Cæsar cannot command his troops. These are both very ugly facts."

Antony shows at his best in the hour of danger and disaster. He drew off his shattered forces westward with skill and courage. He was still strong in cavalry, but of infantry he had only one legion ‡ (the 5th) in tolerable order; of the others § only a remnant survived, and many of the men were without arms. But as early as the 5th of May ‖ he had reached the coast and approached the Gallic frontier. Here he was joined by Ventidius Bassus at the head of three veteran legions.¶ Ventidius had passed the Apennines from Ancona, doubtless with the connivance of Octavian, and overtook Antony at Vada Sabatia, a little west of Genoa. Decimus Brutus, who had marched in pursuit, lay on May 5th at Dertona, some fifty miles north-east of Antony, and with the Apennines between them.

* *Ad Fam.*, xi., 13, 1.

† *Ad Fam.*, xi., 10, 4.

‡ *Ad Fam.*, x., 34, a, 1.

§ The number is uncertain, but Antony's letter (*Phil.*, viii., 8, 25) claims rewards for six legions.

‖ *Ad Fam.*, xi., 10, 3.

¶ *Ad Fam.*, x., 34, a, 1.

An attempt of Antony to throw troops across the
range and occupy Pollentia was anticipated by
Decimus.* Antony now hastened to cross the
Maritime Alps and take refuge with Lepidus. He
and his army endured great privations in the passage, but by the 11th his advanced May, 43 B.C.
guard was at Forum Julii (Fréjus), and
he himself arrived there on the 15th. Lepidus had
advanced from his headquarters near Avignon, †
as far as Forum Voconii, about twenty-four miles
from Antony. From this place he wrote on the
21st a letter to the Senate protesting his fidelity.
On the 28th he and his army declared for Antony :
with their united forces they then turned on Plancus,
who had started from his headquarters by the Isara
on the 20th to support Lepidus, and was only forty
miles off when the reconciliation between Antony
and Lepidus occurred. Laterensis, the lieutenant
of Lepidus, on the strength of whose assurances
Plancus had advanced, killed himself in disgust at
the treason of which he had been the unconscious
instrument. Plancus made good his retreat again
behind the Isara. He writes from thence to Cicero
on the 6th of June, and says that he expects Decimus
Brutus to join him in three days' time.

Pollio and his powerful army followed the lead of
Lepidus, but Plancus held out for some weeks
longer. His last letter to Cicero is dated July 27th,
and is full of declarations of affection and loyalty.

---

* *Ad Fam.*, xi., 13.

† He describes himself (*Ad Fam.*, x., 34) as marching "ab con-
fluente Rhodano," *i.e.*, from where the Durance joins the Rhone.

It must always be doubtful whether his attitude at
this time was merely assumed in order to lure Decimus Brutus to his destruction, or whether Plancus
really remained undecided to the last moment.
Decimus during the latter half of May occupied
Eporedia, Vercellæ, and Pollentia; he thus commanded the entrance both to the pass through the
Cottian Alps (Mont Cenis) and to that through the
Graian Alps (Little St. Bernard); by either of these
he could join hands with Plancus. From a purely
military point of view, Decimus' best course would
have been to retreat to the north-east of the Cisalpine
province, so as to be able to fall back in the last resort
through Illyricum on the support of his namesake in
Macedonia. But by such a retreat he would have left
Plancus unsupported, and would have sadly discour-
aged the republicans in Rome. He resolved therefore to cross the Alps, and the two armies seem
actually to have effected a junction before Plancus
finally deserted the cause. This desertion ended
the conflict in the West. Decimus' legions of recruits proved, as he had expected, untrustworthy;
they were conscious of their inability to face the
veterans, and as soon as these were united against
them they submitted without a blow. Their commander attempted to escape eastward, but was over-
taken and put to death by Antony's orders early in
September.

The revival of the war which they had believed to
be ended was a bitter disappointment for the Republicans of Rome. Cicero remained at his post as leader
of the House and practical head of the central

government, and he was still supported by the
Senate. On the last day of June Lepidus was declared an enemy by a unanimous vote.* The news
from the East was uniformly good. Cicero did all
that man could do to avert the impending ruin.
He adopted every suggestion in favour of the
soldiers who still remained loyal.† He procured
supplies of money for Decimus Brutus, ‡ who was in
sore need, and summoned Cornificius from Africa
and Marcus Brutus and Cassius from the East, § to
bring their forces to bear on the critical point in
northern Italy. The last letter of Cicero which is
preserved to us is one addressed to Cassius very
early in July, and only one later than this (that of
Plancus on July 27th) remains from a correspondent
of Cicero. Thus the light of contemporary evidence which we have enjoyed so long, fails us, and
for the remaining months we have nothing to guide
us but the untrustworthy accounts of later authors.
We know, however, that Cornificius, Marcus Brutus,
and Cassius never arrived, and the fate of Italy was
left to be determined by the armies of the West.

Meanwhile the policy of Octavian was being
rapidly revealed. As early as the 17th of June,
Cicero had written to Decimus ‖ " Of Marcus Brutus
we have no certain news; I never cease urging him
in private letters to come, as you have suggested, and

---

* *Ad Fam.*, xii., 10, 1.

† *Ad Fam.*, xi., 21, 5.

‡ *Ad Fam.*, xi., 24, 2.

§ *Ad Fam.*, xi., 14 and 25 ; xii., 9.

‖ *Ad Fam.*, xi., 25, 2.

bear his part in the war. Would that he were here already ! we should then have less to fear on account of the mischief at home, which is no light matter." This "mischief at home" is the claim which Octavian was already making to be appointed consul for the remaining months of the year.

Plutarch asserts * that Octavian proposed to Cicero that he should join him in the movement, and that the two should be consuls together on the understanding that he would defer in all things to Cicero's advice. Plutarch even gives us to understand that Cicero was caught by the bait, and favoured the young Cæsar's candidature. All this is very improbable. What is certain is that Octavian's request was refused by the Senate. The leader of a deputation of centurions, who had been sent to press his claim, thereupon struck his hand upon his sword-hilt and said, " If you will not give it, this shall give it."

His words proved true, Octavian left August, 43 B.C. Decimus Brutus to shift for himself and marched with his army upon Rome.

The city was without defence except for a few soldiers who had been sent from Africa, and these went over to Octavian. He was elected consul on the 19th of August, and at once seized on the Treasury, the contents of which he divided among his soldiers. He likewise established a court for the trial of his father's assassins, who were all condemned in their absence. He then set forth again with his army to meet Lepidus and Antony. There can be little doubt that he had long been in secret com-

* Plutarch, *Cic.*, 45 and 46.

munication with them. Plancus had written to Cicero in July * : " That Antony is alive to-day, that Lepidus has joined him, that they have formidable armies, that they are full of hope and daring—you may set all this down to Cæsar." It seems probable that Lepidus had not received Antony without first coming to an understanding with him as to a reconciliation with Octavian. Toward the end of October the three chiefs met in an island of the river near Bononia, and the bargain was soon struck. It was agreed to have a Proscription even more bloody than that of Sulla, and Cicero was to be the first victim. Plutarch tells us that Octavian contended for two days for the life of Cicero. On the third day each of the three surrendered his own friends to the animosity of his colleagues. Shakespeare has made the scene live before us :

Ant. These many then shall die, their names are pricked ;
        Your brother too must die ; consent you, Lepidus ?
Lep. I do consent——
Oct. Prick him down, Antony.
Lep. Upon condition Publius shall not live,
        Who is your sister's son, Mark Antony.
Ant. He shall not live ; look with a spot I damn him.

We hear nothing of Cicero during Octavian's presence in Rome. Now that military force had overpowered the commonwealth, the statesman must have felt that he had received his discharge. Plutarch says that he was in his villa at Tusculum when he received tidings of his proscription. He made a faint attempt to escape by sea, but landed again and

---

* *Ad Fam.*, x., 24, 6.

returned to another villa at Caieta. "Let me die," Livy reports that he said, "in the country which I have so often saved." Next day on the urgency of his attendants he allowed himself once more to be borne in a litter towards the sea; but the assassins, sent by Antony, overtook him on the way. His faithful slaves would fain have fought for him to the last, but he forbade all resistance and commanded them to set the litter on the ground. Sitting there with his chin resting on his left hand, an attitude, says Plutarch, which was habitual to him, he quietly awaited the stroke. His head and the hand which had penned the *Second Philippic* were hung on the Rostra in the Roman Forum.

A year and a half before the end, in counting up the chances to his friend Atticus, Cicero had said *: "Must I then take refuge in a camp? It were better to die a thousand times. I have lived long enough." He was saved at least from another Civil War in which he could only have been a helpless spectator. Cicero's work was indeed over, and the tragedy of his death was the natural outcome of his splendid failure. He had staked all on one cast. The policy of the State during the brief months while he was at the helm had been vigorous, straightforward, and unhesitating. He had protested against all half-measures and scorned all ambiguous words. He accepted the internecine conflict between the Republic of the Liberators and the revived Cæsarism of Antony. There was no door of escape, no place left in the State for him and Antony together.

* *Ad Att.*, xiv., 22, 2.

What manner of man Cicero was, I have attempted to show from his own mouth. Happily the materials for a judgment, which I have been able to present to my readers, are copious ; else it would be impossible to appreciate the lights and shadows of a career so varied, or to estimate at its true value a temperament so sensitive, a character so many-sided, a will so much determined by human sympathies and human weakness. We may contrast Cicero in this respect with his great contemporaries, Cato and Cæsar. Cato knew no guide of action except his own stern conception of duty. He was unalterably faithful to the Republic, and was ready to make any sacrifice for it, except the sacrifice of that inopportune rigidity which prevented his ideal being realised in practice. Cæsar pursued no ideals but only practical objects. Whatever means, good or bad, he found ready to his hand from time to time, he used them with consummate skill, in the first place to further his own ambition to be absolute master, and in the next place to suppress certain crying evils and to realise certain definite improvements in administration. He secured Italy from the most pressing danger on her frontier, and he elicited a strong, humane, and orderly government from the confusions of the Civil War. For the sake of these objects, without scruple or remorse, he renounced as unattainable all the nobler fruits of statesmanship, and inexorably crushed out all the possibilities of a worthier future for his nation and for the world. Cato and Cæsar are each of them thorough, positive, one-sided ; they act, rightly or wrongly, without hesitation and without misgiving; their intentions and their motives are sufficiently obvious from their actions.

But the character of Cicero eludes any such precise definition. He had personal ambitions, though they were not unlimited like those of Cæsar. He was no less loyal to the Republic than was Cato, loyal with all the passionate attachment of an enthusiastic nature to the great ideals of liberty and patriotism. But he aspired to be a practical statesman, to adapt his principles to the necessities of the time, and to modify his action so as to secure the greatest possible amount of good under the given circumstances. There were times in Cicero's life, when the requirements of a sage and patriotic opportunism and those of fidelity to principle seemed irreconcilable. At such times the infinite perplexities of the political situation bewildered him; and who might not have shared his bewilderment? He had not the power of shutting his eyes to all considerations but one; on the contrary, his vivid imagination presented every possible aspect of a problem to his mind, and he was always trying to view a question from a dozen sides at once. This habit led sometimes to confusion or inconsistency of statement, sometimes, again, to hesitancy in action.

Cicero made many mistakes as a politician. His forecast is often wrong; he is often taken by surprise; sometimes by the over-refining of his own subtle intellect, sometimes by applying the casuistry of his Greek book-learning too readily to the practical conduct of affairs, he allows himself to be led astray, where a man of less discursive mind might have shaped his course better. But we must never forget that during the greater part of his political life he had no choice before him but a choice of evils. The critics who have blamed him most bitterly would find it hard to define how, believing as he believed, Cicero ought to have acted. Cicero accepted it as the first axiom of politics, that " some sort of Free State " is the necessary condition of a noble and honourable existence; and that it is the last calamity for a people permanently to renounce this ideal and to substitute for it the slave's ideal of a good master. Englishmen and Americans, worthy of their birthright, are not likely to disagree with Cicero's judgment. If this be indeed the cardinal doctrine of the political faith, then Cicero was sound in the faith. At any rate this was the creed in which he lived, and to maintain this he laid down his life. For such a man to accept as sufficient the solution which Cæsar attempted to force on the world, would have been treason against the best light of his soul and conscience. But it was no less true, that to accept in its fulness the doctrine and policy of Cato was to court defeat and to take refuge in mere counsels of despair. Can we wonder, and shall we withhold our sympathy, if an honest man in so inextricable a situation was the prey of doubts and scruples? if he halted between two opinions and was sometimes at a loss to discover where the path of honour and duty lay ? Cicero sought that path diligently, and when at last it was made clear to him, he pursued it, in spite of danger and suffering, to its goal on the beach of Caieta.

The weaknesses and inconsistencies of Cicero lie on the surface of his character, and they are pitilessly displayed before us by the preservation of his most secret letters. In his case the veil is withdrawn which for most of us shrouds from the eyes of the world the multiplicities of our motives, the perplexities of our judgment, the delusions of our anticipations, and the inconsecutiveness of our action. His memory has thus been subjected to a test of unprecedented sharpness. Nevertheless the faithful friends who resolved to present to the world his confidential utterances, unspoiled by editorial garbling, have not only earned our gratitude by the gift of a unique historical monument, but have judged most nobly and most truly what was due to the reputation of Cicero. As it was in his life-time, so it has been with his memory : those who have known him most intimately have commonly loved him best. The reader must judge whether he rightly claims a place as a " hero of his nation " ; at least he was the exponent of its best thoughts and noblest aspirations, its faithful servant in life and its constant martyr in death.

The calm retrospective judgment, perhaps not untinged with remorse, of Cæsar Augustus sums up fairly and honestly the story of Cicero's life. " It happened many years after," writes Plutarch,* " that Augustus once found one of his grandsons with a work of Cicero's in his hands. The boy was fright-

* Plutarch, *Cic.*, 49.

ened and hid the book under his gown ; but Cæsar took it from him, and standing there motionless he read through a great part of the book; then he gave it back to the boy, and said : ' This was a great orator, my child ; a great orator, and a man who loved his country well.' "

INDEX.

HEROES OF THE NATIONS

❡ *The following are the first volumes of this well-known series to be issued at the cheaper price of 7s. 6d. net. It is the hope of the Publishers eventually to re-issue the whole series at this price.*

Each 7s. 6d. net.

NELSON, AND THE NAVAL SUPREMACY OF ENGLAND. By W. CLARK RUSSELL.

GUSTAVUS ADOLPHUS, AND THE STRUGGLE OF PROTESTANTISM FOR EXISTENCE. By C. R. L. FLETCHER, M.A., late Fellow of All Souls' College, Oxford.

PERICLES, AND THE GOLDEN AGE OF ATHENS. By EVELYN ABBOTT, M.A., Fellow of Balliol College, Oxford.

THEODORIC THE GOTH, THE BARBARIAN CHAMPION OF CIVILISATION. By THOMAS HODGKIN, D.C.L., author of "Italy and Her Invaders," etc.

HENRY OF NAVARRE, AND THE HUGUENOTS IN FRANCE. By P. F. WILLERT, M.A., Fellow of Exeter College, Oxford.

PRINCE HENRY (THE NAVIGATOR) OF
PORTUGAL, AND THE AGE OF DIS-
COVERY IN EUROPE. By C. R. BEAZLEY,
M.A., Merton College, Oxford.

LOUIS XIV AND THE ZENITH OF THE
FRENCH MONARCHY. By ARTHUR
HASSALL, M.A., Student of Christ Church,
Oxford.

LORENZO DE' MEDICI, AND FLORENCE
IN THE FIFTEENTH CENTURY. By
EDWARD ARMSTRONG, M.A., Fellow of Queen's
College, Oxford.

OLIVER CROMWELL, AND THE RULE
OF THE PURITANS. By Professor C. H.
FIRTH, M.A., Balliol College, Oxford.

WILLIAM PITT, EARL OF CHATHAM
(1708-1778), OR THE GROWTH AND
DIVISION OF THE BRITISH EMPIRE.
By WALFORD DAVIS GREEN.

HENRY V, THE TYPICAL MEDIÆVAL
HERO. By CHARLES L. KINGSFORD.

EDWARD PLANTAGENET (EDWARD I),
THE ENGLISH JUSTINIAN, OR, THE
MAKING OF THE COMMON LAW. By
Professor EDWARD JENKS, M.A.

AUGUSTUS CÆSAR AND THE ORGANI-
SATION OF THE EMPIRE OF ROME.
By J. B. Firth, Translator of " The Letters
of Pliny," etc.

CONSTANTINE THE GREAT, THE
REORGANISATION OF THE EMPIRE
AND THE TRIUMPH OF THE CHURCH.
By J. B. Firth, author of " Augustus Cæsar."

MOHAMMED, AND THE RISE OF ISLAM.
By Professor D. S. Margoliouth, New
College, Oxford.

MARLBOROUGH, AND THE RISE OF THE
BRITISH ARMY. By C. T. Atkinson, M.A.,
Fellow and Lecturer, Exeter College, Oxford.

JULIUS CÆSAR. By W. Warde Fowler,
M.A., Fellow of Lincoln College, Oxford.

NAPOLEON, WARRIOR AND RULER, AND
THE MILITARY SUPREMACY OF REVO-
LUTIONARY FRANCE. By W. O'Connor
Morris.

CICERO AND THE FALL OF THE ROMAN
REPUBLIC. By J. L. Strachan-Davidson,
M.A., Fellow of Balliol College, Oxford.

ABRAHAM LINCOLN, AND THE DOWN-
FALL OF AMERICAN SLAVERY. By
Noah Brooks.

BISMARCK, AND THE NEW GERMAN EMPIRE: HOW IT AROSE AND WHAT IT DISPLACED. By J. W. HEADLAM, M.A., Fellow of King's College, Cambridge.

ALEXANDER THE GREAT, AND THE MERGING OF EAST AND WEST. By BENJAMIN IDE WHEELER.

CHARLEMAGNE, THE HERO OF TWO NATIONS. By H. W. C. DAVIS, M.A., Fellow of Balliol College, Oxford.

FREDERICK THE GREAT, AND THE RISE OF PRUSSIA. By W. F. REDDAWAY, M.A., King's College, Cambridge.

WILLIAM THE CONQUEROR, AND THE RULE OF THE NORMANS. By F. M. STENTON, M:A.Oxon.

Each 10s. 6d. net.

SIR PHILIP SIDNEY. By H. R. Fox Bourne.

JOHN WYCLIF, LAST OF THE SCHOOLMEN, FIRST OF THE ENGLISH RE- FORMERS. By Lewis Sergeant.

JULIAN THE PHILOSOPHER, AND THE LAST STRUGGLE OF PAGANISM AGAINST CHRISTIANITY. By Alice Gardner, Lecturer and Asso- ciate of Newnham College, Cambridge.

CHARLES XII, AND THE COLLAPSE OF THE SWEDISH EMPIRE, 1682- 1719. By R. Nisbet Bain, author of "The Life of Gustavus III."

JEANNE D'ARC, THE MAID OF FRANCE. By Mrs. M. O. W. Oliphant.

CHRISTOPHER COLUMBUS, HIS LIFE AND VOYAGES. By Washington Irving.

v